Gay Plays: Five

Playing by the Rules Rod Dungate, **Plague of Innocence** Noël Greig,
Beautiful Thing Jonathan Harvey, **Snow Orchid** Joe Pintauro

Beautiful Thing – Jonathan Harvey
'An excellent, heart-warming play . . . fresh, funny and hopeful.' *The Observer*

Playing by the Rules – Rod Dungate
'There's such humour in it, such affection and such energy . . . the action is swift, sharp,
boisterous and ebullient.' *Plays and Players*

Plague of Innocence – Noël Greig
'Daringly complex and sophisticated, it represents young people's theatre at its most
intelligent.' *Times Educational Supplement*

Snow Orchid – Joe Pintauro
'Pintauro reveals a talent for dramatising grand passions with almost operatic vigour. He
unleashes a volcanic uproar of affection, obscenities and physical abuse worthy of *Raging
Bull*.' Frank Rich, *New York Times*

Volume Five in Methuen's highly successful series of *Gay Plays* provides another outstanding
selection by playwright Michael Wilcox. Included here are George Devine winner, Jonathan
Harvey's *Beautiful Thing*; *Playing by the Rules* by 'invigorating and gutsy new playwright' (*Time
Out*) Rod Dungate; the award-winning *Plague of Innocence*, originally written for the Sheffield
Crucible Theatre-in-Education company, by Noël Greig; and American writer Joe
Pintauro's *Snow Orchid*.

Michael Wilcox's plays include: *Accounts, Lent, Massage, Rents, Green Fingers* and *Time
Windows*. He has also written opera libretti for John Metcalf's *Tornrak* (Welsh National
Opera, 1991), Edward McGuire's *Cullercoats Tommy* (Northern Stage, 1993), and, with
Jeremy Sams, a new libretto for Chabrier's *The Reluctant King* (Opera North, 1994). His
autobiographical journal, *Outlaw in the Hills* is published by Methuen. Michael is Literary
Adviser to both Northern Stage and Live Theatre companies.

Gay Plays: Five

Playing by the Rules
Rod Dungate

Plague of Innocence
Noël Greig

Beautiful Thing
Jonathan Harvey

Snow Orchid
Joe Pintauro

Selected and Introduced by Michael Wilcox

Methuen Drama

Methuen New Theatrescripts

This volume first published in Great Britain in 1994
by Methuen Drama

Methuen Publishing Ltd
215 Vauxhall Bridge Road
London SW1V 1EJ

www.methuen.co.uk

ISBN 0 413 68760 0

Methuen Publishing Ltd reg. number 3543167

A CIP catalogue record for this book is available at the British Library.

Front cover: Poster for Ron Dungate's *Playing by the Rules* at Birmingham Rep.
Photo: Stephen Redler

Typeset by Wilmaset Ltd, Birkenhead, Wirral
Transferred to digital printing 2003

Contents

Introduction

The Methuen *Gay Plays* series is now ten years old and in that time I've read hundreds of plays about gay people and on gay issues. Most have been set in that Never Never Land of 'The Present Time'. It has been rare to read a script set outside the lifetime of its author. Favourite themes have been 'coming out' and, in recent years, AIDS. Most of the playwrights have been under 35 years of age and many have been in their twenties. I have only ever received one play about lesbians. This was not a matter of policy on my part, but the division between Gay and Lesbian writing seems to have become more pronounced as the years have passed.

Ten years have seen the arrival of the iniquitous 'Clause 28' that shamelessly discriminates against gay people. As Derek Jarman lay dying, Parliament voted against an equal age of consent for gay men. So we now have absurd legislation that permits heterosexual and lesbian sex at 16, but homosexuals remain criminals until their eighteenth birthdays. The homophobic filth uttered by some MPs in the debate was truly sickening. Homosexuals are still dismissed automatically from the British Armed Forces, but a few Gay police officers (and is there anyone who doesn't know a Gay policeman?) are now out and on the beat. At last there is legal awareness of male rape. There is also an increased visibility of Gay businesses and Gay people in general, compared to ten years ago. But whether the Pink Pound really has the economic clout that is sometimes claimed remains questionable.

Many of the plays I received ten years ago depicted homosexuals as victims of prejudice, violence and moral outrage. Suicide or tragic accident at the final curtain was not uncommon. There was, too often for my stomach, a special pleading for sympathy. If prejudice, violence and moral outrage are still evident in everyday life, on the stage and in the cinema there has been a shift in perspective. In the hugely popular film *Four Weddings and a Funeral*, the gay couple played by Simon Callow and John Hannah have the most durable and sympathetic relationship in the film. John Hannah is sound, intelligent, and a true friend in need. His funeral oration is deeply touching and, incidentally, has had an astonishing impact on the sales of Auden's poems. All this is a million miles from the traditional and demeaning camp queens of British comedy. Jonathan Harvey's play *Beautiful Thing* comes as a similar breath of fresh air. Two teenage boys learn about loving each other without the guilt and fear of earlier generations being visited upon them. Instead, a pragmatic and sweet natured innocence is alive and well and living in south east London. Was such a play conceivable ten years ago?

The other side of the coin exists in *Playing by the Rules*, in which Rod Dungate revisits the world of rent boys that I explored in *Rents* in the mid-seventies. Nothing much seems to have changed. The same tedious, kinky punters still treat lads like disposable Kleenex. One striking difference is that in *Rents* my two rent boys had full time occupations in addition to prostitution. By the 1990s, many of the huge number of unemployed young men, who want to take a pride in themselves and dress well and have some sort of roof over their heads, see the rent game as a respectable alternative to thieving. Whether they perceive themselves as being gay or not is less of an issue than a need for money as a means of basic survival.

Theatre in Education (TIE) companies throughout Britain have been performing AIDS related programmes to schools and colleges, to provide information and promote safer sexual habits. Most of the time, the storylines have concentrated on heterosexual transmission of HIV. This is both a response to Clause 28, which legislates against positive images of homosexuality in schools, or even on local authority property at any time of the day or night, and partly to counterbalance Gay Plague hysteria. At a recent seminar on AIDS on the stage at London's Theatre Museum, representatives from Gay Sweatshop protested strongly about the number of heterosexual AIDS plays being toured to schools. For purely political and legal reasons the experience of gay people was too often a footnote in such plays, rather than their central focus. However, Noël Greig's *Plague of Innocence* is an exceptional example of TIE work, both in form and content. Those who saw the original production found the experience overwhelming and unforgettable. In the form of a dramatic poem, Greig depicts the closing seconds of the century. He doesn't specify the number of actors or the distribution of lines or include any stage directions. That such a piece should be written and presented as part of a TIE programme says much for the generally unheralded and unsung work of hundreds of poorly paid theatre workers who perform regularly in non-theatre venues throughout Britain.

More conventional in form is Joe Pintauro's *Snow Orchid*. A group of Joe's shorter plays, *Wild Blue* appeared in *Gay Plays: Four*. This stunning, full-length play received a magnificent production at the Gate Theatre by the London Gay Theatre Company, hence the two introductions later in this edition by both director, Tim Luscombe, and the playwright. As with other plays included here, much of the action centres around two young men, reminding us that plays about old homosexuals are not that common. One of the many things I admire about this play is the way homosexuality is only one aspect of a dense tapestry of themes, which is something I was searching for and wrote about in my introduction to the first volume of *Gay Plays* a decade ago.

Michael Wilcox
August 1994

Playing by the Rules

Rod Dungate

Characters

Danny, *15 years old, small, can look very young*
Sean, *17 years old, camp*
Steve, *18 years old, pleasant looking, inspires confidence*
Tony, *17 years old, mixed race, pleasant but not as outgoing as the others, hidden violence*
Ape, *19 or 20, Tony's half brother, very friendly, very strong, butch looking, not nearly as quick on the uptake as the others*
Julie, *17 years old, Steve's girl-friend, and Sean's best friend*

The first performance of *Playing by the Rules* was at Birmingham Repertory Theatre Studio on Wednesday 9 September 1992, with the following cast:

Danny	Ian Pepperell
Sean	James Dreyfus
Steve	David Phelan
Tony	Jason Yates
Ape	Robin Pirongs
Julie	Michelle Joseph

Directed by Anthony Clark
Designed by Ruari Murchison
Lighting Designer Symon Harner

The production was revived at Birmingham Repertory Theatre, with the same company, in this slightly rewritten version, on Wednesday 31 March 1993 and transferred to the Drill Hall, London, on Tuesday 27 April 1993.

Playing by the Rules was winner of 1992 Central TV's *Eileen Anderson* Award for the best new play in the Central TV region and Mentorn Film's *First Night* Award.

Note on the style

There are a few general points that I should like to make about the way I see the play 'working'. It may be useful if these are kept in mind.

It is of paramount importance that the meeting point between the audience and the play is the boys' and Julie's performance. Only they use direct address: they may sometimes do this while playing another character, but it must be clear that *they*, and not the characters they are playing, are addressing the audience. It must also be clear that the *actor* is not directly addressing the audience.

The lines which appear in bold italics are the ones which it seems to me are direct address lines. However, sometimes, the boys and Julie speak directly to each other, 'stepping out of the scene' to do so; this may be to comment on the scene or to make a joke that has occurred to them. These lines are also written in bold italics. It should be kept in mind, though, that 'italicisation' is a flexible font!

Danny *never* uses direct address after the introduction.

We should be aware that when the boys present other characters to us, it is their version of the character we see.

The acting space is flexible. Characters do not have to make entrances into 'scenes' nor exit from them. They can drop in and out as required.

Playing by the Rules is divided into Six Days, an Introduction and an Epilogue. The six days are themselves divided into twenty-seven sections, numbered consecutively. It is important to note that, within any one day, the action must flow *without any break, absolutely smoothly*, from one section to another. While keeping this in mind, it may be helpful to delineate one section from the next, say with lighting, sound, or physically in the acting space. From one day to another, it is desirable that there is a clear break.

Thank you for taking note of all this.

Note on this text

In order to retain an element of the atmosphere of the original productions, this text is based on the use of the acting space as directed by Anthony Clark in Ruari Murchison's designs.

A large metal 'bridge' was suspended over the acting space: actors reached it by two ladders placed one at each end. On the rear wall, two shells of motor cars 'emerged' at different heights; these were also reached by ladders. A third car shell was at ground level. At the rear of the space, a dustbin, halved lengthways, operated as a seat. The rear wall was partly covered with mirror-tiles.

Actors did not always leave the acting space when not in a scene: they could view the action while leaning on the cars or ladders, sitting in the cars or on the bridge, or standing at the edges of the space.

Lighting, music and other effects were prominent.

Introduction – The Streets

Music with a strong rhythm. The six characters come in and strike uncompromising tableaux to do with the stories in the play, sometimes in pairs, sometimes on their own. Music fades. Most of this introduction is direct address.

Tony   Boys playing.

Steve   Shutting eyes won't make us go away.
Nor hands held up in horror –

All   that's hypocrisy.
It's our story;

Steve   we'll tell it in our way,

Danny   Saying what we want –

All   what we want to say!

Julie   Cars,

Steve   lights,

Danny   a carpet,

Sean   ladders,

Ape   a mirror –

All   Watch it, you'll crack it!!

Ape   Just checking it out, OK?

Tony   It's for us,

Sean   at least for the next couple of hours.
And you are the audience –

Danny   clients –

Julie   punters.

Ape   For the usual?

All   Yea!!

Ape   Too many people about.

All   Never stopped you before!

Sean   – He's done it in the middle of a roundabout.

Steve   And though the punter usually calls the tune
D'you mind going along with our game?

Tony   Here we can bend the rules of space and time.

Steve   Our rules are:

Sean   To tell the truth –

Julie You don't know how!

Sean   Shut it!

Julie   Make me.

Ape   God!

Tony   Shrewth! –

Julie To learn you something,

Sean   and to have a laugh.

Ape Shall I tell 'em a joke?

Tony   Don't be daft.

Ape I'm going to play.

Steve   And me.

Sean   And her.

Julie   And him.

Ape And you.

Steve   And Danny.

Danny   Fifteen years of age.

Danny has collected a hold all and come back into the action.

Steve In care they talk of cash for boys who're bold,
He's heard our City's streets are paved with gold;
So today he's legged it. Look now! – a sorry sight! –
No bread, alone, and nowhere to spend the night.

One – The Streets (Tuesday 4)

Stillness. **Danny**, *is standing alone: he is clearly not at ease. Sean comes in; he is carrying a large carrier bag from a department store. He walks past* **Danny** *and greets him in a friendly manner.*

Sean   Hi!

Danny   Hi!

Sean   Busy?

Danny   Yea.

Steve *comes up behind* **Sean** *and grabs him in a neck-lock.*

Steve   Your bread.

Sean   None left.

Steve   What you got in there?

Sean   Nothing.

Steve   Tell us.

Sean   It's a secret.

Steve *lets* **Sean** *go as they both laugh.*

Steve   *Sean . . . on her way back from a shopping expedition.*

Sean   *Mr Action-Man Steve . . . the first time he's taken me from behind.*

Steve (*to* **Danny**)   I haven't seen you here before.

Danny   No.

Sean ⎱
Steve ⎰ *Mint chicken.*

Julie *comes on and crosses to* **Steve**.

Julie   Hiya.

Steve ⎱
Sean ⎰ *Julie.*

Sean   *My best friend.*

Steve   Hi.

Sean   *She's Steve's girlfriend.*

Steve *kisses her.*

It's a messy business.

Julie   *I work in a cake-shop.*

Sean
Steve } *She's a tart.*

Julie *Takes one to recognise one.* (**Julie** *speaks to* **Danny**.) You working?

Danny What's it to you?

Steve (*to* **Julie**) I missed you.

Julie I missed you too.

Steve Folks throw you out again?

Julie Missed having you next to me.

Steve Missed having you. I'll take tonight off – let's go back to the flat!

Julie Yes, please!

Sean She could come with me.

Steve We're going back to the flat.

Sean (*to* **Julie**) Why don't you come with me. (*To* **Ape** *who is crossing the acting-space.*) Ape! (*To* **Julie**.) I'm going late night shopping.

Julie Where to? (**Julie** *giggles.*)

Sean *Ape, look – the strong silent type.* Ape! Are you going back to the bijou residence?

Ape What's that?

Sean My flat, Einstein.

Ape Oh. Yea.

Sean Good. You can carry this.

Ape *looks into the bag.*

He's all right, Ape; but half the time we don't know where he is – the other half the time he doesn't know where he is.

Ape I'm not walking about with this.

Sean You'll do as you're told. It'll only take you five minutes. (*To* **Julie**.) I've seen some great clothes in the Pavilions: I'll get you something if you come with me.

Ape (*to* **Danny**) They're mad this lot!

Danny Right.

Sean (*to* **Julie**, *trying to persuade her*) Come on.

Julie I ain't seen Steve for weeks.

Sean You haven't seen me neither. I'll get you a present and a bottle of gin. Come on. As for you there's a Vets' Convention at the ICC – go and help them fist a few bullocks.

All but Steve *He needs the money!*

Steve *I need the money.*

Julie All right, then.

Sean Great.

Julie But give us a kiss first.

Sean Yuk! Yuk! Yuk!

She kisses him.

Julie Have you missed me too?

Ape Wanna watch out, Steve – Sean's on the turn.

Sean I could sue you for libel.

Julie (*to* **Steve**) See you. (*Kisses him.*) Pick me up at Sean's. (*To* **Ape**.) See you later, Ape.

Ape Great.

Julie (*a public whisper to* **Ape**) We'll all get rat-arsed.

Steve You drink too much.

Sean
Julie } *Hark who's talking.*

Julie *and* **Sean** *are gone, giggling loudly.*

Ape I was looking for Tony.

All (not **Ape**) *Ape's brother.*

Ape Anybody seen Tony?

Sean She's been out all afternoon playing the arcades.

Ape King's looking for him.

Steve *has put on the King wear and mounted the bridge. Everyone joins in the 'Mr King' at the beginning of the following lines.*

Steve *Mr King, once on the scene, is now a man of money,*

Sean *Mr King, views the scene, like bumble bees view honey,*

Julie *Mr King, once was seen on roads and racks and dilly –*

Ape *So why's the air surrounding him*

All *always so fucking chilly?*

Sean *and* **Julie** *depart.*

Steve/King Seen Tony?

Ape 'Aven't seen him, Mr King. D'you want me to get him?

Steve/King Thought you hadn't seen him.

Ape   Oh.

Steve/King   Pillock.

Ape   I know where he hangs out.

Steve/King   Pillock.

Ape *goes.* **Danny** *comes into* **King***'s view.*

Haven't seen you here before.

Danny   No.

Steve/King   New, eh?

Danny   Fifteen quid.

Steve/King   What for?

Danny   The usual.

Steve/King   Who says I'm buying?

Danny   Sorry.

Steve/King   (*he holds out i.d.*)   Vice squad.

Danny *runs away.* **King** *laughs.*

Steve   *King's a wanker.*

Tony *arrives.*

Steve/King   Hiding from me, Tony?

Tony   Mr King.

Steve/King   Know him?

Tony   Never seen him before.

Steve/King   Smart little arse – but a bit wet behind the ears still. Find out who he is.

Tony   Not getting fed up with me, are you?

Ape   *Mr King, on the scene, only looks for Tony.*

Steve   *And Tony thinks he'll care for him – a notion all too phoney.*

Steve/King   I'm parked round the corner.

Steve *removes the King wear. In the meantime,* **Sean***, putting the final touches to his Vicar wear comes in – he carries a pink rubber glove. He tries to attract* **Steve***'s attention.* **Ape** *crosses to him.*

Ape   *Some punters are professionals . . .*

Sean   *. . . amateurs, like this geezer stand out like a sore prick.*

Ape   D'you want business?

Sean/Vicar   No thank you.

Ape   Right, Vicar.

Sean/Vicar   That is to say . . .

Ape   Where's your car?

Sean/Vicar   You misunderstand me.

Ape   No I don't.

Sean/Vicar   You see . . .

Ape   I get you, Vicar.

Sean/Vicar   No, no. That young man,

Ape   Right.

Sean/Vicar   He's my nephew.

Ape   What? Victor, Vicar?

Sean/Vicar   Victor . . . Victor.

Steve   *Victor's my working name.*

Ape   *But 'Vicar' 's not his!*

Sean/Vicar   Don't keep calling me Vicar. His mother, my sister you know, she's very worried. Could you ask him to have a word with me. Please.

Ape   No sweat.

Sean/Vicar   Bless you son.

Ape   One thing, though . . .

Sean/Vicar   What?

Ape   For Christ's sake look in the shop window

Ape *calls up to* **Steve.**

Punter for you. Said he's your uncle!

Steve *comes off the bridge, to the* **Vicar.**

Sean/Vicar   Hello, Victor.

Steve   Hi.

Sean/Vicar   D'you fancy a meal?

Steve   Where?

Sean/Vicar   How about the Spaghetti House round the corner?

Steve   Poxy dive. I'll come to the Regency Highup.

Sean/Vicar   I can't afford that.

Steve   Tough, then.

Sean/Vicar   I just want to talk to you.

Steve   And the rest.

Sean/Vicar   Not this evening.

Steve   Fifty.

Sean/Vicar   It's too much.

Steve   I can't go out for less than that.

Sean/Vicar   I don't earn that much.

Steve   Then take it out your collection plate, Vicar.

Sean/Vicar   I just did – and don't keep calling me Vicar. (*He takes out his purse and begins to extract some notes.*) Thirty was all I could take.

Steve   Put that away, dick-head. D'you want us both done?

Sean/Vicar   Sorry, master.

Tony   *Eyes always skinned for porkers – they can't wait to do you for importuning.*

Julie   *It's the only long word most of 'em know.*

Sean/Vicar   Don't call me dick-head.

Steve   Right you are . . . Vicar.

Sean/Vicar   How much of your valuable time can you give me for thirty?

Steve   Here, eight o'clock. I'll eat your stinking spaghetti. No more.

Sean/Vicar   Bless you.

Sean   *Steve can be a real hard madam when she wants to.*

Steve (*to* **Sean**)   I'm not in business for pleasure. (*To Audience.*) *I'm an entrepreneur.*

All   *Spirit of the Age.*

Tony *comes on as another punter. Takes out a cigarette.*

Steve   *A professional.* Want a light?

Tony *takes a long look at him.*

Tony/Punt   No thanks.

He takes a deliberate look in **Ape***'s direction.*

Ape   Looking for a light?

Tony/Punt   Thanks.

Ape *gives him a light. They move off together.*

Steve   *Quick and discreet.*

Danny *comes back.*

Steve   You've come back.

Danny   So?

Steve   So you OK?

Danny   What's it to you?

Steve   Just asking.

Danny   I'm fine.

Steve   You sure you know what you're doing?

Danny   Course.

Steve   First time out?

Danny Piss off.

Steve Who d'you think you're kidding?

Danny Fuck off.

Steve What's your name?

Danny Danny.

Steve See what I mean?

Danny What?

Steve Don't give out your real name unless you know who you're talking to. Dick-head. How much you made tonight?

Danny That's my business.

Steve I bet you haven't done a single punter.

Danny I'm not out here for me tan.

Steve Steve.

Danny I thought you said you don't tell anyone your name.

Steve I know who I'm talking to don't I?

Ape *has put on Punter-wear.*

Danny Could you spare me a pound? – I've lost me fare and I've got to get to Northfield.

Ape/Punter *looks in* **Steve**'s *direction.* **Steve** *has to get* **Danny** *out the way.*

Ape/Punt Victor.

Steve Sure.

They go to the punter's car.

Danny Wanker!!

Danny *is left on his own. He climbs on to the bridge.* **Sean** *and* **Julie** *bring on cushions and bits and pieces to suggest Sean's flat.*

Sean *You want to work the streets, you got to get to know the streets, and you got to get to know what makes them tick. Danny is on what I think you call a steep learning curve . . .*

Two – Sean's Flat (Tuesday 4)

Julie *. . . Me and Sean, on the other hand, are on a steep slippery slope.*

Julie *and* **Sean** *have been drinking some time. They are used to drinking, and can carry it quite well.*

Julie This bottle's finished.

Sean I got another one. It's in that carrier.

Julie *looks in a carrier.*

Julie 'Ere, what's 'escargot'? (*She pronounces it wrongly.*)

Sean It's French. Escargot. Snails.

Julie   Oooh, la, la. French. What they taste like?

Sean   Dunno.

Julie   Can we eat 'em now?

Sean   Don't know how to cook them.

Julie   What you get them for then? Henry?

Sean   Henry never eats here. The odd drink, that's all.

Julie   Not getting much for his money then is he?

Sean   Thanks a million.

Julie   What's in 'ere we can eat?

Sean   Loads.

Julie   I don't know where you get the dosh from.

Sean   Easy come, easy go! Come on, hurry up, I'm dying of thirst.

Julie   Liar.

Sean   Liar yourself.

Julie   Where's those sandwiches?

Sean *gets a carrier and hands it to her. At the same time he takes the carrier she was investigating and puts it away somewhere.*

Sean   If you haven't got any food at Steve's you can take some of this.

Julie   Thanks. But you know Steve – he'll be well stocked up. And it's all paid for.

Sean   No wonder he has to work so hard!

Julie   'Ere, this is nice.

It's an Art Nouveau-style lamp. Woman holding globe or the like.

Can we plug it in?

Sean   No plug on it. 'Ave to get one. You going back to Steve then?

Julie   Yea. Might as well. Four weeks at home and the novelty wears off. Anyway, Mum's on the way out now . . . Definite . . . Pickled as a fucking jar of walnuts. If you had a plug we could get the lamp going.

Sean *goes for plugs.*

Sean   My Ma never drinks.

Julie   Mine drank anything she could get her hands on. Forty fags a day. She used to say to me: 'Keep looking for that pot of gold at the end of the rainbow, girl.' Always pissed when she said it of course. Your dearly beloved Mother Superior searched me out while I was there.

Sean   You didn't tell her where I am did you?

Julie   You are joking. Her come round here, then you in court for murder.

Sean Chance'd be a fine thing. Raise a hand against one of God's anointed and it's thunderbolt time.

Sean *returns. He has a small carrier and two lots of material. He shows* **Julie** *the cloth.*

What you think of these?

Julie For me birthday present?

Sean You can choose.

Julie They're gorgeous.

Sean This one. I thought that too. I'd like to see her blown up by a fucking thunderbolt.

Julie That's awful.

Sean Me Dad chucked me out, locked the front door behind me, vented me things through me bedroom window and all she could do was her drama queen – 'Oh surely to God, Sean, if you could just stop your airs and graces, he'd have you back tomorrow.'

Sean ⎫
Julie ⎭ 'Hail Mary full of grace . . .'

Squeals of laughter. They come to a halt.

Sean Plugs.

Sean *empties plugs and screwdrivers out.* **Julie** *starts putting the plug on.*

Sean Going to find your pot of gold with Steve, then?

Julie I wouldn't't'a thought so.

Sean You keep coming back.

Julie Well . . . I love him all right.

Sean What's Steve like in bed?

Julie You fancy him?

Sean Not my type.

Julie He's all right. I've had better. I've had worse. He's good at cooking.

Sean D'you have an orgasm?

Julie You know a lot about it.

Sean I listen to 'Woman's Hour'.

Julie Sometimes.

Sean With Steve?

Julie Sometimes.

Sean Does it hurt?

Julie When I have an orgasm?

Sean When you screw.

Julie Course not. I wouldn't do it if it did. I like putting plugs on.

Sean *is back with another carrier.*

Sean   Here's one I did earlier.

He's holding up a matching lamp.

Julie   They look nice as a pair.

Sean   Suppose you didn't have a choice about doing it, and he wanted you to?

Julie   I'd bite his dick off. Why?

Sean   It doesn't matter.

Julie   Sean? . . .

Sean   Look, look, look. Your glass is empty. Never win the hostess of the year award that way, will I?

Julie   Sean!

Sean   That's my name.

Julie   Sean!!! Are you having problems with Henry?

Sean   Course not. He keeps me here.

Julie   So?

Sean   So I can't be having problems with him.

Julie   That's bleeding Irish if you ask me.

Sean   No one did, dear.

Julie   What's it like when you make love?

Sean   When we fuck d'you mean? A quick bang – not much to write to Mother about there. D'you know, he's the only man's never wanted to watch me coming.

Julie   Does he wear protection?

Sean   No.

Julie   I thought you'd know better.

Sean   He doesn't go with no one else.

Julie   You're a fool.

Sean   The boys don't bother half the time – except to barter.

Julie   I make sure Steve's got pocketfuls. Henry's just using you.

Sean   Where else would I get a flat like this, darling?

Julie   D'you have to call him 'Councillor'?

Sean   Have to call him 'Your Worship' next year when he's Lord Mayor.

Julie   Drop you then.

Sean   No. He likes me too much. Putty in my hands.

Julie   Likes's not very much for what he gets from you.

Sean   Fucks's not very much for what I give him. I've been fucked one way or another since I was twelve and always for less than I get now. At least I'm not selling my arse to strangers on the street. Henry wants me to go to college. He'll get me in and keep me there. I can keep Tony.

Julie   Tony! Tony'll get you thrown out – he's trouble. He's mad. Even when he was fostered they gave him back.

Sean   I love Tony.

Julie   He's straight.

Sean   Huh! He's rent. I dream about him every night. He'll come round. I think about waking up and seeing his beautiful body next to me. I dream about holding him in my arms and cuddling him, 'til all his worries're cuddled away.

Julie   You read too many 'Woman's Owns'.

Julie *plugs the lamps in.*

Look at that – very sophisticated. Just watch out Ape doesn't break them.

Sean   Ape treats beautiful things with respect.

Loud sirens pass, far below.

Julie   *It would seem, far below, that our City has finally woken up.*

Sean   *Safely above this urban hunting ground, Julie and me continue our journey into happy inebriation . . .*

Sean *and* **Julie** *'freeze' in the flat.*

Three – The Streets (Tuesday 4)

Danny *falls from the ladder. His nose is bleeding. He crosses to the dustbin seat and sits dejectedly.* **Steve** *comes back in.*

Steve   Hungry?

Danny   No.

Steve   Thought you might be.

Danny   Well I'm not.

Steve   Had an accident?

Danny   What d'you think?

Steve   Looks like it.

Danny   Shows how much you know.

Steve   So what happened?

Danny   Black kid jumped me.

Steve   What'd he look like?

Danny   What's it to you?

Steve   We know most of the kids round here. We'll sort him out, maybe.

Danny   Just a kid. I don't know. In a group.

Steve *has opened the sandwich.*

Steve   You don't like ham then.

Danny   I didn't say that.

Steve   You said you didn't want it.

Danny   I said I wasn't hungry.

Steve   So you do want it?

Danny   No.

Steve   Right.

Danny   Unless you're going to waste it.

Steve   Legged it from 'The Conifers', haven't you?

Danny   No.

Steve   Cut the crap. I know you from there. I was just finishing when you came in. Stroppy little cock you was. Screws couldn't handle you, that's why I remember you.

Danny   You won't say anything will you?

Steve   What d'you think I am? Don't go away, I'm just going to throw this in the bin.

Danny   Don't.

Steve   Why not?

Danny   I am hungry.

Steve   Say please to nice Steve, then.

Danny   Please.

Steve   No. Say, 'Please nice Steve.'

Danny   Please nice Steve.

Steve   Now say thank you.

Danny   Thank you.

But **Steve** *has not completely let go of the sandwich. He snatches it back.*

Steve   But before I let you have it you got to tell me the truth how you messed up your face.

Danny   I was getting cold. My legs ached. I was sitting down in that hotel down there –

Steve   'The Fleur de Lily'.

Danny The waiters chucked me out. I wasn't doing no harm. One of them had me by the arm, and I went to knee him one, and I fell down the steps.

Steve Fucking cheek – half of them used to be on the slipper themselves.

Steve *is amused, then he notices* **Danny** *is not.*

Right now, you're thinking it might just be that 'The Conifers' isn't so bad. Isn't that right? (**Danny** *nods.*) Yea. I tell you how I remember 'The Conifers': I remember having to share rooms with kids I hated the sight of, of nowhere being your own private place; I remember the bastards always on your back, always wanting to know what you're doing. I remember fights over the telly, fights over who's sitting in what fucking chair, fights over who fucking started fights. Did you have nightmares? Remember them. Did you get bullied? Remember that and how it suits the poxy screws. Remember what it's like to be ashamed to go out in what you're wearing, to see nothing, to do nothing, to own nothing, to feel like nothing, to grow up believing you're going to end up nothing. You were living in care but did you ever meet one person who ever cared?

Danny *is sobbing.*

Danny One. He was punished for it. Sent away. I hate it. I hate it.

Steve Every day of every month of every year remember that and swear you'll never go down that road again. That's the start: it's Number One first, last and in between. In the meantime, I'll see you all right. But no more giving me a hard time, and telling me fairies. Right?

Danny Yea.

Steve Come on. Go and wash your face – we'll find somewhere for you to stay. We'll get something proper to eat and find a party. Sound good?

Danny *starts to run off.*

Where you going?

Danny New Street bogs.

Steve Go back to the 'Fleur de Lily'. Any trouble, say you're a friend of Steve's. I'll wait here.

As **Danny** *goes,* **Sean,** *as the Vicar Punter, returns.*

Sean/Vicar Hello, Victor.

Steve Oh, it's you.

Sean/Vicar You did say eight o'clock.

Steve Yea. Right.

Sean/Vicar I've booked a table for us. At the Highup.

Steve Blimey! Splashing out.

Sean/Vicar I'm going to put it on my Co-op visa card.

Steve Am I dressed for it?

Sean/Vicar You look fine. Shall we go?

Steve (*looking in a shop window*) Perhaps I should've put a different jacket on.

Sean/Vicar That one's fine.

Steve Perhaps I should go and brush me hair.

Sean/Vicar Your hair's wonderful.

Steve Perhaps I should go for a piss first.

Sean/Vicar They do have lavatories there. What's up? Have you lost your appetite?

Steve No, nothing's up. Let's be going then.

Sean/Vicar Good. If anyone sees us, remember you're my nephew.

Just as they move off, **Danny** *returns.*

Danny Steve!!

Steve (*to* **Vicar**) Just a sec, Uncle Beverley.

Sean/Vicar Don't call me Uncle Beverley.

Steve Right you are, Vicar. (*To* **Danny**. **Sean** *returns to his flat removing the Vicar-wear.*) Just off for a bit. Be back nine-thirty, ten. See you here then.

Danny OK.

Steve All in a day's work. Chin up. Uncle Beverley!!

Steve *runs off in the direction we imagine the* **Vicar** *to have taken.* **Danny** *has time to kill.* **Tony** *is on the bridge.*

Tony *For what seems like hour after hour after hour, Danny trudges the City Streets. From the windswept, bare-bones, market, slippery with cabbage leaves and slimed with broken flower-heads, through piss-stench passages, soggy with newspapers, and round the City's concrete collar.*

Ape Hi there, kid! Wanna lift?

Sean Need your bus-fare kid?

Julie You can't sit there!

Ape Would you like a bed for the night?

Tony *Desperate, he settles down amid Wimpy packets, Kentucky Fried cardboard, and bus tickets in the friendly doorway of an Army Recruiting office.*

Steve *returns.*

Steve You look a right fucking dosser there! Come on, let's go to Sean's.

Four – Sean's Flat (Tuesday 4)

They are all in Sean's flat. Music is playing.

Steve I said you'd put him up for a bit. You don't mind do you Sean?

Sean Oh hello. Can't have you sleeping in doorways can we, dear?

Danny Thanks.

Sean Just anybody's then.

Julie You should know.

Sean Bitch.

Ape You could have Tony's bed tonight.

Sean Is he with King?

Ape Or I'll sleep in Tony's bed and you can have the sofa – you'll fit on it better'n me.

Julie Carry on like this and you'll soon be a madam, nice red light in the window. No need to step out the door at all then.

Sean This is Julie, Danny.

Steve Sean's always been a madam.

Sean Lady, darling; don't forget it.

Julie Welcome to the madhouse, Danny.

Danny Thanks.

Julie You sure he knows what it's for? – He looks like he's just out of nappies.

Steve You're pissed.

Julie Sean's been leading me astray.

Sean I'm innocent, your honour; she dragged me across the kitchen and poured it down me throat.

Julie Oh dear, look at that face. He doesn't approve.

Sean No sense of humour.

Julie Come on, let's go and wash up the glasses. (*A loud whisper to* **Sean** *as she goes.*) We'll finish the bottle in the kitchen.

Sean You'll come to a bad ending, d'you realise that?

And laughing, they go.

Ape OK if I have a bath, Sean?

Sean You're costing me a fortune.

Ape I'm going for a bath.

Steve No need, Sean's already got one.

Ape I know. Oh. Yea.

And he goes too.

Steve I wish she wouldn't drink like that.

Danny It's all right.

Steve We're expecting a baby. But don't say anything – Julie don't want anyone to know.

Danny Why?

Steve I'd better get her home.

Danny Steve.

Steve   Yea?

Danny   Thanks.

Steve   I'll come and see you tomorrow; get you some new clothes.

Danny   You don't have to.

Steve   Right: but I want to. I only have to do what I want to. That's what it's like on the outside. Come on Julie, let's get going.

Julie   Oh, I'm enjoying meself!

Steve   Get your things.

Julie   You'll have to carry this – I'm too pissed. Bye Sean.

Sean   Bye slaggy.

They go. **Danny** *begins to take things out of his hold all – a pair of trainers, an inappropriate shirt, a pair of pyjamas.* **Sean** *appears with pillows and duvet.*

Sean   Are you gay? I am. Tony, you haven't met him yet, and Steve say they aren't but I bet they are really, and Ape, well, he's anybody's guess. Actually, he's anybody's – we're trying to give him away. Is this your first time out? I don't go on the slipper now because I'm kept here by a nice man who got me this flat. I'm his secret bit on the side. I'm the only totally out gay person here at the moment. Are you gay?

Danny *nods.*

Good. That'll be nice because we can chat. How old are you?

Danny   Fifteen.

Sean   You'd best say you're twenty-one from now on. Unless you're talking to punters and if they're that type you can tell them you're thirteen-and-a-half. And another thing, and this is important, you'll have to get rid of these pyjamas. No self-respecting gay wears pyjamas. Except old gay people. What else you got?

Sean *goes for the hold all.*

Danny   No, don't.

Sean   Clean knickers and socks. That's very organised, at least you won't be smelly. We'll find you somewhere to put your things tomorrow. Aaah! What have we got here? I don't believe it! I don't. I don't. I don't. What's his name? (**Sean** *is suddenly holding up a teddy bear.*) Tell me. Tell me. What's his name?

Danny   He hasn't got one.

Sean   Liar . . . I'll pull his arm off!

Danny   Aberdeen.

Sean   He can't be called Aberdeen.

Danny   He is.

Sean   Aber-fucking-deen.

Sean *runs out. He returns immediately.*

Sean   Aber-fucking-deen's brother.

Sean *is holding aloft an identical teddy bear. Only* **Sean***'s is immaculately dressed. He introduces the bears to each other.*

Sean   How d'you do, Aberdeen old chap. I'm Zebedee. Boing!! Oh, my God, look. They're trying to have sex. Stop it at once. I'll make Aberdeen a new outfit if you like. He could have a kilt. Kilts are very sexy. Zebedee, stop it, get down!!! What's up? – You don't look very happy.

Danny   This evening I didn't know where I was going to go or what I was going to do. Then I met Steve. And then he bought me a spring roll and chips, and then we came here, and now you've made me a bed, and Steve says he's coming round tomorrow.

Sean   So what?

Danny   And you don't even take the piss about Aberdeen.

Sean   I couldn't possibly do that. Zebedee would never speak to me again. Would you Zeb? Bonk!! Bonk!! Oh God he's at it again. Get off! He's a fucking nymphomaniac. Filthy beast.

Danny   I'm scared you'll all suddenly disappear.

Sean *gives* **Danny** *a reassuring little kiss on the top of his head and goes.*

Sean   Goodnight.

Five – Sean's Flat (Friday 7)

During the following, **Danny** *changes into his new outfit.*

Tony   *Tuesday,*

Ape   *Wednesday,*

Steve   *Thursday,*

Sean   *Friday.*

Steve   *Only four days and already Danny has had more fun than he had in all the years in 'The Conifers'.*

Sean   *First the mornings . . . yawning chasms of inactivity . . .*

Danny   Anyone want tea?

Ape   What's the time for Christ's sake?

Tony   Quarter past fucking eleven.

Ape   Go back to bed.

Sean   A lady needs her beauty sleep.

Danny   Oh, right.

Steve   *Danny needed a little time to adjust to the routine of night-work hours. The day really starts with afternoons . . . precise pockets of energetic discovery . . .*

Sean   *mimes – with occasional improvised interjections – his journey as he describes it; he is clearly shoplifting as he goes.*

Sean   *The clothes shop in the Pavilions – pop up to the cake-shop to say hello to Julie –*

Julie   Hello.

Sean ⎱
Danny ⎰ Hello.

Sean   *Indulge, waistline permitting, in a cream gateau.*

Danny   Can I have a doughnut?

Sean   No! *Into HMV, Virgin, across the road to Rackhams, test the perfumes.*

Sean   *climbs onto the bridge.*

Up the escalator to chat up the lovely Terence in menswear on the first. Hello Terence.

Tony ⎱
Ape ⎰ Hello Sean.

Sean   *Corporation Street, Chamberlaine Square – see if any students are bathing in the fountain, Broad Street and into the Highup for cocktails.*

Danny   They won't serve us.

Sean   Don't care. *We'll make a scene, they hate that. Get my laughs either way.* Get me a drink!!

Tony   *And the evenings . . . sprawling horizons of Aladdin entrance-ways marked with pulsating rainbows: babel night-worlds of sand-blasted mirrors, replenished glasses and live music — on and on and on.*

Steve   *Who could enter this world an orphan?*

Sean   *Danny was ushered in for better or for worse —*

Danny (**Danny** *is trying on his new jacket*)   I love this —

Sean   *— by his new found family, dressed with careful attention to detail —*

Ape ⎫
Tony ⎬ *— by his guide and mentor.*
Sean ⎭

Steve   *But Danny is completely broke:*
So he's hardly an awesome bloke:
And by Friday he began to say . . .

Danny   I really think, and I mean it, that it's time I started work so I can pay my way.

Steve   *I'm not keen for him to start so soon, but Danny's an obstinate little bugger, so I ask Tony to teach him a trick or two.*

Tony, **Sean**, *and* **Ape** *are in* **Sean***'s flat teaching* **Danny** *the ropes.* **Steve** *hands* **Danny** *a pizza in a box, then climbs onto the bridge to watch.*

Tony   Pretend to go and stand at a bus-stop.

Danny   Any one in particular?

Tony   Choose the quietest one. Punters'll always sniff you out. And if the porkers come, you can always get on a bus.

Danny   It might not be going where I want to go.

Tony   Dick. You just cross the Circus and come back to one of the other corners. Imagine you're standing at a bus-stop then.

Danny   This feels silly.

Tony   Steve said I had to teach you some of the tricks before he'd let you on the slipper.

Danny   Why's it called 'on the slipper'?

Tony   I dunno. It don't fucking matter.

Danny   I only asked.

Sean   Because when you walk round the run, it's shaped like a slipper.

Tony   Bollocks. It's because there was a bog there called 'The Slipper'.

Steve *They're both wrong. It's because in Victorian times, the boys didn't wear boots but soft shoes called slippers.*

Ape *That's crap Steve.*

Steve
Tony } *What is it then?*
Sean

Ape *I can't remember but I know it isn't that!*

Ape *leaves the flat.*

Tony Look!!! Just stick your hands in your pockets and look casual.

Danny I'm still eating my pizza.

Tony Then fucking get rid of it. (**Danny** *gets rid of the pizza.* **Tony** *prods* **Sean**.) Oi, go and make us some coffee will you? Keep your eyes peeled. (**Danny** *walks to the bus-stop and waits.*) Now – your punter's coming towards you.

Tony *walks towards Danny's bus-stop.*

Danny You've trodden in my pizza.

Tony*'s reaction is over the top.* **Danny** *moves the pizza out of the way.*

Tony You want to do this or not, donkey?

Danny Sorry.

Tony A first time punter's the worst, but you can get more off him. Half the time he won't say nothing. He'll be scared, he sees his name spread across the front page of his local, but he wants you more than he doesn't want that – but only a little bit. So you've got to make it easy.

Sean D'you want a coffee, Danny?

Tony Fuck off Sean.

Sean But you said make it.

Danny No thanks, Sean.

Tony Fucking hell.

Tony *treads in the pizza again.*

Sean Oh, for fuck's sake Tony, you're treading tomato all over the carpet.

Danny Should I say something?

Sean It's not you messing it up.

Tony If it looks like the punter isn't going to.

Danny Okay. (*Acts.*) Can I help you?

Tony What a dick! You're supposed to be a rent-boy not a receptionist.

Sean I dunno. I can just see her painting her nails. Something pastel for you dear.

Tony   You – shut the fuck up! Just say 'Cold, isn't it?' or 'Isn't it quiet – or wet – or anything.' Just start a conversation.

Sean   I always stick to deep red myself, more dramatic.

Tony   Cut the crap, I told you.

Sean   Pick your feet up so I can wash this mess off.

Tony   Try it.

Danny   It's like drama.

Tony   That's right. My drama teacher paid a fiver every time he sucked my dick.

Danny   Fucking hell!

Tony   Shocked?

Danny   Mine never paid nothing.

Sean   You've trod this right in. Always make 'em pay my dear: and always get the money first.

Tony   Look, I'm hovering around, perhaps been up the street twice. How you going to make the approach?

Sean   'Is that a shotgun in your pocket, or are you just pleased to see me?'

Tony   Fool!!

Sean   I can do amazing things with a dish cloth.

Tony   Shut up!! Off you go.

Danny   Excuse me, could you spare me a pound? – I've lost me fare and I've got to get to Northfield.

Tony   He'll think a pound's your asking price. Do another one.

Danny   I'm lost, can you tell me how I get to the coach station?

Sean   You haven't got a light have you?

Tony   Have you got the time?

Danny   I've had me money stolen.

Tony   Where's the ICC?

Sean   Could you change a pound for me?

Danny   D'you know where I could get something to eat?

Ape *has been watching for a bit.*

Ape   Bathroom's free.

Sean   They won't understand that one.

Ape   They're having you on.

Tony   Ape only has to hang his prick out and they all come running.

Sean   And he either fucks them or beats them to death with it.

Ape   Look for cars with only one geezer in. Stick to the regulars – just ask if they want business – they know what you're talking about.

Sean   That's what we love about you Ape – real style.

Tony   How can he stick to regulars if he's new?

Ape   He's new – the regulars'll find him quick enough. (*To* **Danny**.) Just you be careful.

Danny   I'll be all right.

Tony   He'll be all right. Stop frightening the kid.

Danny   I'm not scared.

Tony   We watch out for each other.

Sean   We're a family.

Steve *comes down from the bridge.*

Steve   *You learn the rules of the game – then you're okay.*

Tony   *It's a short life on the street –*

Ape   *Just like being a swimmer or an athlete –*

Sean   *So number one rule of the game –*

Steve   *Maximise your profit while you can, 'cause you can be sure every other bugger's trying to do the same.*
Just look at him, he reminds me of my baby brother.

Sean   *Take care when you're setting out your stall,*

Steve   *By your carefully tended casual look you stand or fall,*
It's a twenty-first century business . . . appearance is all.

Tony   *If I could look that young again, knowing what I know now, I'd make a fortune.*

Steve   Present for you.

Danny   What?

Steve   Shut your eyes. (**Danny** *shuts his eyes.* **Steve** *places a baseball cap jauntily on his head. – As fashions change, this could be any other little fashionable accoutrement.*) Daa daaa! (*Everyone laughs.*)

Tony   One beaudacious dude.

Sean   I think it should go more like this.

Danny *goes to a mirror to look.*

Danny   Sound.

Steve   You look wicked.

Danny   I've never had really nice gear before.

Steve   I'll get some more for you.

Tony   You won't need. He'll be buying his own in a day or two, won't you kid?

Tony *moves away.* **Danny** *speaks quietly to Steve.*

Danny You're supposed to be saving up for the baby.

Steve Don't worry kiddo. I'm the best. I can earn five hundred a week when I want.

Sean
Ape } Eat my shorts man!!
Tony

Steve You'll change your fucking tune, you tossers, when I'm out of here.

Danny Pay for me own gear soon. Should I wear it sideways?

Ape Lots of the punters'll want you. Class ones too. You'll find your Sugar.

Danny Like Sean?

Tony Henry's not class. He's a big fat slob.

Sean It's his flat!!

Danny Are these better with the belt or without?

Steve You sure you want to do this?

Danny Course.

Steve Sean don't mind you staying here.

Sean I don't.

Steve I'll see you don't starve.

Danny I'm not going back to 'The Conifers'. They're better with, aren't they?

Steve You wouldn't have to.

Danny I've got to stand on me own two feet.

Steve Who says?

Danny You did.

Steve We all have regulars we like Danny. But there's lots of others. Punters who try to piss off without paying, arse-holes who want you all night for a fiver. Tossers with stinking breath or aftershave so cheap you need a gas mask.

Danny Worse than Tony's farts?

Steve No – but a close second. There are punters with pricks so nasty you'd want gloves to touch them.

Danny I wouldn't go down on them.

Steve How d'you know? I've known other tarts get so hungry they'd sell their arse for a Kentucky Fried.

Tony And then they're overpriced some of 'em.

Danny Have you sold yours?

Warning sounds come from the others.

Tony No one's had my arse, kiddo and no one's going to. I'm class.

Danny If it's so bad, why d'you all do it, then?

Steve   Tony secretly dreams –

Tony   *– Of owning fast cars when I'm old enough; sexy women; for little people to say 'That's Tony – he's one powerful, powerful man.'*

Steve   Ape, because he know's he's thick –

Ape   *– But that don't stop me feeling like a piece of shit when I sign on. A bit of rough trade's always good for a few quid. I'm not washing up in no fucking kitchen!*

Steve   Sean's different – he's brainy – he could get a job –

Sean   *– But I want to have fun.*

Steve   *As for me – it's easy money – I'll take it while I can.*

Ape   *Steve wants to live in a thatched cottage with roses up the wall . . .*

Sean   *And little Julie in her Pantry baking bread and children playing in the garden.*

Tony   *He saw a picture like it in a colouring book his brother gave him one Christmas when they were all still living together.* I've just farted.

Exaggerated gasps and so on from everyone.

Sean   *So Danny, –*

Ape   *– Our latest recruit –*

Tony   *– What does he want?*

Danny   Should I wear the jacket open or done up?

Steve *moves over to* **Danny** *and does the jacket up. He stands back and looks. He moves in again and undoes the jacket, steps back and looks.*

Sean   *Steve likes the jacket best undone.*

Steve   Who are you?

Danny   Grant.

Ape/Steve
Sean/Tony } Nice to meet you Grant!

Six – The Streets (Friday 7)

Sean, Tony, Ape *run to the cars –* **Ape** *to the one on floor level – he will put on Ivor wear.* **Danny** *has his back to the cars and stays centre, until his final conversation with* **Ivor**, *when he gets in the car.*

Sean/Punt   Hello there.

Danny   Grant!

Sean/Punt   Jump in.

Move to **Tony/Punter**.

Tony/Punt   Want a lift?

Danny   Thanks.

Move to **Ivor**.

Ape/Ivor   Get in.

Move to **Sean/Punter**.

Sean/Punt   I like to be stroked.

Danny   Okay.

Sean/Punt   With two hands.

Danny   Right.

Sean/Punt   Here's a tenner in your pocket.

Danny   Okay.

Sean/Punt   Do it gently.

Danny   Just as you like.

Sean/Punt   While you talk to me, Grant.

Danny   Okay.

Sound of a zip being undone.
Move to **Tony/Punter**.

Tony/Punt   Can you give a good blow?

Danny   Try me.

Tony/Punt   How much?

Danny   Thirty.

Tony/Punt   Twenty – but no coat on.

Danny   D'you want to bite me tits, then?

Tony/Punt   Rubber – you idiot.

Danny   No.

Tony/Punt   Twenty-five.

Danny   I'm not swallowing it.

Tony/Punt   It's perfectly safe, I'm a dentist. Open wide.

Sound of a zip being undone.
Move to **Ape/Ivor**

Ape/Ivor   You're new. What's your name?

Danny   Grant.

Ape/Ivor   I'm on my way home.

Danny   That's okay.

Ape/Ivor   How much time have you got?

Danny   I've got to meet me friends at half-ten.

Ape/Ivor   How old are you Grant?

Danny   Fiftee – . . . Thirteen-and-a-half.

Ape/Ivor   Oh, good. Do your seat belt up then – we don't want to break the law.

Sound of seat belt being done up. Back to the first car.

Sean/Punt   Oh! . . . That's good. Faster. Faster . . . Squeeze me . . . Harder . . . No! Hard!! Aaah.

Danny   Hard enough?

Sean/Punt   Gorgeous.

To the second car.

Tony/Punt   Take it right in.

Danny   You're hurting me.

Tony/Punt   Don't stop. What a lovely neck you've got.

Danny   You're pulling my hair.

Tony/Punt   Suck. Suck you bastard.

To the third car.

Ape/Ivor   Aren't the trees nice at this time of year?

Danny   We've got trees like this in our garden at home.

Ape/Ivor   You must live in a big house then.

Danny   It's a mansion. In the country. My Dad's an atomic scientist, but he's mad. He beats me up.

Ape/Ivor   You should tell the Social Services.

Danny   He said he'd kill me if I did, Mister.

Ape/Ivor   Call me Ivor.

Danny   I'm very unhappy, Ivor.

Sound of **Sean/Punter** *having an orgasm.*

Sean/Punt   Wonderful. Wonderful.

Sound of the dentist having an orgasm.

Tony/Punt   Now swallow. Come on, swallow.

Move to **Ape/Ivor**.

Ape/Ivor   Would you like a chocolate?

Move to **Sean/Punter**.

Sean/Punt   I'll drop you back.

Danny   Thanks.

Sean/Punt   That was good. – See you around.

Danny   I'll be here.

Move to the dentist.

Tony/Punt   There, that wasn't so bad, was it?

He shouts out.

Danny   My twenty-five.

Tony/Punt   What's the rush? Two crisp tens and a five look, and a five for the teeth marks you little tosser.

Danny   I just hope your old lady's short sighted.

And finally back in Ivor's car. **Danny** *joins* **Ivor.**

Ape/Ivor   Your Daddy shouldn't make you unhappy. Childhood should be a happy time.

Danny   I wish I could be happy.

Ape/Ivor   I'd like to make you happy.

Danny   I'd like to make you happy too.

Ape/Ivor   If I can make you happy, then that makes me happy, son.

Seven – Ivor's House (Friday 7)

Sean   *As they turn into Ivor's driveway,*

Tony   *Danny gets his first glimpse of the house . . .*

Danny   Fucking hell.

Ape/Ivor   Don't swear please.

Sean   *Ivor doesn't like bad language . . .*

Ape/Ivor   It indicates a lack of imagination.

Tony   *Ivor unlocks his huge panelled front door and steps inside.*

Ape/Ivor   Well don't stand in the doorway, come in.

Danny *expresses surprise, wonder and admiration.*

What d'you think?

Danny   It's . . . wicked!

Ape/Ivor   And I bet you are too. Come here. (*He cuddles him.*) You look like a little street urchin, d'you know that?

Danny   Is that bad, Ivor?

Ape/Ivor   It's very good when there's an angel striving to burst out.

Danny   D'you like my cap? I had one like this before. It was a present from my Mum, but she left because my Dad hit her. And when he saw it, he went ape-shit – he took a knife and ripped it into shreds. I was so scared. He hates me, see, because he's fat, and he's jealous because I do weight training.

Ape/Ivor   You mustn't overdo it – you're still a youngster. Your delicate physique could become distorted by too many muscles.

Danny   I only do it a bit. Just to keep in shape. I'll show you.

Danny *has sat on the floor and is taking off shoes and socks. He is going to do exercises.*

Ape/Ivor   Don't do that!

Danny   It's okay, honest. I do a little work out like this every day. My doctor says it keeps my asthma attacks away.

Ape/Ivor   That's all right then.

Danny *intersperses his exercises with the removal of his clothes.*

Ape/Ivor   Why don't I get us a drink?

Danny   Okay.

Ape/Ivor   What would you like? Fanta? 7Up? Tango? Coke? Or I could get you a milk shake.

Danny   Scotch please.

Ape/Ivor   Oh, you bad boy.

Danny   Could you put my jacket somewhere safe? – I only just got it.

Danny's shirt comes next – and so on.

Ape/Ivor   D'you want anything in it?

Danny   Rocks.

Ape/Ivor   Nothing else?

Danny   Diet Lilt.

Ivor   I'll tell you what, I'll put some lemonade in it as next best. Yes?

Danny   Yes.

Ape/Ivor   And some ice?

Danny   Rocks. D'you want to take my pants off for me?

Ape/Ivor   That wouldn't be at all right. (**Ivor** *returns.*) Warm enough?

Danny   Yes. Your carpet's so soft. My hands disappear into it. In 'The Conifers' the carpets were as thin as blankets and the blankets were like carpets.

Ape/Ivor   'The Conifers?'

Danny Once, when my Dad had to do a really hush hush thing – to do with nuclear bombs I think – I had to go to a boarding school for a bit.

Ape/Ivor Come and get your drink, little one.

Danny *goes for the drink.*

You're as scrumptious as caviar, you know.

Danny We used to have caviar every Sunday at home. For tea.

He tries his drink. It's stronger than he thought.

Ape/Ivor Don't drink it if you don't like it.

Danny Would you like me to blow you now?

Danny *goes to undo Ivor's trousers. There is a moment of anticipation before* **Ivor** *reacts.*

Ape/Ivor Get off!!!

Ivor's *reaction is extremely sudden and violent. He sends* **Danny** *reeling.* **Danny** *curls into a ball to protect himself.*

Danny Don't hit me.

Ape/Ivor No. Don't do that. I won't hit you. Honestly, it's all right. It doesn't matter.

Danny I'm sorry.

Ape/Ivor You mustn't do that.

Danny I thought it was what you wanted.

Ape/Ivor All I want is for you to have a happy time here. You don't have to do anything you don't want to do – understood? (*He waits for a reaction.*) Understood? Good. We'll see about getting you that bath you asked for.

Sean *Did you hear Danny ask for a bath?*

Danny Thanks – not too hot.

Tony *and* **Sean** *turn the dustbin seat over: inside it is painted like a bath. They produce the required items, including taps, from a bucket. During the scene they blow bubbles.*

Ape/Ivor You get yourself another drink while I run it for you. And no more scenes please. *If Ivor wasn't so nice, you'd think he was a bit weird wouldn't you?*

Sean *Danny does nothing for a while except drink two scotches and watch cartoons on Ivor's video. Then –*

Ape/Ivor It's time you were in your bath, you little monkey.

Danny *gets undressed and into the bath.*

I've put bubble bath in for you.

Danny I feel like I'm in an advert on the telly.

Ape/Ivor It's Mutant Ninja Turtle (*Change this as necessary.*) bubble bath.

Danny 'Smy favourite.

Tony *The ledge that goes round the bath is crammed full . . .*

Ape/Ivor You just enjoy yourself and have a good play.

Tony   *There's a Jaws that swishes its tail and opens and closes its mouth. There's a blue elephant that swims by turning its ears round.*

Sean   *There's an action man with no clothes that does a piss when you squeeze it.*

Ape/Ivor   I didn't know it did that.

Sean   *There's a submarine that goes up and down with lots of seamen in it.*

Tony   *And a green water pistol with gold stars on it.*

Sean   *It's a good job it's a big bath really.*

Ape/Ivor   Don't you squirt that thing at me.

Danny   Put your hands up.

Ape/Ivor   Don't you dare.

Danny   One more word and it's curtains for you.

Ape/Ivor   Mercy. Mercy.

Danny   Give me one good reason why I shouldn't finish you off now.

Ape/Ivor   I'm too young to die.

Danny   Not good enough. Psssh. Psssh. Psssh.

Ape/Ivor   Oh God! Don't shoot.

Danny   Psssh, psssh.

Ape/Ivor   I'm on the way out. Finish me now.

Danny   Psssh. There's no more water in it.

Ape/Ivor   I'm soaked.

Danny   You're dead.

Ape/Ivor   Don't splash, child. Bend over and let me wash your hair. What on earth have you been playing at? You should see the dirt in this. The water's getting cold. Time to get out.

Sean   *Ivor takes his hand and helps him from the bath and begins to dry him in the biggest, whitest, fluffiest, towel he has ever seen.*

Ivor *gently towels* **Danny** *dry.* **Steve** *speaks out of the near-darkness.*

Steve   *In his fifteen years Danny has learnt about being clean. He has been scrubbed almost bare by care workers, been made to stand under hot and cold showers, been punished in cold baths and hot baths; he has played vicious wet towel games in communal showers, has rubbed boys down and been rubbed down in numerous changing rooms, he has been hosed down several times in 'The Conifers' garden — playing instead of working; he has even been doused with disinfectant when he had crab lice. In 'The Conifers' they dunked his head down the bog — several times. He has even, on one occasion — two — been roughly strip-*

searched. What he has never realised, till this moment, is that anyone – any man – could treat him so gently.

Danny   Can you stop drying me?

Ape/Ivor   Why? – Don't you like it?

Danny   It's not that. It's just, it's just – oh God, I can't hold it back any longer, I can't –

He grabs **Ivor** *and presses himself hard against him. While he comes,* **Ivor** *holds him tightly.*

Danny   Sorry.

Ape/Ivor   Better? Now, run down stairs and get dressed.

Tony   *Danny has done his job well: but he hasn't quite learnt everything there is to know.*

Ivor *has disappeared. While* **Danny** *dresses, and unseen by* **Danny**, **Ivor** *brings back on* **Danny**'s *jacket. While* **Danny** *dresses,* **Danny** *says . . .*

Danny   Ivor! Ivor! I'm sorry Ivor. I didn't know what you wanted!!

He goes to collect his jacket and finds a tube of Smarties and a Bounty bar with them. He is not pleased. **Ivor**'s *house, the bath and so on, has been cleared away while* **Danny** *dressed.*

Eight – The Streets (Friday 7)

Danny *pours out the Smarties and some rolled up paper falls out with them. On investigation, this turns out to be thirty pounds. He's well pleased. He eats some of the Smarties while attacking the Bounty. No money, but a small card in this. He reads it.*

Danny   Ivor Stanwick, 267 2672: Solicitor and Commissioner of Oaths.

He carefully places this in his pocket. He is about to stuff the Bounty into his mouth when **Ape** *appears.*

Wannit?

Ape   Ta.

Nine – Sean's Flat (Friday 7)

Ape, **Tony**, **Sean** *stand round* **Danny** *who gives nothing away.*

Tony   Well?

Danny   Well, what?

Sean   Well . . . What?

Danny   What?!

Ape   Come on.

Danny *slowly puts his hand to his pocket, then quickly brings out the cash.*

Danny   Loads o' money! My treat tonight. Where we going?

Sean   Let's go to 'The George'.

Tony   I'm banned.

Sean   'The Zealand Bar'.

Tony   I'm banned there too.

Sean   'Folly's'?

Tony   And there.

Sean   Is there anywhere you aren't banned from?

Tony   'The Duke's Head'.

Ape   I'm banned there.

Sean   Fucking Hell. Anyone banned from 'The Unicorn'?

There is a chorus of 'No'.

Good.

Tony   I don't want to go there though. I always have to do it for the landlord.

Sean   Freddie Kruger lives!! Where then?

Steve *has arrived with* **Julie**.

Steve   What about 'The Nighthawk'?

Ape   I'm not going there!

Sean   Why not?

Ape   Too queenie.

Danny   What is it?

Sean   Gay club.

Julie   Great disco.

Sean   You'll love it dear.

Tony   We'll never get him in.

Ten – The Nighthawk, Reception (Friday 7)

Muted disco music can be heard. **Tony** *has put on George wear:* **George** *is the bouncer.*

To/George   Who's your new boy then Steve?

Steve   Danny.

To/George   Hello Danny.

Danny   Hi.

To/George   I hope we get on well, Danny, 'cause you're going to have to stay out here.

Sean   Why?

To/George   Because he ain't left school yet, that's why.

Sean   No one'll notice.

Steve   We'll make sure he don't buy any drinks, George.

To/George   It's more than me job's worth.

Steve   What you worried about? Porkers only ever come in here to pick up chicken themselves.

To/George   When I say no, I mean no.

There is a chorus of 'Eat my shorts man'.

Watch your lip.

Sean   What time's your break George?

To/George   And no sneaking in when me back's turned. (*With his back turned, quietly to* **Sean**.) Half eleven. I'll come and find you.

Julie   Have you no shame?

Sean   Necessity is the mother of deception.

Music is suddenly loud.

Eleven – The Nighthawk, Disco (Friday 7)

Several 'rooms' of 'The Nighthawk' are used. These are all suggested by the volume and nature of the music, and by lighting.

Steve   D'you like it?

Danny   It's the one.

Steve (*to* **Danny**)   Let's have a dance.

Julie   I want a drink.

Sean   What d'you want, girl?

Julie   Steve can get them.

Danny   No, I'll get them.

Tony   They won't serve you.

Steve   I was going to dance.

Julie   I don't want to dance.

Steve   Danny does.

Danny   No I don't.

Sean   I thought that's why we came here.

Steve   You told me you liked dancing.

Tony   Anyone show him dancing – I'll show him.

Julie   You fell over last night.

Danny   I want tonight to be on me.

Tony   He's rolling in it.

Ape, *now in Rupert wear, approaches Danny. Rupert is in leather.*

Ape/Rup   Hi ya kid.

Danny   Hi.

Ape/Rup   Cute.

Danny   Yea?

Ape/Rup   I'm Tex.

Sean/Steve/Julie/Tony   Fuck off Rupert!!!

Ape/Rup   OK! I can take a hint.

He wanders away.

Sean   That's Rupert, dear.

Danny   He said his name's Tex.

Sean/Steve/Julie/Tony   He's a wanker.

Danny   Crap cap.

Sean   S and M.

Danny   What?

Sean   Sexual gratification by liberation through pain.

Danny   Ugh!

Steve   Don't knock it. It's an optional extra.

Sean   Makes my eyes water.

Steve   Whips.

Tony   Canes.

Julie   Handcuffs.

Steve   Blindfolds.

Tony   Ropes.

Julie   Masks.

Steve   Needles.

Sean   Zips.

Steve   Who's for what?

Danny   I'll get 'em.

Sean   Come on honey, save your money: I'll dance with you. (*To* **Steve**.) Large G and T.

Danny   Lager.

Tony   Sol.

Julie   Baby boy can get the next lot.

Steve *and* **Julie** *get the drinks.* **Sean** *and* **Danny** *go off to dance.*

Danny   I don't think Julie likes me, does she?

Sean   You're imagining it.

Danny   She was all right this afternoon.

Sean   Her Mum's dying – you got to make allowances.

Danny   I can't remember my Mum.

Sean   Wish I could say the same.

Danny   Steve gets nicer and nicer.

Sean   He's the best thing that's happened to Julie.

Danny   I'm not surprised.

Sean   Don't knock her. She's okay.

Elsewhere, **Rupert** *bumps into* **Tony** *who is dancing.*

Ape/Rup   Nice mover.

Tony   More'n I can say for you.

Ape/Rup   Not a lot wrong with my dancing.

Tony   Not a lot right with it. Give us a spin, Rupert.

Tony *executes a flash spin.* **Rupert** *copies – he's not at all bad at it.* **Tony** *applauds vigorously.* **Rupert** *tosses* **Tony** *some poppers which* **Tony** *uses immediately. We return to* **Sean** *and* **Danny** *in a quieter part of the club.*

Danny   Why don't Julie like me?

Sean   She thinks you're on the make.

Danny   I'm not.

Sean   Julie and me was both suspended from our poxy school when we was fourteen and it was her taught me how to fight.

Danny   Were you bad?!

Sean   I was a working boy – earning but guilty – where's the fun in that? Julie taught me we have to make the most of what we got. I made a secret pact with the Devil. I promised him every time I got fucked, I'd name a priest or teacher he could have the soul of.

Danny   Don't that frighten you?

Sean   I don't believe in no bogey person! Julie's had to fight really hard for everything she's got. Ever tried to get a bone off of a dog?

Danny   Only once!!

Sean   That's Julie – on a good day! Remember that.

Danny   I couldn't've managed without Steve.

Sean   How much d'you make this evening?

Danny   Seventy.

Sean   Julie don't earn much more than that in a week. Remember that, too.

Danny   I can fight too, you know.

Elsewhere, **Julie** *is trying to get* **Steve** *to dance.*

Julie   Come on.

Steve   Thought you didn't want to dance.

Julie   I do now.

Steve   Make up your mind.

Julie   Come on.

Steve   Okay. We can see if Danny's all right.

Julie   He's with Sean. Come on!

Steve   I'll get you a lager.

Elsewhere, **Tony** *is dancing on his own.* **Ape** *is on the bridge now wearing King wear.*

Tony   Oh, Mr King, I didn't see you there.

Ape/King   Now you see me, now you don't.

Tony   Didn't know you came down here.

Ape/King   Good. Don't like to be too predictable. People find out what you're up to then.

Tony   What you up to Mr King?

Ape/King   Been talking to a friend today – an overseas associate. Ever heard of Amsterdam?

Tony   Oh yea.

Ape/King   Pleasure City some say. Your name came up in conversation.

Tony   Mine?

Ape/King   Yours. A little chat, Tony.

Tony   Sure.

Ape/King   We should have a bite to eat, see what we can come up with. Have these.

He drops him a polythene bag containing little coloured pills.

Tony   Thanks a million Mr King. Lovely, lovely Rainbow Makers.

Ape/King   Give me a ring at the Royale.

Ape/King *has gone. But* **Sean** *has seen the tail end of this conversation. He has watched the rainbow makers being passed to* **Tony***. Sean turns to go away, not wishing* **Tony** *to know what he has seen, however,* **Tony** *spots him.*

Tony   Sean! Guess who I've just seen?

Sean   Prince Edward?

Tony   Mr King.

Sean   I was close, then.

Tony   No honest.

Sean   Be careful, Tony.

Tony You don't know anything about him.

Steve *and* **Julie** *join* **Tony** *and* **Sean.** **Rupert** *spots* **Danny** *on his own and approaches him.*

Steve About who?

Sean ⎱ King.
Tony ⎰ Mind yours.

Steve King's a wanker.

Julie Ain't Danny with you?

Sean She's cruising.

Steve Not on his own!

Sean He'll be all right.

Tony Can't go cramping his style.

Steve You're hopeless.

Rupert *moves in on* **Danny.**

Ape/Rup On your lonesome?

Danny No.

Ape/Rup I'm Tex.

Danny You're Rupert.

Ape/Rup Cute.

Danny Fuck off.

Ape/Rup Don't move away.

Danny Leave me alone.

Ape/Rup Dance with me.

Danny Please let me go.

Ape/Rup What a well built boy.

Danny Leave me alone.

Ape/Rup Can't resist.

Danny My friends'll be back in a minute.

Ape/Rup (*rubbing himself against* **Danny***'s bum*) Snugger than a bugger in a rug.

Danny Let me go, please.

Ape/Rup Nice sausage for me breakfast too.

Danny FUCK OFF!!

All hell breaks loose.

Ape/Rup }   Shut your mouth brat!
Steve }   Danny needs help.

Steve }   Let him go you prat.
Danny }   Steve!

Ape/Rup }   Little prick like you going to make me?
Julie   }   Be careful Steve.
Sean   }   You all right Danny?

Steve }   Another crack and you'll get my fist down your throat.
Julie }   Sean, stop them can't you.
Tony }   Wild party time.

Danny   }   Steve, let him go now.
Ape/Rup }   Kid's pimp are you?

Steve *and* **Ape/Rupert** *start to fight.* **Julie** *and* **Sean**, *and then* **Danny**, *even, then* **Tony** *join in.* **Rupert** *is hassled off.*

Sean   Stick that up your arse Rupert!!

Twelve – Sean's Flat (Tuesday 11)

Sean   *Danny's only a week away from 'The Conifers' – but it could as well be a lifetime.*

Steve   *He made a good start on Friday, and despite the unfortunate hiccough in 'The Nighthawk', nothing daunted, excelled himself on Saturday. On Sunday Ivor had him round for tea –*

Tony   *Had him for tea!*

Sean   *He drummed up a little business on Monday, but tonight he is off the street . . .*

Danny   Ivor's meeting me to take me to a restaurant.

Sean   Make sure it's somewhere decent.

Tony   He's going to be worth a bit.

Ape   Take it careful.

Steve   He looked phoney to me. D'you want me to take you out?

Danny   I phoned him.

Steve   He'll be all right – loads of kids down New Street only just out their prams.

Danny   I like him.

Tony   Loads of handbag.

Danny   He's mine.

Steve   Come clubbing after?

Danny   'The Nighthawk'?

Steve   'DD's'.

Danny   What's that?

Steve   'Dan Dare's'.

Sean   It's a younger crowd. It's better.

Danny   I didn't like the other place.

Steve   It's better.

Tony   I got to see King. I might come down after.

Ape   I'm out of it tonight.

Ape *goes. As he goes . . .*

All   You're out of it everynight.

Sean   Julie's coming round for a fitting. We'll come down later.

Steve   No. She don't really like it. We'll be back by 11.30.

Steve   Don't forget. 'DD's'. Outside. 10.30.

Danny   10.30. Outside. 'Danny Dare's'. Yes, Grandad.

Steve   Fuck off!

Thirteen – La Pinacoteca (Tuesday 11)

Ape   *Ivor spoils Danny. In a romantic corner of* . . .

Ape *has difficulty with the Italian words.* **Sean** *makes an excellent Italian waiter. One half of the dustbin seat is brought forward and a table top and cloth placed on it.*

Sean   *La Pinacoteca, discreetly candle-lit and 'it takes all sorts as far as we're concerned'* . . .

Ape   *Ivor and Danny are served a sumptuous supper* . . .

Sean   *Antipasto Misto, followed by Tortellini alla Panna, followed by Bistecca alla Florentina with Uccellini in Umido: and for sweet – Monte Bianco.*

Ape/Ivor   Have you enjoyed yourself?

Danny   Murder.

Ape/Ivor   You've had enough?

Danny   Couldn't eat another thing.

Ape/Ivor   I don't know where you put it all.

Danny   What's this called?

Ape/Ivor   Cointreau.

Danny   It's very sophisticated.

Ape/Ivor   It is.

Danny   What's yours?

Ape/Ivor   Drambuie.

Danny   Can I have a taste?

Ape/Ivor   Sure.

He tastes Ivor's drink.

Danny   Ugh! That's horrible.

He finishes his Cointreau.

Ape/Ivor   You're not supposed to gulp it down.

Danny   Sorry.

Ape/Ivor   What about my offer?

Danny   I said I'd think about it.

Ape/Ivor   You've had all evening.

Danny   I need to think about it.

Ape/Ivor   Don't take too long.

Danny   What's that supposed to mean?

Ape/Ivor   Plenty of other fish in the sea.

Danny   Yea?

Ape/Ivor   Meals like this don't come cheap, you know.

Danny   So? You said to come here.

Ape/Ivor   It was my treat.

Danny   I've enjoyed it.

Ape/Ivor   Why not just say yes, then?

Danny   It's a big step.

Ape/Ivor   Mine's a very big house. Too big for just me. You'd enjoy yourself. Space, good food, as much drink as you want. Free all day. Holidays. Abroad even. You like me don't you?

Danny   Of course.

Ape/Ivor   Well then.

Danny   What's the time?

Ape/Ivor   Bored?

Danny   I only asked the time, for God's sake.

Ape/Ivor   About nine. Going somewhere?

Danny   I gotta meet Steve.

Ape/Ivor   I take you out and now you rush off.

Danny   I'm not rushing. Be reasonable.

Ape/Ivor   Who's Steve?

Danny   My friend.

Ape/Ivor   Is that why you won't say yes?

Danny   No.

Ape/Ivor   Does that mean 'yes'?

Danny   No.

Ape/Ivor   Is he your special friend?

Danny   Yes.

Ape/Ivor   Your lover?

Danny   No. He's my best mate if you must know.

Ape/Ivor   Why's he so special?

Danny   He looked after me.

Ape/Ivor   I could look after you. Think how much I could do for you. You'd want for nothing.

Danny   I said I'd meet him 9.30.

Ape/Ivor (*burst of ferocious anger*)   Then why don't you piss off to him then?

Danny   Just gone nine did you say?

Ape/Ivor   Get a watch for God's sake.

Danny   Could never afford one.

Ape/Ivor   It is four minutes and thirty-seven seconds past nine . . . precisely.

Danny   That's a very nice watch.

Ape/Ivor   I only have nice things.

Danny   Smart.

Ape/Ivor   It was given to me by a client.

Danny   Smart.

Ape/Ivor   I couldn't part with it.

Danny   I'd best be going.

Ape/Ivor   Don't.

Danny   I have to.

Ape/Ivor   Just a few more minutes.

Danny   It's a very smart watch.

Ape/Ivor   Why don't you try it on?

Danny *puts out his arm:* **Ivor** *puts the watch on it.*

Danny   Looks wicked, don't it? Perhaps Steve won't mind waiting an hour or so.

Ivor *takes hold of* **Danny***'s hand.*

Ape/Ivor   I could drop you back down.

Danny   We'd better go then, hadn't we?

Fourteen – King's Room (Tuesday 11)

Sean   *At the Royale King does not go for Ivor's sentimental fripperies.*

Tony *and* **King** *pick up the glasses from the restaurant table.*

Sean/King   Don't swig your drink, pillock, bring it with you.

Tony   Sorry.

The table is removed and **King***'s room set up.* **Tony** *starts to dance:* **King***'s manner causes him to stop.*

Sean/King   Have you enjoyed yourself?

Tony   Great meal, Mr King.

Sean/King You've had enough?

Tony Couldn't have eaten another thing.

Sean/King I don't know where you put it all.

Tony Hollow legs – that's what me old bid used to say.

Sean/King What happened to your old Mum?

Tony Jumped in front of a train on the way to work. Told one of her workmates she couldn't cope with me and Ape no more. Ape always was an handful. Still is. You know Ape, don't you?

Sean/King Seen him around, yes. Working, is he?

Tony He gets by.

Sean/King How about you?

Tony I manage.

Sean/King But could always do with a little bit more, I expect.

Tony Suppose so, yea.

Sean/King Look, I'm not going to beat about the bush, you heard most of it over dinner. I'm determined to clean up in this city. No room any more for the individuals and the amateurs – now's the age of the trans-national business. You wanna get on, you have to maximise your business potential – that's what I'm into. With my European partner, Gunter. I'm getting capital and muscle to get going from him, and I'm going to be unstoppable. I'm not messing.

Tony Never thought you was. What's he getting – your partner?

Sean/King Among other things – you!

Tony Me?

Sean/King You and a long line of other willing and able young men with a spirit of adventure.

Tony To Amsterdam?

Sean/King The very place.

Tony I haven't said I want to go.

Sean/King Chance of a lifetime.

Tony But . . . I don't know no one.

Sean/King You'll know Gunter. I'll introduce you.

Tony All me mates live here.

Sean/King   Tossers and wankers. Steve – a jumped up prick with pretensions. Your brother – half-brother – thick as pig shit. And Sean – fucking little nancy prancing about. They're done for once I get going. You're better off out of it.

Tony   I don't know.

Sean/King   Fabulous place, Amsterdam. Pleasure city. Bars, clubs, music. Nightlife the envy of the world. Makes Birmingham look like the fucking Teddy Bear's picnic. You'll love it – even extend your sell-by date by a couple of years. Who's the new kid staying with you?

Tony   Danny.

Sean/King   Nice little arse. Tell him I want to meet him.

Tony   Want him in the business?

Sean/King   Want him to replace you.

Tony   I won't tell him.

Sean/King   You'll do as you're fucking told.

Tony   I fucking won't man!!!

We could expect **King** *to be angry. When he speaks, his voice is ice-cold.*

Sean/King   Don't go losing your temper with me, Tony. Let's weigh up the situation shall we? Tony doesn't want to go to Amsterdam and I want him to. Tony doesn't want to let Danny come in to his place, and I want him to. Tony doesn't like to do as he's told and I like him to. So what does Tony like? Besides bright lights, bars, music, and tarts with twats like railway tunnels? He likes rainbows doesn't he? – Or at least, that what makes rainbows.

King *holds up a plastic bag of tablets.*

Lovely Rainbow Makers. My very good business associate, Gunter, has a readily available supply. So available, he'll share it with you at cost . . . an extra source of income for you. Very lucrative. Lovely, lovely Rainbow Makers.

Tony *sees the trap.* **King** *may or may not put on music.*

Blackies're good dancers, aren't they, Tony? D'you dance? Sorry?

Tony *makes a barely audible response.*

Sorry, could hardly hear you.

Tony   Yea.

Sean/King   Yea?

Tony   I'm a very good dancer.

Sean/King   I'm a very good dancer . . .

Tony   Mr King.

Sean/King   Let's have a look then, see how you'll fit into Amsterdam nightlife.

Tony *dances with encouragement from* **King** *– a Rainbow Maker.*

Sean/King   I think we should liven this up a bit, don't you? Open up.

Tony *dances a bit faster.* **King** *offers a pill,* **Tony** *opens his mouth.* **King** *pops in a Rainbow Maker. He kisses him very hard. He throws* **Tony** *down.*

Strip!

Fifteen – Dan Dare's (Tuesday 11)

Loud music. **Steve** *gives* **Danny** *a drink.*

Danny   What's this?

Steve   Diamond White.

Danny   What is it?

Steve   A sophisticated cider. You'll like it.

Danny   What you got?

Steve   Grolsch.

Danny   Why didn't you get me that too?

Steve   Because Grolsch is for big grown-up men and White for little tarts who ask too many questions . . . And who turn up late!!!

Danny   'S Ivor's fault.

Steve   I hope you charged him overtime.

Danny *shows him the watch.*

Did you nick this?

Danny   No I didn't!!

Steve   He never give it to you.

Danny   He did. It came from a client of his. Blue, innit?

Steve   D'you know what this is worth? You sure he give it to you?

Danny   I told you.

Steve   It's a fucking Rolex.

Danny   So?

Steve   So what you been doing for him? You been selling your arse?

Danny   What goes on between Ivor and me is private and confidential.

Steve   Listen to me. I been at this game a lot longer'n you and I know what punters want, what they can have, and what they'll make do with. But you got to keep your feet on the ground, otherwise you aren't safe.

Danny   I don't understand a word you're saying.

Steve   Look. (**Steve** *produces condoms from his pocket.*) If you're being fucked, are you using these?

Danny   Ivor doesn't go with nobody else.

Steve   Jesus Christ kid, you'll be using that line yourself at least once a week.

Danny   You're making a fuss about nothing.

Steve   Listen to me, Danny.

Steve *grabs hold of* **Danny**.

Danny   You're spilling my drink.

Steve   Listen!! For God's sake. Look around you. What d'you see?

Danny   Don't be stupid.

Steve   What d'you see?

Danny   Lot a guys. Having a party.

Steve   Nearly all of 'em gay. I'm probably the only bloke in here that's not gay. And while we're all dancing and laughing and drinking AIDS is in here too, dancing and drinking and laughing with us. How many people here? Give me a guess.

Danny   Four hundred. Five hundred? I dunno.

Steve   Say four hundred. Look at 'em carefully. In a couple of years, not one, not two, not ten, *dozens* of 'em's going to be dead. Know anyone who's died?

Danny   No.

Steve   I do. And I know kids your age walking around with a for-sure death sentence hanging over them. Imagine what that feels like.

Danny   You're frightening me.

Steve *lets* **Danny** *go*.

Steve   Really? You still got a lot to learn, Danny. Punters don't really care for you – you got to look out for yourself.

Danny   Ivor cares. He's asked me to go and live with him.

Steve   Are you going?

Danny   What d'you think?

Steve   Do you like him?

Danny   He's all right. He's rich.

Steve   He must like you to give you that watch. Let's see it again.

Steve *looks closely at the watch.*

Thought so. It's a fake.

Danny   Ivor wouldn't wear fakes.

Steve   Well, this is a fake. Definite.

Danny   Why?

Steve It's the numbers.

Danny What do you know?

Steve Honest.

Danny I'll ask Sean – he knows.

Steve Something very pasty about a geezer with a fake Rolex.

Steve *gives* **Danny** *a light, friendly smack on the cheeks with both hands. It signals 'You're green to fall for Ivor's little trick,' combined with 'I know what goes on around here – don't even begin to think you do.'* **Steve** *dances.* **Danny** *joins him.*

Sixteen – Sean's Flat (Tuesday 11)

Julie *has a top on, which is in the process of being made.* **Sean** *is pinning a sleeve in. They are both drinking.*

Sean Stand still. I can't pin this if you keep moving.

Julie I was looking at me watch.

Sean Put it up again and bend it round.

Julie He's late.

Sean You have been back a week.

Julie You're not supposed to keep a lady waiting.

Sean You're no lady –

Julie So he always keeps me waiting.

Sean He's probably busy.

Julie Still out clubbing you mean.

Sean How loose d'you want the cuff?

Julie Did they say if they was going clubbing?

Sean How loose d'you want this cuff?

Julie How about doing it so it does up?

Sean Naffaroony, darling.

Julie Have it your own way.

Sean I'm the one with taste! They said they might go for a quick couple. Danny's been with Ivor, he might have got held up.

Julie Has he found a Daddy already?

Sean You'll have to ask him.

Julie Fucking fast worker.

Sean *gives her a warning glance, so she changes the topic.*

What you going to do at the back?

Sean   Pleat it from the shoulders and double vents I thought – very butch. Take it in at the waist so you wear it with a belt – show your tits off.

Julie   You're a genius at this Sean.

Sean   Leave it out.

Julie   No, honest. D'you remember Damion went to Art College? He wasn't half as good as you. You could go.

Sean   Leave it out.

Julie   You could.

Sean   You're beginning to sound like Henry. He even said he'd get me a place in a Sixth Form College.

Julie   Oh yea? Promises, promises.

Sean   He could do it. He's on the Education Committee; he's got a lot of clout.

Julie   Then for fuck's sake take him up on it while you can.

Sean   Leave it out.

Julie   Is Danny gay?

Sean   Yes.

Julie   Is he after Steve?

Sean   Not that I'm aware of.

Julie   They spend a lot of time together.

Sean   So do we; don't mean I'm after your body.

Julie   You're a pouffe.

Sean   You're a tart!! You worried about Steve?

Julie   You must be joking!

Sean   So what you leading up to?

Julie   You, Sean. Look at you. Danny's a fast worker, I can see that much. Got Steve running around after him. Got you keeping house for him.

Sean   Let's get this off shall we? He's just a kid, Julie. Steve helps everyone. Treats us all like we're his fucking brothers – right pain sometimes!

Julie   But what about you?

Sean   I like having Danny here, so as far as I'm concerned, he can stay as long as he likes.

Julie   You said he's gay.

Sean   So what?

Julie   All boys together?

Sean   Perhaps.

Julie So what's Henry going to say when he finds out you're fucking a boy every night who still wears nappies.

Sean Julie! I'm your best friend. Don't –

Julie I'm only –

Sean Don't say any more. Don't let's fall out. Please.

Julie When's this going to be ready?

With a very loud 'Taraa' **Steve** *and* **Danny** *enter the flat.* **Danny** *picks a piece of the pattern and holds it against himself.*

Danny Oooh, I could just do with something made out of this. Dead sexy.

Sean Put it down.

Steve Take no notice – he's pissed.

Julie Had a glass of lager did she?

Danny No. Diamond Whites. They're very nice.

Sean God, she'll be wetting the bed tonight.

Steve (*to* **Julie**) Hi, Julie.

He goes to kiss her.

Julie You were supposed to be here an hour ago.

Steve Got held up.

Danny Music!! I want to dance.

Steve Whacko Jacko here was late – then we had trouble getting in.

Danny (*mimicking the camp voice of the door attendant*) 'Bent like all the rest of us round here!'

Sean What's he on about?

Steve Danny! – You're legless.

Danny Music! I want to dance. (*To* **Sean**.) Look at my watch.

Julie (*to* **Steve**) You take me for granted.

Steve I've been showing Danny the ropes.

Sean It's a very nice watch. Now sit down.

Danny I can't. The room goes round when I shut my eyes.

Sean You don't have to shut your eyes when you sit down.

Danny When I sit down they shut by themselves.

Julie He needs his nanny.

Sean It'll be tears before bedtime.

Danny Let's have some music, Seannie. I wanna dance.

Steve Danny, just shut up for a minute will you.

Sean Sit!!!

Danny *sits.*

Steve (*to* **Julie**)   Didn't do it on purpose. Honest.

Julie   Well, lucky for you, it took Sean a long time to try me birthday present. You're forgiven.

There is a short kiss.

Can you remember being like that at his age? You ought to try to make him sick before he goes to bed.

Ape *comes in.*

Ape   What gives?

Danny   Come and dance with me.

Ape   There's no music.

Steve   I'll put some on.

Sean   Don't put it on too loud – I'm getting complaints from the neighbours.

Danny   Come on.

Danny *makes* **Ape** *dance with him.*

Julie   Can we make it a threesome?

Danny   Yea! Where's the sounds?

Steve   Coming.

Steve *puts it too loud.*

Sean   Turn it down!!!

As soon as the music starts, **Danny** *stops dancing.*

Danny   D'you like my watch? It's a Rolex.

Ape   Wicked.

Julie   Lucky boy.

Danny   My punter give it me.

Steve   I told you, it's a fake.

Danny   Ivor wouldn't have fakes.

Steve   It's a fake.

Danny   It isn't.

Steve   Yes it is.

Danny   No it isn't.

Steve   Yes it is.

Danny   No it isn't.

Sean   Leave it out Steve. (*To* **Danny**.) He's winding you up.

Ape   Dance!!!!

Danny   Watch this. Come on Steve. Like in the club.

They begin part of some routine – there's an enthusiastic response from the two onlookers. They join in.

Your Daddy here this evening?

Sean   No. Yesterday, you drunken sod.

Danny   What's he like?

Sean   Very sophisticated. French looking.

Steve   He was born in Dudley!

Sean   Fuck off!

Danny   No, what's he *like*?

Sean   Oh. You name it he likes it. He's a fabulous lover. I can hardly move when he's been round. And very rich.

Danny   Ivor's going to keep me. He's rich.

Steve   He's a wanker.

Danny   He give me this Rolex.

Steve   Fake Rolex.

Tony *comes in.*

Tony   Fucking hell.

Sean   Come and join in.

Tony   What? – And look like a prat.

Julie   It's Dan's dance.

Sean *tries to bring* **Tony** *into the dance.* **Tony** *dances on his own.*

Tony   This is dancing man. This is how you dance.

Ape/Steve/Sean/Danny/Julie   Eat my shorts man.

Steve   Ape's got it.

Tony   No white trash can dance.

Steve   You ain't a black man.

Tony   Fuck you – !!

Danny   You're half and half.

Tony   Fancy yourself, don't you?

Danny   What you mean?

Tony   Look at you!

Danny   Look at me what?

Tony   Cock-sucking prick teaser.

Danny   How can I suck cocks and be a tease?

Tony   Suck mine.

Steve Leave it out, Tony.

Tony I want to see if he can do it.

Steve Leave it out.

Tony Wanna see a black man's dick, little boy?

Steve 'S enough.

Tony Get your fucking hands off me.

They begin to fight.

Steve Get off Danny's back, arsehole.

Tony Don't tell me what to do.

Steve I'll knock some fucking sense into you.

Tony Come on then!

Tony *produces a flick-knife.*

Julie Shit.

Tony Come and take me on then.

Ape Where d'you get that?

Tony Gotta be tooled up. A dude's only safe if he's well tooled up.

Ape You're crazy man.

Tony What if I am?

Sean Give it to me . . . We're all friends here . . . Give it here, Tone.

Sean *puts his hand out to take the knife.* **Tony** *is going to hand it over. Suddenly he lashes out.* **Sean**'s *hand is cut.*

Tony Get away.

Sean Fucking hell, you cut me. (*He shouts out in pain.*)

Tony Shouldn't've got in the way.

Ape Steady.

Julie You all right, Sean?

Tony (*to* **Danny**) Going to suck my dick now boy?

Steve Don't move Danny.

Ape Don't anybody move.

Tony Big Brother to the rescue.

A moment.

You should see your faces.

Tony *throws the knife down.*

Sean You cut my fucking hand.

Tony Let's have a look. Just a scratch. Accidents happen. Forgive me?

He kisses **Sean** *on the lips then pushes him away with a laugh.* **Sean** *was expecting tenderness and is deeply hurt.*

There's no music. I wanna dance.

Music is put on very loudly. **Tony** *jumps on to a piece of furniture and strips off his jacket and shirt. He strips off his trousers. All this must be done sexily.*

Tony   Who wants to see what's in my pants?

Ape   We do.

As **Tony** *repeats his line, he gets more and more upset.*

Who wants to see what's in my pants?

Ape   We do.

Tony   Who wants to see what's in my pants?

Ape/Steve/Danny/Julie   We do.

Tony *reaches into his underpants and produces a small bundle of notes. He screws them apart and throws them into the air. Money floats to the floor.*

End of first half

Seventeen – Sean's Flat (Tuesday 18)

There is the sound of mechanical laughter. Lights up. **Julie** *is eating cream cakes,* **Sean** *has a half-eaten one on a plate. The laughter turns out to be a set of chattering teeth.*[1]

Sean   They're gross.

Julie   Girls at work give 'em to me, for me birthday. Eat your cake.

Sean   Don't want it.

Julie   For fuck's sake Sean. You got to snap out of it. He'll come back when he's ready.

Ape (**Ape** *is lying on the bridge*)   *Julie's talking about Tony. After he'd scrunched up the money, he stripped off but there wasn't no fun in it. He was acting like a crazy man.*

Steve (*speaking from one corner*)   *He disappeared in the middle of the night and hasn't been seen anywhere since. No one we know knows where he is.*

Ape   *He's been gone a whole week.*

Julie   He's a survivor – he'll turn up.

Sean   I don't want him to turn up – I want to know where he is.

Julie   You're better off without him.

Sean   You keep on saying that.

Julie   It's the truth.

Sean   No it's not.

Julie   Why won't you see he sponges off you?

Sean   I'm lonely without him.

Julie   That's crap. You've got all of us.

Sean   Doesn't count.

Julie   You've got me!

Sean   You go in and out at the wrong places ducky.

Julie   That's better. How about Henry?

Sean   I really, really love him.

Julie   Henry?

Sean   Tony!! I really love him. I could help him; he just needs loving by somebody who really cares about him.

---

[1]The teeth were later changed to a clockwork 'crawling' toy. If this is substituted for teeth some minor alterations to subsequent lines need to be made.

Julie Lovey-dovey fucking crap. If you ever hear me going on about Steve like that, for God's sake put me out me misery.

Sean Worried about losing him though, aren't you?

Julie Steve likes doing it with women, Sean. Danny might be a poisonous little rat trying to get his teeth into Steve, but no way can he give Steve what Steve wants more than anything else in the world.

Sean Babies.

Julie I don't think so.

Sean You're a hard bitch, aren't you?

Julie When I want to be.

Sean Wish I could be a hard bitch.

Julie Throw out your spongers then.

Sean They need me.

Julie No. You need them: they give you something to do.

Sean God I hate you sometimes.

Julie You know what's wrong with you Sean?

Sean Julie! – Leave it out! I –

Julie You're going soft! You've stopped – wanting things!

Sean Whatever I want I get!

Julie How is things with Henry?

Sean He's still fucking fucking me, if that's what you want to know. At least he never turns up late.

Julie He loves you.

Sean No. He only likes me because I'm good for him. 'Who'd want to cuddle someone as old and fat as me?' he says. Well, he's right! – Who would? So he can fucking well pay for it. It's a purely financial arrangement.

Julie And Danny?

Steve *comes in with a bunch of flowers.*

Steve Happy Birthday.

Julie Where've you been? I've been waiting hours.

Steve I've got something else for you. I got Danny to wait while they wrapped it up.

Sean I wondered where he was.

Steve I took him shopping.

Julie Spending more bleeding money on him?

Steve Not much.

Julie Too fucking much whatever it was.

Steve   I'm just helping him out – that's all!

Julie   Danny's taking you –

Steve   Leave it out, will you.

Sean   Leave it out both of you.

Steve   I brought you a present, Julie – hurry up Danny!!

Danny *comes in carrying a large, gift-wrapped parcel. His appearance has changed dramatically. He is wearing a completely new outfit with new hairstyle. He looks like a young man, now, rather than a lost little boy.*

Danny   Coming. Hi. Happy Birthday Julie – it's from Steve. I got you a card look.

Julie   Thanks.

Sean   One beaudacious dude.

Danny   D'you like it?

Sean   It's very sexy, dear. I hope you're going to put up your prices.

Danny   Steve says he's fed up with the hassle of getting me in the clubs. Do I look eighteen now?

Steve *has opened the box, and taken from it a gigantic teddy bear.*

Steve   'Hello Mum'. D'you like it?

Sean   Fuck me sideways with the Rotunda.[1]

Julie   You'll have to think up a name for this one.

Steve   Can't you?

Julie   Sean's better.

Steve   I can change it if you don't like it. I think it's great.

Julie   Thanks. (*They kiss.*) Where we going tonight?

Steve   Where d'you want to go?

Julie   Spencer's?

Steve   I'll pick you up about ten.

Julie   No you bleeding won't pick me up about ten. We'll go now.

Steve   I got to work.

Julie   It's my birthday; I want you to take me out.

Steve   I got to earn enough so you can have a good time.

Julie   We'll use my money.

Steve   No.

---

[1] The Rotunda is a tall, circular office block tower: this phallic-looking building has formed an important part in Birmingham's sky-line. At the time of writing, there are now however, plans to demolish it. Sean is welcome to create his own expletive at this point . . . I am, after all, indebted to the cast for this one!

Sean Stop bickering you two.

Julie Keep out of it Sean. What's wrong with it?

Steve Nothing's wrong with it, but –

Julie Well?

Steve I got to treat you, it wouldn't be a treat otherwise.

Julie Bleeding treat spending an evening with you.

Sean She's right, Steve.

Steve Keep out of it Sean. I'll pick you up earlier, then – about nine.

Julie Not good enough. You spend more time with that little squirt than you do me! Gone on the turn have you?

Steve Don't be so fucking stupid.

Sean She's got a point Steve.

Julie⎫
Steve⎭ Keep out of it Sean.

Julie Oh! – Fucking go out if you have to.

Steve I'll be here at nine.

Julie Just don't start moaning if I'm pissed out me head.

Sean Come on, let's get us a gin. We'll leave the men to their work. (*To* **Steve**, *confidentially*.) Make sure you're here to pick us up.

The boys go.

Oh, fuck 'em Julie. I got something for you.

He collects his bits and pieces together eventually breaking into 'Happy Birthday, dear slaggie', goes out, comes back in and hands her the jacket, it is folded up. She takes it and holds it against herself.

Julie It's gorgeous.

Sean Happy Birthday.

Julie Thanks.

She kisses him.

Sean Yuk! Yuk! Yuk!

Julie I'm going to get drunk tonight.

Sean We don't need men to enjoy ourselves.

Julie Pity you're not straight.

Sean Wouldn't that spoil the fun?

Eighteen – The Streets (Tuesday 18)

Danny   I don't think Julie likes me. She'll stop you watching out for me.

Steve   You've got your shirt buttoned up too far.

Sean, *in Vicar wear, approaches* **Danny**. *He has an unlit cigarette in his hand.*

Sean/Vicar   Have you got a light?

Danny   Sorry. Don't smoke.

Sean/Vicar   Neither do I really.

Danny *wanders away*, **Steve** *approaches.*

Sean/Vicar   Hello Victor. Well, how much?

Steve   What for?

Sean/Vicar   All night?

Steve   Can't help you. Go round the corner. Say Victor sent you – Cardiff Dave. Short light brown hair.

Sean/Vicar   Does he take switch?

Steve   He takes anything. Obliging lad.

The **Vicar** *wanders away.*

What d'you turn him down for?

Danny   Why did you?

Sean   *Bad for business to be turning punters away.*
Normally the rule is seize every opportunity you can,
The offer could be the last. – Who knows? You may
Spend empty-handed hours standing in drizzle or sheltering from
            rain.

Ape/Ivor *has appeared on the bridge.*

Danny   Ivor!

Steve   *Some nights are like that. You're lucky if you earn 30p. Mind you, what I'd do for you for 30p you might as well do for yourself.*

Danny   Ivor!

Ape/Ivor   Danny.

Danny   We going to a restaurant?

Ape/Ivor   Sorry. Can't tonight.

Danny   But you promised!

Ape/Ivor   I said I'd try. It's not possible any more.

Danny   Why?

Steve   *Danny is learning one of Life's most important lessons.*

Ape/Ivor   Circumstances have changed.

Danny How?

Ape/Ivor You're not the boy I thought you were.

Danny You asked me to live with you.

Ape/Ivor It wouldn't work. I've changed my mind.

Danny You can't. You said you loved me.

Steve *Namely, that you can't rely on Human Nature: or, to put it another way –*

Ape/Ivor (*to* **Danny**, *giving him some money*) Take this. What d'you have to grow up for?

Danny What'd I do wrong?

Steve *– To put it another way, there's not a single fucker you can really trust.* You made a scene.

Danny Why doesn't he like me any more?

Steve Never make a scene on the street, not with the punters, not with the other renters. Never. It has the punters doing a ton to get away.

Danny He said he'd keep me. He said he loved me.

Steve Life's tough, innit?

Danny What I do wrong?

Steve You've spoilt his game.

Danny I really liked him.

Steve That's part of his game too.

Danny I'll sell his watch.

Steve I'll put you in touch with someone.

Danny You said it's a fake.

Steve Maybe it's real. You're better off without him. Look – you get picked up, you get chatted up, they tell you they love you, then they get bored with you and drop you back where they picked you up. Don't mix your business with your pleasure. Get on with the job and keep your eyes on the till. See you later . . . Ten o'clock.

Danny 'DD's'?

Steve 'The 'Hawk'. See if you can get in on your own.

Steve *goes off,* **Sean,** *wearing King wear, appears on the bridge.*

Sean/King Seen Tony, kid?

Danny No one's seen him for a week.

Sean/King Pity. He'll turn up. You're Danny aren't you?

Danny No, I'm Grant.

Sean/King You're Danny. Know who I am?

Danny Mr King.

Sean/King Tony'll be back. Wanna make some cash then?

Nineteen – King's Room (Tuesday 18)

During the following narrative, **Sean** *passes the King wear from his position on the bridge to* **Steve** *on the ground.* **Steve** *puts it on.*

Steve   *King takes Danny to a quiet little club he knows with no questions asked and buys him several sophisticated drinks.*

Sean   *He weans him from Sol, which, says King, is only for toe-rags, and buys him first Dos Equis and later, Urquell.*

Steve   *By the time they reach King's room, Danny is decidedly the worse for wear.*

Steve *is now playing* **King**.

Steve/King   You a bit pissed?

Danny   No.

Steve/King   That's bad, that is. Takes the edge off your technique. What sort of technique you got?

Danny   What sort you like?

Steve/King   (*he means the answer, not the technique*)   Good one.

Danny   Is that the bog?

Steve/King   I want to talk to you.

Danny   Can I have a piss first?

Steve/King   I'm setting up a new business. And I think you could be a great asset to me.

Danny *sits down.*

Danny   Oh yea?

Steve/King   How would you like a nice flat of your own, your own telly, a CD?

Danny   Me own bedroom?

Steve/King   Your own flat.

Danny   Nicam VCR?

Steve/King   If you liked.

Danny   What's the catch?

Steve/King   No catch: piece of piss. Just a few little . . . projects. It's all very simple. I'll explain.

Danny   Okay. But quick!

Steve/King   It's your one-boy outfits – and I speak from experience you know – they operate only from one day to the next, taking it as it comes. Dangerous position to be in, uncertain . . . like the City's great water features – sometimes gushing forth water high into the air, the next day, just a widdley little trickle. However, looking at it from the outside, I can see it's a simple thing to put right. You need a business plan, a strategy to smooth out the ups and downs. You follow me?

Danny   In a way.

Steve/King Take the economy now. In recession? – You're in trouble. Fluctuating interest rates? – You're in trouble. Punters having problems with the mortgage, the business, the car repayments? – You're in trouble – and how!, it never rains but it pours. You're in a free market – what d'you do? You slash prices – your income disappears like water dripping through your fingers. Now my way, you hit a muddy puddle, I act as your friendly bank manager – I sub you against your earning potential from a reservoir we have built up by rigorous cost centre analysis and you pay it back only on very favourable terms only when you're in full production again.

Danny Sounds okay.

Steve/King I have a genuine desire to participate in WC – wealth creation, to be a part of our City's economic regeneration backed up by my Dutch partner, Gunter. International Convention Centre now, all sorts from Europe and beyond. Strategically placed ads in selected publications to exploit advantageous networks without saturating the market . . . High level diplomats, legal eagles, politicians galore, businessmen away from their wives, policemen, members of Her Majesty's Armed forces, even visiting royalty. They do like to have someone nice to take out – 'Meet Daniel, my personal secretary.' You'll have to dress the part, of course, none of this tarty rubbish you've got on.

Danny Steve's just bought me these.

Steve/King Tosser had no taste when I was having him years ago. Then, after your client has seen the delights of International Birmingham in your charming company you can take him back to your residence and he can taste the delights of your charming body. In no time at all, that pissing little trickle of punters has swollen into a river . . . no, a flood . . . no, no, a deluge of wealthy clients. And they pay me well for getting a well behaved, well trained, well dressed boy, and I pay you very well for being that well behaved, well trained, well dressed boy. Sound good?

Danny Well . . .

Steve/King Something worry you?

Danny The punter –

Steve/King Client.

Danny The client pays you. We don't get paid direct?

Steve/King That's right. Wonderful isn't it?

Danny And you get a rake-off.

Steve/King A small agency fee. We have overheads.

Danny *rises.*

Steve/King Just one more thing.

Danny *remains standing, trying to take the pressure off his bladder.*

Steve/King Some clients, of course, like boys . . . younger. Younger than you.

Danny Course.

Steve/King   Now younger boys become less young. So I need a regular stream of fresh spring chicken on tap for my broody old cockerels . . . Or should I say cocks?

Danny   Cocks, Mr King.

Steve/King   Could you help in this department at all. I'd have thought with your background . . .

Danny   Er . . .

Steve/King   Good commission of course.

Danny   In 'The Conifers', the Social and Life Skills counsellor used to say 'Anything is possible given the will to do it.'

Steve/King   Useful things, social and life skills. I think we have agreement on all points don't we?

Danny   Oh, yes. Definitely.

Steve/King   Good. Just excuse me a moment while I pop to the bathroom. Not in a hurry for it are you?

Steve/King *goes into the bathroom.* **Danny**, *on his own can show his true discomfort.*

Steve/King   I'm getting a good little team together, Danny. Glad to have you as a member. You okay out there?

Danny   Fine thanks.

Steve/King   Good. Shan't be a couple of shakes. It's not anyone can start a business, Daniel. Oooh, I needed this piss, Daniel, what a relief! . . . Know what I mean? In business, first you got to have a dream, then you got to turn that dream into a vision, then you got to have a mission to succeed. I've got a mission statement, Daniel, to inspire my workforce. Can you guess what it is?

Danny   No.

Steve/King   Go on.

Danny   You tell me.

Steve/King   All right then. Boyz 'R' Us. Boyz with a 'z' of course. There. Bathroom's all yours.

Sean   *So Danny makes a dash for the bathroom, wondering if he can make it in time but the little boys' room is not quite vacated.*

Danny *has rushed off as* **King** *has walked in.* **King** *lies down on the floor, as* **Danny** *rushes back in. The acting space has become the bathroom.*

Steve/King   I've seen the seedy side you know. Now I just want to clean the whole act up.

Danny   Mr King, you're lying in the bath.

Steve/King   So I am.

Danny   You got no clothes on.

Steve/King   Glad you noticed.

Danny   Something I can do for you?

Steve/King   I thought you was dying for a piss.

Danny   Oh! Right. D'you want the bath plug in or out?

King   It's that sort of attention to detail keeps the punters coming back.

Danny *rushes up on to the bridge where* **Ape** *and* **Sean** *are drinking cans of lager. They hand* **Danny** *a can.* **Ape** *upends his can, and golden slash comes out and lands on* **King**.

Lovely, lovely, lovely.

Sean *upends his. Slash falls onto* **King**.

Lovely, lovely, lovely.

Danny *upends his. His slash, however, is short.*

Love – Hey!, remind me to tell you about performance indicators.

Twenty – The Streets (Tuesday 18)

It's raining. Cars can be heard passing by in the wet. **Steve** *is standing on a corner. He is looking out for lone men in cars. He does this very surreptitiously for some time.* **Sean** *in Punter wear appears on the bridge.*

Steve   Excuse me. Got the time?

Sean/Punt   Twenty-five past nine.

He walks on. Not a punter after all.

Steve (*he mimics him quietly to himself*)   Twenty-five past nine. Beep, beep, beep. On the third stroke it will be nine twenty-five precisely. Beep, beep, beep. On the third stroke it will be nine twenty-five –

Ape *is standing behind* **Steve**.

Ape   First sign of madness.

Steve   You should know.

Ape   I don't talk to meself.

Steve   But you're stark, raving bonkers.

Steve *laughs.* **Ape** *would normally laugh – he doesn't.*

Fucking night-and-a-half this is.

Ape   Nothing doing?

Steve   'Aven't seen no one, not all night.

Ape   Not even the vicar?

Steve   It's the rain.

Ape   There's going to be a crack-down. It's in the paper.

Steve   Bugger, shit, fart. Who's been stirring this time?

Ape   A chief superintendent porker. Danny got business, I saw him go off with King.

Steve   So? Tony's not here.

Ape   King got inside Tony. He got inside his head. He'll do the same to Danny. You watch. No getting your leg over then.

Steve *looks at* **Ape**. *Suddenly, without warning* **Steve** *lands a punch on* **Ape**. **Ape** *staggers back, it was so unexpected. The two boys look at each other in fury.* **Ape** *slowly turns his back, wrapping his arms round himself. He might sit down.*

Steve   You fucking deserved that, pillock.

Ape   Yea.

Steve   Pillock. You should learn to stay out of trouble.

Ape (*he turns and looks at* **Steve**)   Yea. Maybe I should.

Wait.

Steve   Pillock.

Ape   Pillock, yourself.

The last two lines have given them a breathing space.

Steve   Hurt me hand look.

Ape   Sorry. My fault.

Steve *watches a couple of cars go past.*

My Mum killed herself, d'you know that?

Steve   Yea, Tony says.

Ape   It was my fault. She said that in a letter she wrote. Before she jumped. – Tony read it me. They put us in a home together.

Steve   I know.

Ape   When I was nine, Tony got picked to live with a family, but they didn't want me, only him. I started peeing the bed. I couldn't stop it. They sent me to a trick cyclist – it made fuck all difference. The kids all knew. Them kids, fingers pointing at me, calling names. I hate being laughed at.

Steve   D'you hate our jokes?

Ape   Yea. I feel like that again.

Steve   Not going to start pissing the bed again? – Better warn Sean.

Ape *looks at* **Steve**. *It's not* **Steve**'s *nature to say 'sorry' but if it were, he would: he gives him a friendly punch instead.*

Where are all the bastards?

Ape   They're cleaning us up.

Steve   Fuck this for a game of soldiers – I'm getting soaked. Coming for a drink?

Ape *shakes his head.*

Meeting Danny later – you could come as chaperon.

Ape What's that?

Steve (*not laughing*) It don't matter. Ape . . . what's up?

Ape Tony. I been everywhere I know he goes, and he's not there and he hasn't been there. I asked everyone, nobody hasn't seen him.

Steve He's just chilling out somewhere.

Ape He always tells me where he goes.

Steve Well, he just hasn't this time.

Ape He *always* does. I need advance warning, he says, I'm a bit slow.

Steve He might've forgot.

Ape We got a friend who's got his savings. He hasn't taken those. We had his earnings Tuesday night so he didn't have no money.

Steve He's a survivor. He'll turn up.

Ape He might be dead.

Steve Now you're losing control.

Ape He could 'a topped hisself.

Steve That's silly Ape.

Ape Me Mum did.

Steve He's hiding.

Ape He might be in the sewers. He had a favourite film he saw. In the war. These people all hid from the Germans in the sewers. They connect up across England.

Steve Ape, you're not thinking of going down them?

Ape Got to.

Steve You mustn't. It's dangerous. You'll get lost. It's raining – you'll drown down there.

Ape It's okay – I got a torch.

Steve Ape, it's not okay. They're hundreds of miles long.

Ape You're not going to put me off.

Steve There're rats down there, big as cats and dogs.

Ape I'm not scared.

Steve Ape – he won't be down there.

Ape Where else could he be?

Steve Look, I'll make you a promise if you promise me you won't go into the sewers tonight.

Ape What?

Steve   I think Tony'll turn up in a day or two. But if he don't, I got a mate'll lend me his car on Sunday. If he hasn't turned up, I'll take you looking for him. If we don't find him then, we'll all put our heads together. Fair enough?

Ape   I dunno.

Steve   Have you tried the Cannon Hill?

Ape   No.

Steve   Pillock. That'd be a good start wouldn't it?

Twenty-One – King's Room (Tuesday 18)

Sean   *Mr King at salesmanship is more than simply able,*
Mr King recapitulates the offer on the table.

Steve *and* **Sean** *both as* **King** *speak from the floor to* **Danny** *who is on the bridge.* **Steve** *and* **Sean** *do not wear King wear for this short section. The end of one line overlaps with the beginning of the next.*

Steve/King   Think it over, won't you. It's a good one.

Sean/King   Luxury apartment, push-button everything, taxis whenever you want them . . .

Steve/King   Money coming in faster than you can spend it, a Swiss bank account . . .

Sean/King   Wicked clothes, nobbiest restaurants, full drinks bar . . .

Steve/King   Gold rings, motor cars, silver watches – gifts from grateful clients . . .

Danny   I'll talk to you tomorrow.

Steve/King   I'll even get you a mobile phone!

Danny   A mobile! – Murder! – That'd give 'The Conifer' dumbos something to talk about.

Danny *begins to descend from the bridge.*

Steve   *I turn up late for meeting Danny at 'The 'Hawk'. I want to see if his new mature look works. He's nervous, but plucky. Takes the plunge –*

Danny *jumps from the bridge.*

Twenty-Two – The Nighthawk (Tuesday 18)

There is loud disco music and lighting as Danny jumps from the ladder.

Steve   *Straight in. No problem. How about that?*

Danny *dances for a bit.* **Rupert** *approaches* **Danny**.

Ape/Rup   Hi there, cutie pants.

Danny   Boil your head.

Ape/Rup   No one to dance with?

Danny   BO.

Ape/Rup   I like BO.

Danny   Kinky.

Ape/Rup   Wanna dance with me?

Danny   I thought you was banned.

Ape/Rup   I'm their best customer. Dance?

Danny   Keep your hands to yourself then.

Ape/Rup   Not my hands you need worry about.

Danny   What you got all that leather on for?

Ape/Rup   It feels sexy – next to my skin.

Danny   Kinky! D'you think I'd look good in it?

Ape/Rup   Like you were made for it.

Danny   D'you think I got a good body? I do weight training.

Ape/Rup   It's a gorgeous body.

Danny   I dance good, don't I?

Ape/Rup   Yes.

Danny   You go in for all chains and ropes and whipping and that, don't you?

Ape/Rup   When you're bad, you have to be punished.

Danny   D'you think I'm bad?

Ape/Rup   I'm sure you could be.

Danny *laughs at this and does a flourish of some sort which requires a lot of wiggling of hips and bum.*
Steve *arrives.*

Oh, yes. That's very bad.

Steve   You. Fuck off!

Ape/Rup   What's up?

Steve   I said 'Fuck off.'

Danny   We was only dancing.

Ape/Rup   Just keeping him warm for you.

Steve   The day you keep him warm, I'll have your balls off.

Ape/Rup   Charming.

Danny   Don't make a scene.

Steve   Danny: you got to learn to steer clear of shit like Rupert. He's poison.

Ape/Rup   Speak for yourself dear.

Steve   Shut it.

Ape/Rup   Perhaps you should keep him on a lead.

Danny   A leather one!

Ape/Rup   Woof! Woof!

Steve   Still living with your mother, Rupert?

Ape/Rup   See you some other time, cutie.

Steve   Like fuck you will.

Ape/Rup (*as he goes*)   Woof! Woof! (*He turns and pants, tongue out.*)

Steve   Don't you do that again.

Danny   What?

Steve   Messing with an arse-hole like that.

Danny   We was only dancing, Steve. Keep your hair on.

Steve   You may think you learnt a lot in the last couple a weeks –

Danny   I have –

Steve   Yes, you have.

Danny   Yes, I have.

They are very, very angry. They have to wait while their anger subsides.

Danny   Steve. I do like you.

Steve   I like you too.

Steve *flicks some stray hair back off* **Danny**'*s face, or even back onto his face – it doesn't matter which.* **Danny**'*s arms gradually go round* **Steve**'*s waist. They dance close together.* **Julie** *and* **Sean** *arrive.*

Julie   Steve!

Steve   Julie!

Julie   You fucking bastard.

Steve   I was just –

Julie   You must think I'm stupid! – God! – I am stupid.

Steve   I don't know what –

Julie   I'm not stupid, Steve.

Sean   They was only –

Julie   You in on it too then Sean? Tell everyone, have you Steve? – Everyone except me!! (*She turns on* **Danny**.) You! – You're the worst bastard of all. Little bastard. Little bastard.

She's grabbed him and is shaking him.

Steve   Get off him!

Steve *tries to pull her off.*

Julie   Get off me. Let me go you fucking queer.

Steve   Calm down will you!

Sean   Shut up, Julie. You'll get us all thrown out!

Julie   Get off me!

Steve *has her one side,* **Sean** *has her the other. She calms down.*

Sean   Right. Let's sort this out.

Danny   Shall I get the drinks in?

Sean   You – shut up!

Julie (*fairly under her breath*)   Fucking little bastard.

Steve   I don't know what all the fuss is about.

Julie   Don't you?

Steve   I just forgot the time.

Sean   It's Julie's birthday, Steve.

Steve   I know that!

Julie   Funny way of showing it.

Steve   I was just coming to get you. You know me!

Julie   I do now.

Steve   I like your jacket.

Julie   Cut the crap!

Steve   I do – honest!

Danny   Yea, it is.

Julie (*to* **Danny**)   Piss off! (*To* **Steve**.) Steve – you ain't no fucking queer. You and me – we're all right. I dunno what that little shit's done to you –

Steve   He hasn't done anything.

Danny (*he plays an ace*)   He thinks I'm the best dancer!

Julie   I'm going.

Steve   Where?

Julie   Anywhere that little shit isn't. It's my birthday – I'm going to enjoy myself.

Sean   You can't just leave Julie.

Julie (*to* **Steve**)   I'll wait for you outside. (*To* **Sean**, *returning the jacket to him*.) I'd 'a' thought you'd 'a' let me know. You better take this back. (*To* **Steve**.) Two minutes – then I'm off!

She goes.

Danny   Don't worry Steve. Life's tough. She'll get over it.

Steve   I love Julie.

Danny (*now overplaying his hand*)   Julie's just an old slag.

Sean *slaps* **Danny** *hard.*

Steve   Talk some sense into him, Sean, for God's sake.

Danny (*he's almost screaming with rage*)   You hit me, I hate you!

He goes.

Steve   Where you going?

Danny   To find somebody who likes me.

Steve   Stay here.

Danny   I'm going to dance with Rupert and you can't stop me.

He's gone.

Steve   Well, I hope you're happy now Sean.

Sean   What d'you mean?

Steve   This mess. It's your fault.

Sean   No it isn't.

Steve   If you didn't keep winding Julie up . . .

Sean   I don't fucking wind her up. She gets wound up because you're such a bastard to her.

Steve   Just because I turn up a few minutes late?

Sean   Are you really this thick or are you just putting it on?

Steve   I'll fucking thump –

Sean   For a start, you didn't turn up, we came here for you. Second it wasn't a few minutes it was more than an hour. Third you always treat her like a piece of shit and fourth she really does love you. And what's more, prick-head, I entertain your girlfriend every night because you're too selfish to, I put up your waifs and strays for you because you don't like them living on the streets, I let you have parties in my flat. And last of all you lie to us all and Julie gives me her fucking birthday present back.

Steve   You're a right pain, Sean. Why don't you fuck off and leave me in peace.

Sean   No. Just for once, you do the fucking off. I'm staying where I am.

Steve   Mind you don't take root then. I'm going to look for Danny.

Twenty-Three – Sean's Flat (Tuesday 18)

Danny *and* **Steve** *are isolated in a small pool of light. It is private, intimate. They remove their jackets, lie down perhaps.*

Danny   You're very quiet.

Steve   I think I like you more than anyone I've ever met.

Danny   More than Julie?

Steve   Don't laugh at me.

Danny   I'm not.

Steve   I can't even think about no one else.

Danny   That's okay.

Steve   Is it?

Danny   (*he laughs at this discovery*)   The light's dancing in your eyes.

Steve In the club tonight . . .

Danny In the club tonight . . .

Steve In the club tonight, I wanted to cuddle you very tight.

Danny How tight?

Danny *links* **Steve***'s arm round himself.*

Steve Tighter.

Danny Do it then. Even tighter.

Steve You wouldn't be able to breathe.

They are very close together, arms around each other, breathing hard.

Danny Steve.

They kiss once, lightly. Then **Danny** *reaches up for* **Steve** *again, and they kiss for much longer. Then* **Steve** *kisses* **Danny***'s face, ears, neck as they caress each others' bodies.*

Danny Stop!

Steve What's up?

Danny Undress me. Quickly. Shoes. Socks. Shirt. Trousers. (**Steve** *runs his hands up* **Danny***'s body then brings them to rest inside the waistband of* **Danny***'s briefs.*) Take them off. (**Steve** *does so.*) This is me. Say hello.

Steve Hello you. (*Another kiss.*) Put the duvet and pillows on the floor.

Danny *brings in duvet, pillows and a sheet. He improvises a bed while* **Steve** *quickly undresses. They get into the bed and begin to make love for a moment.* **Steve** *is on top of* **Danny***, supporting his weight.*

Danny Stop.

Steve What is it now?

Danny In 'The Conifers' –

Steve Don't talk about that now.

Danny Yes. For a minute.

Steve *rolls off* **Danny***, and they lie on their sides.* **Danny** *is struggling to say something,* **Steve** *remains in just enough contact to encourage and support him.*

In 'The Conifers' there was this boy called Mike. We liked being together. We spent all our free time together and all the nights we could. We liked doing it, don't get me wrong, but we liked just lying together with each other too, and we liked going out together and we liked eating our dinner together. The other boys knew about us, but not a one of them never said nothing.

Then there was all the scandals in the other Centres. Everyone nervous. But Mike and me, we couldn't, couldn't stop being with each other. Every day, all day, all night, every night it was all we wanted. He's the only person I've ever loved.

Then one of Mike's room-mates grassed us up. They moved him out so fast I didn't know he was going.

Steve   Wankers.

Danny   Wankers made me stand by the front door and watch him go. Made me open the car door for him to get in. Made me shake his hand. Made me say goodbye. Said it would help me grow into a real man. But I whispered him a private message that nobody knew about. After that, they wouldn't allow me no male friends back to the house. I wasn't allowed to ever be alone with another boy. They said I was at risk.

What I whispered to Mike was –

Danny ⎱   'I won't ever fall in love with anyone else.'
Steve ⎰   'I love you.'

Steve   You're not on your own any more.

For the first time in the play, two people make love.

Twenty-Four – Sean's Flat (Sunday 23)

Sean *and* **Ape** *sail in on two loaded supermarket trolleys. They distribute stuff around because . . .* **Sean,** **Danny** *and* **Ape** *are surrounded by clothes and all sorts of other things.* **Sean** *has a pad on which he's noting things down.* **Ape** *is dressed in his usual tee-shirt and jacket, but has no shoes, socks or trousers on.* **Danny** *is dressed in underpants with a towel round him.*

Danny Forty-seven shirts.

Sean I've already done the shirts.

Ape You've got twenty-one tea-cloths, you've got six big towels and seven little ones.

Sean There's a big one missing.

Ape Here it is.

He takes the towel from around **Danny***'s waist.*

Danny Why you got this?

Sean It's wallpaper.

Danny You got twelve rolls of it.

Sean I was going to do the bedroom, but they ran out before I got enough.

Danny It might come in handy for Steve. He's going to decorate the flat when we move in.

Sean What's Julie going to do?

Danny Who cares? She's a slag.

Sean Hey! Remember what happened last time.

Ape Here's a tea-set.

Danny Five packs of felt-tips. Two boxes of pencils, nine rulers.

Ape How long's Steve been gone out now?

Sean Ape! – You only asked that half-an-hour ago.

Danny Eight watches, five digital and three with hands.

Ape Ten watches, I got two more here.

Danny Are they digital?

Sean No.

Ape Well, how long?

Sean Ape: Steve's now been gone for three-and-a-half hours. He's going all round Birmingham and you know him, he won't come back till it gets too dark or till he finds Tony.

Ape He promised.

Danny And he always keeps his promises. One bean bag.

He throws the bag to **Ape**.

Sean   Careful. That's my favourite pouffe.

There's a loud bashing on the door and ringing of the bell.

Danny   Who's that?

Sean *looks scared – hides under the duvet.* **Danny** *instinctively follows suit.* **Ape** *is left standing. He feels he should hide too – there is only room for his head. Banging again. Letter-box opening.*

Julie   Let me in Sean. I know you're in there. Let me in, you bastard.

Ape   It's Julie
Sean   Arse-holed by the sound of it.

I want to come in so I can throttle Danny-boy. You hear that, you fucking little turd. You fucking had it.

Danny   Oh, fuck!!

So what? Hurry up! – I'm dying for a piss. I'm going to have your balls off Danny. You hear me!

I can hear you in there. (*Bangs the door.*)

Ape   You'll have to go.
Sean   Out the back way. JUST A MINUTE JULIE, I HAVEN'T GOT ANYTHING ON.
Ape   Hang on, let me get me trousers on.
Danny   She'll see me on the balcony.
Ape   They all join up. You'll have to run along.
Sean   JUST COMING NOW. When you get round the corner, the next flat's empty. Break through that.
Danny   Suppose –
Sean: Go!

Sean *pushes* **Danny** *out.*

Sean   It's all right, Julie, for Christ's sake. I'm coming now.

He opens the door. **Julie** *rushes in.*

Julie   Where are they – the bastards?

Sean   They're out.

Julie   Where?

Ape   Steve's lent a car and's gone looking for Tony.

Julie   And the little turd?

Ape   He went round the corner –

Sean   To get some bread.

Julie   He was here. You let him go. You bastard. Bastard, bastard, bastard.

She has picked up a cushion and is beating **Sean** *with it.*

Sean   Fuck off!!

Ape Come and sit down.

He picks her up; she struggles.

Julie Put me down you fucking Ape.

Ape That's me.

He plants her onto the bean bag in the trolley.

Sean Blimey!

Julie I hate you!

Sean No you don't.

Julie Yes I do! I hate him and I specially hate you. And I hate Steve and most I hate Danny. They staying here?

Ape Yes.

Sean No.

Julie Yes or no?

Sean Yes and no.

Julie Which?

She looks threatening.

Sean Yes they are at the moment, but no, they won't be much longer.

Ape *tips* **Julie** *out of the trolley.*

Julie They moving in together somewhere?

Sean No.

Ape Yes.

Julie The fuckers! I'll kill 'em both. Got any knives? (*She starts rooting around inside a box of cutlery.*) Where's your carving knives?

She goes into the kitchen for knives – we hear the clattering of cutlery. **Sean** *and* **Ape** *are panicking that they may have knives in one of the trolleys – they are carrying out a rapid check.*

I'll wait till they come back. No fucking knives!!!! No, wait! – This is better. I'll bash their poxy brains in.

She returns, she has picked up a base-ball bat. She's taking practice swipes at the furniture.

Sean (*to* **Ape**) For God's sake get it off her.

They use the trolleys as shields.

Ape She's dangerous, man.

Julie (*to* **Ape**) Come near me and I'll smash your brain in too.

Ape (*to* **Sean**) She means it.

Sean You haven't got one.

Julie (*she shouts at the top of her voice*) Bastards!!!!

*She throws the bat away. Throws herself into a chair. Pulls out a half-bottle of drink and swigs at it. She holds the bottle in **Sean**'s direction.*

Want some pouffe?

Sean   Got me own, slag. (*Several bottles.*)

Julie   Fucking place looks like a fucking bomb's hit it.

Sean   I've been teaching Ape 'Hunt the Thimble'.

Julie   What you up to?

Sean   My collection.

Julie   What you doing?

Ape   We're counting it.

Sean   To see what it's worth.

Julie   Selling it?

Ape   Giving it away.

Julie   What you up to?

Ape   Aiden came round.

Sean   My probation officer.

Ape   Ex-probation officer.

Sean   Ape thumped him.

Julie   You fucking liar.

Ape   Did.

Sean   Wallop.

They act out highlights from the story.

Ape (Aiden)   'Take it easy, kid.'

Sean (Ape)   'I can take it easy. I can take it not easy. You're fucked mate.'

Julie   You're in trouble.

Ape   He was tonguing Sean.

Sean   I seduced him! He fancies me. (**Sean.**) 'You like me. That's why you came here. Kiss me.' (**Aiden.**) 'No.' (**Sean.**) 'Yes, I want it, you want it. Kiss me.'

Ape (Aiden)   'You are so beautiful.'

Ape *has grabbed* **Sean.** *They kiss as they perform.*

Sean (Sean)   'I feel so safe with you.'

Ape (Aiden)   'Such beautiful hair. Such a beautiful body. An angel, an angel.'

He grabs **Sean**'s *dick.*

Sean   Ow!! Don't overdo it.

They are heartily amused by their performances.

Julie   Eat my shorts man.

Sean   He'd seen my collection stupid. Said I'd go to prison.

Sean (Aiden)   'You've been in front of the bench twice for shop-lifting. Are you listening? I can't keep this quiet, I simply can't.'

Ape (Aiden)   'By the time this gets to court you could be eighteen.'

Sean (Aiden)   'You're a man, and no amount of prancing about like a girl'll change that. It's a custodial for sure.'

Ape   And you know what he (*ie* **Sean**) said? (**Sean.**) 'Fucking bollocks cunting tough!'

Sean   I did.

Ape   So then he seduced him.

Sean   And Ape saw and walloped him.

Ape   Wallop.

Sean (Ape)   'You're fucked mate.'

Ape (Ape)   'A piggy PO with his tongue half-way down a kid's throat and his hand inside the kid's pants.'

Sean (Aiden)   'Your story won't stick.'

Ape (Ape)   'But some of the mud will.'

Sean   Wallop.

Ape (Ape)   'You're fucked mate.'

Sean   Wicked.

Sean ⎫
Ape ⎬   Yo! Yo! Yo!

Sean   I'm not going to no fucking prison.

Ape   We know what they do to gays.

Their highly energetic performance has worked – **Julie** *has cheered up somewhat.*

Ape   Ouch!

Ape inspects his foot.

Sean   You look like shit, girl. You should go home. Even if it's only a couple of days.

Julie   I want to see Steve.

Sean   It won't do you no good. Steve's in love.

Ape   He is.

Julie   If I could see him, I could talk sense into him.

Sean   Don't Julie. It'd hurt you seeing them together.

Julie   I told meself I never wanted to see him as long as I lived.

Ape   Go home like Sean says.

Julie   I can't. The police're after me, too. I broke into the cake shop – past the dogs and everything. That night, when I left you in the club. I wrecked the place. Ripped up the serviettes, threw the doyleys around, splattered fruit tarts at the walls, put the plugs in the sinks and left the taps running. Covered the glass lift with spray cream. They know it's me, I know. I don't want them turning up and upsetting me Mum.

Sean   It was five days ago.

Ape   Porkers 'ant come yet, they 'ant coming.

Julie   I want Steve.

Sean   Go home. Take this with you. (*He gives her a bottle of something.*) Cheer yourself up.

Julie shakes with rage.

Julie   Oh yes. That's fucking right. Buy me off! Just like me fucking father when I fell for that stupid baby. Got to have it even if the school expels you. 'God will forgive you for misusing your body but not for wantonly abusing it.' Bought me off with the promise of a bedroom to meself! Huh! Only my Mum saw how ashamed I was. Upset her so, she stopped loving Jesus and started loving the bottle. I know all about being bought off. Shit-brain.

Sean   It's a present.

Julie   Buying me off.

Sean   To make you feel better.

Julie   Buying me off. All me life whenever I want something someone buys me off. Me kid's Dad paid me to keep his name out of it. Me sister went to college and wanted my room for homework, paid me to give it up. Everybody takes everything away from me. I want Steve. It'll be all right. – We'll work it out.

Sean   You're only hurting yourself Julie. Let him go.

Julie   I don't believe this. Even you're on fucking Danny's side. All the little bum boys stick together? You make me sick. You can take this and shove it right up your arse. Perhaps that'll solve your problem with Henry. Tell the bastard Steve to look for me in the canal.

She goes.

Ape   You'll have to go after her.

Sean   Threats. She's drunk.

Ape   No one believed my Mum. She did it. – What about the baby?

Sean   Christ Ape – that's all in Steve's head.

Ape *runs towards the door.* **Sean** *sees he has hurt his foot.*

Sean   You've hurt your foot.

Ape   I think I've trod on a piece of glass.

Sean   Sit down. I'll have a look at it. I got a medicine box here somewhere.

He hunts for it, finds it, starts to tend to **Ape**'s *foot. It takes some time.*

Ape   She going to be all right?

Sean   What a mess we get ourselves into. Her 'n' me'll both end up inside.

Ape You won't go to prison, Sean. I promise.

Sean I hope so Ape. I am scared.

Sean *ministers in silence for a bit.*

If this don't heal up properly, we'll have to get it seen to: it could turn poisonous.

Ape I think the Pakkies're right, you know. I think we go on being born over and over again. They say we can be born as a frog, or a bee, or a mouse or even a tree. D'you know that?

Sean It's reincarnation. We'll have to get rid of the gear.

Ape What they say is that we've all got this special bit in us that is really us, and that carries on. But that there's so much shit going on all the time, that we can't find that bit in us.

Sean How d'you know all this?

Ape Ali. (*Accent on the second syllable.*) He was rich, man. Took me away for a week. We went to Cornwall. To mellow out.

Sean You've never said.

Ape You've never asked. Have you ever noticed that whatever they say –

Sean Asians?

Ape Geezers – all geezers – except renters – they say all sorts at the beginning, but at the end, they only want our body, or our cock, or our gob to go down on 'em, or our tight little arse if it's like yours Scannie. Like your PO wanker.

Sean Right.

Ape Now the reason you can't trust none of the wankers is because they make so much shit because they can't find that special bit of themselves. Did you know that?

Sean Like your soul, I suppose. How you supposed to find it?

Ape Ali said only about six people a year find it.

Sean That's not many.

Ape Right. But, Ali said, they're very special. And they live all by themselves on the tops of mountains. But that's where he's got it wrong.

Sean Why's that?

Ape Because you've found it, Seannie – and you only live in a council block.

Sean Fuck me, Ape! (*An exclamation, not a request!*)

Ape What?

Sean You've just talked philosophy. You're wicked man!

Danny *comes running in.*

Danny Sean! Sean! Look what we've found!

Steve *comes in with* **Tony**.

Sean Tony!! Give me a hug!

He gives **Tony** *a hug.*

We've been so worried. Where've you been? No, don't tell me now, later will do. You look awful. Are you hungry?

Danny   He needs a bath.

Sean (*to* **Tony**)   You sit straight down. I'll run you one.

He runs into the bathroom.

Ape   Tone.

Tony   Ape.

Ape   Where you been?

Tony   Chilling out.

Steve   With the crusties man.

Danny   Smells like he's been with the winos.

Ape   Not Tony's style. He's been with his black brothers and sisters.

Steve   He's got friends in a squat in West Heath.

Danny   You should've let us know where you were. Sean's been murder.

Ape   Not now Danny.

Tony   Yea.

Steve   We've got to celebrate. We'll have a party.

Ape   Sean's had complaints about the noise.

Steve   Any empty flats?

Danny   Let's go on a picnic.

Steve   Piss off.

Danny   That's a celebration.

Ape   Where?

Danny   Cannon Hill.

Sean *bustles back in.*

Sean   There'll be no celebrating in Cannon Hill nor anywhere else until this guy's had a bath. (*He pushes* **Tony** *out.*) The water's running. Pooh! You stink. What the hell have you been doing?

Tony *is gone.*

Danny   We're going to Cannon Hill Park for a picnic.

Sean   Everyone goes there. It's a dump.

Danny I know! I know! There's some hills, just outside the City. D'you remember, Steve? When you was still at 'The Conifers'?

Steve We had an outing there! That's right.

Sean It must be the Lickeys.

Steve That's right. We all went, didn't we? Thirty kids in a coach.

Danny Packed lunch. – Corned beef and cheese-and-tomato sandwiches.

Sean I must make some. I've got three kilos of game pâté and two devilled turkeys.

Ape I'll get some tubes.

Steve Polly Parrot bought everyone ice-lollies.

Danny Mine dropped off its stick and got shoved down me pants.

Steve I remember how you shrieked!

Danny It was cold!

Steve A new kid bought you two to make up for it – you walked around with one in each hand.

Danny That was Mike.

Ape You got the whacky baccy? – I'm out.

Steve In the kitchen.

Danny I'll start the sandwiches.

Steve and **Sean** *are left on their own.*

Sean Did Danny tell you Julie's looking for you?

Steve He mentioned it.

Sean I think it's serious.

Steve This thing between Danny and me . . . Julie's history.

Sean You can't just dump her like that!

Steve She'll survive.

Sean She might kill herself because of you.

Steve It's nothing to do with me, fuck-brain!!

Sean She's my best friend, Steve.

Steve I didn't mean to shout. It's not your fault – you just don't understand. This, what I feel, I haven't ever felt like this before. Never. I liked Julie, Sean, honest, I don't want to hurt her, but, I can't . . . I . . . It's not what . . . You help me Sean. You got to talk to her for me.

She'll listen to you. You can explain. I don't want to see her. I'll end up hitting her if she bad mouths Danny again, I will.

Sean   I can't sort this out for you.

Steve   You sorted out your probation officer.

Sean   Ape 'n' me did it together.

Steve   Then sort out Julie together.

Sean   Aiden was a prat.

Steve   They're all prats.

Steve *starts the following list off. Others* **join in** *as indicated – they do not* **take over***. As they all speak, they open the bonnet of the floor-level car and unfold a green silk as large as the acting space: this covers everything – pillows, cushions, crumpled duvet etc, to form hillocks beneath it.*

+ Tony   POs, care workers,

+ Ape   attendance officers, ed-cyclists, care assistants, porkers,

+ Danny   social workers, teachers, bullies at school, solicitors, shop keepers, store detectives,

+ Sean   vicars, priests, beaks, doctors, royals and farty do-gooders.

Twenty-Five – The Lickeys (Sunday 23)

Sean   *We head in the general direction Steve remembers . . .*

Ape   *But as we get nearer, Danny remembers exactly the spot.*

Danny   Here. Here's definitely where it was. I sat down here and ate me packed lunch. Exactly here. (*He places his bag exactly on the spot.*)

Steve   This is it. I had a piss behind that tree.

Danny *and* **Steve** *take their shirts off.* **Sean** *undoes a button or two.* **Sean** *tends to* **Tony***.*

Sean   Here, take your shirt off.

Tony *doesn't resist. They have cans of lager.*

Steve   The sun here, makes you feel better, don't it?

Sean   Put some of this on you.

Danny   Leave it out, Sean. He don't need any.

Sean   Yes he does. And so do you, so don't laugh. Haven't you heard about the ozone layer, ignorant bastard?

Steve   What about it, prof?

Sean   You won't be laughing when you're dying of skin cancer.

Steve   Cheerful!!

Sean   Put it on then.

Tony *'s done.*

Danny.

Sean *does* **Danny**'s *back.*

Danny Want me to do yours?

Sean No thanks! Two minutes in the sun, me, and I look like an Irishman's knob.

Steve Not a pretty sight.

Sean *leaves* **Danny** *and* **Steve** *to look after each other, he goes and sits in the shade. They fall into silence, enjoying the sun. Drinking.*

Tony You staying like that, Ape?

Ape Take off me jacket.

Tony Never get a tan.

Ape Never catch up with you.

They relapse into silence once more.

Danny Ain't the sun hot?

Sean Einstein.

Steve Beautiful.

Sean Tony, don't stay in the sun too long.

Tony Fuck off.

Sean Please yourself.

Relapse into silence once more. **Steve** *scrunches up a can. Throws it at* **Tony**.

Tony Fuck off.

Tony *lobs it at* **Ape**.

Ape Fuck off.

Ape *puts it aside.* **Steve** *sits up, gives* **Danny** *a not long, not short, kiss.*

Steve I do love you.

He lies down again so that **Danny** *can hold him. This is the first* **Tony** *knows of* **Steve**'s *and* **Danny**'s *relationship.*

Tony (*to* **Ape**) What goes?

Ape True love.

Tony They'll learn.

Ape *throws the empty can at them.*

Steve Fuck off.

They relapse back into silence.

Sean There's not a lot to do, is there?

Ape *reaches out and puts on a radio cassette.*

Steve I need a piss.

Ape   Me too.

Steve   Come on, then. We'll go for a stroll. (*Another spliff comes out.*) I'll have a piss behind my tree again.

Sean   My God, but you're common. I'm going to look for a gents.

Steve   Sean: today is a holiday – you are forbidden to work.

Sean   If I want to piss, I'll piss. If I want to work, I'll work. If I want to do both, I'll do both.

Steve   That's what you think.

Sean   Kiss my arse, bitch!

Steve   Right.

Sean   Help.

Sean *runs off shouting 'Rape!' followed by* **Steve** *and* **Ape**. **Danny** *turns the radio cassette off.*

Danny   Where you been?

Danny *looks around. Finds a sandwich – starts eating it, perhaps has another at the ready.*

Tony   So much space here. (*It seems to worry him.*) Been to Monte Carlo, drove down the West Coast of America, saw the Barrier Reef, went surfing. Motored to the lakes in Scotland, looked down on them from the top of a mountain.

Danny   Where you going next then?

Tony   I been at FitzPatrick's: Car Graveyard. Hid myself among the dead and dying. Drove a thousand cars a thousand miles each. Felt their sorrow, felt them bleeding to death, shared their pain as paint flaked. They . . . wrapped me up . . . took me all the places I wanted to see till I'd seen them all. Now nothing. When I dream – nothing. When I shut my eyes just nothing.

Danny   D'you wanna know what happened to me? I met a man who shared his dream with me. He dreams of us set up in beautiful apartments, only posh clients and so much money you can't spend it all and have foreign bank accounts like the crims do and the company directors.

Tony   You been with King. I'll tell you about King. He's my punter. He doesn't go with no one else. (**Danny** *nearly speaks, but thinks better of it.*) He wants me to go to Amsterdam. That night when you and me had the fight . . . Before that, he took me out and we went to his room. Nothing wrong, nothing strange, done it hundreds of times. Quick blow, nothing to it. That night he says to me, 'We're in for a surprise: a bit of a change. A black man's got style' he says. 'He dresses in style,' he says. 'Let's see if he undresses in style,' he says. He has me take me clothes off – while I do a dance. 'No hurry' he says, 'I like to watch you dance.' 'Very nice,' he keeps saying, 'Very nice.' His dick's up at attention, but I ain't turned on. 'Not interested, you bad boy,' he says. Kneels down, goes to it. 'Just like the old days,' he says. On the bed, still at me. Pulls me head round, down on him too. We stop. He rolls me over. Hands through my hair, down my back, over my arse. 'What a beauty.' Finger feeling, pressing, probing. 'What a beauty.' D'you know what he's going to do now? I know what he's going to do now. No one has my arse, I'm not a pouffe. Roll off the bed. Just turn over, can't get at me then. Can't move. Cold fingers press again. Feel him climb on, weight across my legs. Kiss the back of my neck. 'Ready now boy?' 'Get off me!' 'I don't want you inside me.' No voice. Face in the pillow. Feel his hard prick up against me. I won't let it in. Press tight. No good. Greased up. 'Beautiful arse! Built like a cunt!' Backwards, forwards, backwards, forwards. Feel pillow on face. Crying. Why crying? Hand slips beneath my belly, grabs me, rock hard. 'Beautiful arse, beautiful prick. Black man likes being fucked.' No, no, this can't be. Nod my head, yes. Change position then, to get a better stroke. Fast breath on my neck. In he digs his teeth – comes inside me. I came too.

Sean *comes in. He stops and watches, listens.*

Am I hard now, Danny, telling you this?

Danny I don't know.

Tony Feel me.

Danny No.

Tony Feel me.

Danny Very hard.

Tony Fuck me!

Danny No.

Tony I'll pay you.

Danny No.

Tony Just another punter.

Danny Not a punter.

Tony Please. Fuck me.

Danny Not right.

Tony I'll pay you. Just a job then.

Danny Not a job.

Tony Now. Quick.

Danny No. Not right.

Tony Quick.

Ape *and* **Steve** *come running in.* **Ape** *has his hands together.* **Danny** *runs behind* **Steve** *for protection.*

Steve Look. Look here. Ape's caught a butterfly.

Danny What is it?

Ape A Red Admiral I think.

Danny Let's have a look. Oh yea. Look, its wings are still opening and closing.

Ape Yea.

Danny D'you think it's frightened?

Tony *smacks* **Ape**'s *hand, the butterfly escapes.*

Danny It's getting away.

Ape Catch it.

They try to catch it. **Tony** *looks round, sees* **Sean**. *Laughs.* **Sean** *runs out. It becomes dark. The acting space is lit by stars overhead.*

Twenty-Six – The Lickeys, Night (Sunday 23)

Steve *and* **Danny** *are lying down together,* **Danny**'s *head on* **Steve**'s *chest.* **Steve** *holds him.* **Tony** *and* **Ape** *sit away, back to back.* **Ape** *and* **Tony** *share a joint. The cassette is playing.*

Ape   We haven't seen Sean all evening. 'Ave you upset him?

Tony *doesn't answer – simply puts his hand out for the joint.*

Danny   I can feel your heart beating in my head. It's very loud.

Steve   It's a big heart.

Danny   D'you realise, we haven't seen anyone else up here?

Steve   Don't you like it?

Danny   I love it. I think if I was on my own I'd be scared, but with you, it's great.

Steve   Good.

Danny   Have you thought, there's probably hundreds of creepy things wandering about and we can't see them. They come out in the dark you know. Every time we move we probably kill hundreds.

Steve   Kill a few more then.

They roll over a few times, laughing.

I love you Danny.

Danny   And I love you, too.

Steve   That's the first time you've said that.

Danny   It must be the stars made me say it.

Steve   Does that mean you don't mean it?

Danny   Course I mean it.

Steve   You know like star signs, d'you think they mean anything?

Danny   Load of bollocks in my opinion.

Steve *laughs. The two of them kiss.* **Ape** *sees them.* **Ape** *creeps towards* **Steve** *and* **Danny**. **Ape** *upends the remains of a can of beer over them. Whoops of pleasure. Laughter from* **Ape**, **Steve**, **Danny**.

Steve   You tosser! You bastard!

Danny   I'm soaked.

Steve   I'll do you for this, Ape.

Ape *goes wildly into a chimpanzee impression – it's brilliant! Now we understand how he got his name.* **Danny** *jumps up and joins in.* **Steve** *joins them.* **Tony** *takes out a game rifle and fires at them: he throws grenades.* **Steve** *and* **Danny** *play feeding the chimp. When* **Ape** *comes over they jump on him, and sit on him. It's all great fun.*

Danny   Wait.

Danny *grabs a tube. Shakes it, sprays its contents over* **Ape.**

This'll learn you. (*He's finished with the spray.*) I want to do another one.

Steve   That's enough Danny.

Danny   I want to do it again.

Steve   That's enough.

Danny   Where's his jacket? (*He finds it.*)

Steve   Not his jacket.

Danny   Look at this Ape! (*He has* **Ape**'s *jacket on. He does 'thick' acting.*) I'm a bit slow. I'm a bit thick. I'm a bit like an Ape.

Ape *shouts out, throws* **Steve** *out the way.*

Steve   He's drunk Ape!!

Ape *grabs hold of* **Danny.** *Gets him down.*

Ape   Don't do that!

All hell breaks loose. **Ape** *has* **Danny** *by the throat and is clearly throttling him.* **Steve** *shouts to* **Ape** *to stop and to* **Tony** *to get* **Ape** *off.* **Steve** *struggles with* **Ape** *but is not nearly strong enough.* **Tony** *puts the cassette back on and starts dancing. He has taken up* **Danny**'s *bag and is throwing the contents around as he dances.* **Tony** *has to get* **Ape** *off* **Danny.** *He has his foot on his chest.*

Tony   Fucking shut up! Turn off that row, Steve.

Steve *turns off the cassette.* **Ape** *shuts up. A mobile phone in* **Danny**'s *bag starts to ring.* **Danny** *goes for the bag, but* **Tony** *is quicker. He answers the phone.*

HELLO . . . NO, MR KING, IT'S TONY. (*To* **Danny**.) It's for you.

Steve   Don't answer it.

Danny   I must.

Steve   Danny, please.

Danny   Don't worry. I know what I'm doing. I'm going to make loads for both of us. HELLO, MR KING . . . TOMORROW NIGHT? YEA, THAT'S FINE. (*To* Steve.) It's OKAY. I promise. HIS NAME'S ANDY . . . JUST LIKE YOU ASKED FOR . . . YEA, COURSE . . . HE'S ELEVEN OR TWELVE . . . HE WILL BE ALL RIGHT WON'T HE? . . .

Steve's *and* **Danny**'s *eyes meet.*

Steve   Don't get involved – he'll screw you up . . . get inside your head.

Tony   Empty you out!

Steve   You're coming to live with me: King will want to own you.

They hold the look for a long time. Then, slowly, purposefully, **Danny** *goes back to the call.*

Danny   COURSE I'M LISTENING . . . TOMORROW NIGHT, EIGHT O'CLOCK . . . I KNOW WHERE . . . YEA, GOODNIGHT, MR KING.

Twenty-Seven – Sean's Flat (Tuesday 25)

The green silk which was brought out for the Lickeys is put back into the car bonnet. Everything on it remains on the floor, and we are back in **Sean**'s *flat.* **Steve, Sean, Tony** *and* **Ape** *are completing the packing of* **Sean**'s *collection into boxes and bags. Everything will be piled into the two shopping trolleys.* **Sean** *is dressed only in a plain coloured towelling dressing gown.* **Ape** *is not wearing his jacket.* **Tony** *and* **Ape** *seem to follow each other around, never far apart from each other.*

Sean It's a lot of stuff.

Steve We'll make a couple of journeys.

Ape More'n that I should think.

Steve That's okay.

Sean Someone'll see us.

Tony We could get rid of some to me friends in West Heath – they're well connected.

Sean Aiden will have told the police by now. I know he will.

Steve Even if he has there's no proof once we get rid of this lot.

Ape What's in here?

Steve It's all Danny's clothes.

Steve takes them out.

Sean Can you shift these (*Some stuff.*) Steve? I'll sort those.

Steve No. It's all right. Let me.

Tony I'd burn 'em.

Steve You would!

Sean Don't fight. He isn't worth it. (**Steve** *looks at* **Sean.**) He isn't Steve.

Ape Can we get all the stuff by the door?

Steve I thought I loved Julie. I didn't know the half of it.

Ape Where's Julie?

Tony Good riddance to him I say. He took us all for a ride. Poisonous little rat.

Sean That's what Julie called him.

Tony Well, she was right then, wasn't she?

As **Steve** *speaks, he holds the bag, somehow Aberdeen is in his hand. Aberdeen has a kilt.*

Steve It don't matter what you say, it don't matter what you call him . . . I'm angry, yea, but it . . . but you can't . . . it's with him and with me. It was . . . When you . . . When I . . . Once, I heard about someone swallowed burning coal. I can feel them in me: in my guts.

Tony He's really screwed you up.

Steve He didn't mean it to end up this way.

Bag and bear end up on the floor.

Tony We were happy enough before he came along.

Ape   I want it like that again.

Steve   Sean, this is going to have to stop for your own sake. Look! – You've got nothing left.

This is true. The space is empty, except for **Danny**'s *bag, with Aberdeen lying on it, and elsewhere,* **Zebedee** *who lies forgotten.*

Sean   Sometimes I hardly notice I'm doing it. I find things I don't know nothing about in me carrier. Creosote I found last week. What would I do with creosote? I took it back and got a refund . Sometimes I take things I like and give them away. I like giving people presents. Sometimes it's too easy. Nothing doing then. Sometimes I do it to show I'm better than stuck-up shop assistants. Sometimes I choose to lift stuff that's really hard. That's the buzz. Waiting. Watching. Your heart pounds away. Sometimes I get a hard on. That's really good. Better than sex. I won't go to prison! You hear that all of you? They'd do horrible things to me in prison. I saw this gay on the telly: they made him put on cigarette ash eye-shadow and burnt crayon lip-stick even though it was in the dark. I won't go. I'll kill myself first. Huh! Zebedee and Aber-fucking-deen. (*He moves and picks up* **Zebedee**.) Zebedee was given to me the day I started school. Time he went in the bin. (*He throws* **Zebedee** *away*.) D'you remember what you wanted to do as a kid Ape?

Ape   Drive a dumper truck.

Sean   Tony?

Tony   Racing driver.

Sean   Steve?

Steve   It was silly. A magician.

Sean   I always wanted to build bridges, you know. Big wide bridges to carry motorways over other motorways. Huge curves of roads over more roads, over more roads like at Spaghetti. Railway bridges. Towering metal hammocks slung between high hill tops to lead trains over wide rivers hundreds of feet below and with gigantic rivets holding them together. Imagine working out how all those joins fit. Once, I went on holiday on a canal with a friend and his Mum and Dad and we crossed over a river on the Pontcysylite Aqueduct. And it was funny, you know, because we were all in the boat, and the boat was in the water, and the water was up in the clouds. Oh, God! – I'd like to have built a bridge like that. You could die then, couldn't you, and you'd know you'd done something.

Steve   You could do it.

Sean   No. Not now.

Ape *has crossed to the phone. He makes a call.*

Ape   HELLO . . . COULD I SPEAK TO THE POLICE . . . IS THAT DIGBETH? . . . CAN YOU TELL ME SOMETHING? IF SOMEONE'S DONE A CRIME BUT THEY REPORT SOMEONE WHO'S DOING A MUCH, MUCH MORE SERIOUS ONE, CAN YOU LET THE PERSON OFF THE FIRST ONE? . . . WHAT? . . . OH YEA, MY NAME'S SEAN, SEAN O'HALLORAN . . . THERE'S THIS MAN CALLED MR KING, SEE . . .

Tony *grabs the phone from him and puts it down.*

Tony   You twat! You fucking twat, Ape!!

Ape I'll get him off.

Tony You've screwed up, dick-head. Porkers know King. They're hand in glove. Porkers are on King's payroll. Porkers like King's little boys too.

Steve We don't live in the West Mids for nothing.

Epilogue – The Streets

The boys have moved to the back of the acting-space, they stand in the shadows. Julie is possibly there too. **Danny** *comes in wearing a fashionably smart suit and tie. He is speaking on a mobile phone.*

Danny   Hello, Daniel speaking, may I help you? . . . Oh, Mr King, it's only you . . . What? . . . One of the Westminster mob . . . Sir Richard Boyson . . . I saw him last night – 'E's all right but a bit of a poseur . . . Taking me to a caviar reception Thursday . . . Andy? He won't do what? – The little bastard. I'll sort him out, don't worry. I got a couple more lined up – totally reliable I can assure you . . . I've just come from 'The Conifers', I thought I'd try 'The Oaks' next, I've got some contacts there and after that 'The Silver Birches' . . . Piece of piss, Mr King. Queuing up . . . I've had an idea, by the way, could be good for business . . . See, what I'm thinking is we're paying 'em too much. What they do for twenty, they'll do it for fifteen, what they'll do for thirty, they'll do for twenty. Top ought to be fifty – absolute toppers . . . See – anything we ask 'em to do's a piece of piss: the kids I'm talking to are desperate for money.

He has taken a Rainbow Maker from a special box he carries. He pops it into his mouth.

End

Playing by the Rules

'Why choose to write about male prostitution?' people ask me. – Not a straightforward question to answer: in the first place I don't think there was an actual moment of *choice*, in the second, it's not a play about male prostitution. I remember a chance meeting with Sergeant Keith Donovan of the West Midlands Police who was researching his report *Hidden From View* and Terry Beavington of *Triangles* who at that time was working as a social worker. They talked at length about the 'rent scene' and all of a sudden there's this idea in your head shouting 'Me first! Me first!' No choice about it, you see.

The original production at Birmingham Rep was directed by Anthony Clark: I owe him an enormous debt of gratitude – he was a most supportive and helpful critic at every stage of the play's growth. During my initial discussions with him about the possibility of a play in this general area, the only thing I was certain about was that I wanted the story told from the boys' point of view. It seemed to me then (and I haven't changed my view since) that the boys' view of their lives is the interesting and complex one. If we watch documentaries or read reports in newspapers it is easy for us to cut ourselves off from the truth. – *Aren't the boys sad? Aren't their punters wicked? Why doesn't someone do something about it?*

I was quoted in one newspaper as saying that 'If we gave the boys our sympathy they'd tell us to push off.' (That was the polite version of what I really said!) But do the boys really make informed choices to become prostitutes? Are the punters in fact wicked? 'Who are the punters?' and 'Why do they use the boys?' I began to wonder . . . 'Who gets what out of whom?'

There is something else attractive about placing this story in the acting space. Characters in a play have a habit of affecting us as if they are real people. They refuse to be cut and dried. – And quite right too – they are, after all, flesh and blood. Characters we believe we should dislike have an irritating habit of making us care about them – even if it's only for a short time. On the other hand, characters we should like end up making us cross. Warm flesh and blood characters set us difficult problems and simply won't make life easy for us. I think it makes them chuckle to see our discomfort.

This is why I say my play is not about male prostitution. It's about six people; it's about their fight for survival. I hope the characters demand much more of your attention than the job the boys do.

But as a playwright, I cannot blame my characters for the way the story turns out. I have a responsibility to tell the truth as I see it. Although my story is completely invented, I believe I can vouch for the truth of all individual elements in it – and if that sounds like a challenge, then I am happy to have issued it. The commitment of the entire *Playing by the Rules* team was impressive – they were as keen that we should present the truth as I was. We had two tasks – to tell the story, and to tell the truth. The story, the drama if you like, was our way to present the truth: at every stage we examined the balance between story and truth to the best of our ability.

The acting space is like a large mirror in which Society is reflected. Sometimes it's like a magnifying mirror which lets you see things that might otherwise have remained hidden, sometimes it's like one of those distorting mirrors that makes you laugh at yourself. I hope you will have many different reactions to *Playing by the Rules*, but whatever they are, it might be useful to remember that a mirror, is, after all, a mirror.

Rod Dungate
Birmingham, 1994

Rod Dungate believes the one decision he got right in life was to choose to live in Birmingham. He has a BA in Drama (Bristol University) and an MA in Playwriting Studies (Birmingham University). Earlier in life he trained as a teacher of Drama and Mathematics. Plays include *A Little Light Orienteering, Masque of New Hope, King James' Ear, First Past the Post,* an adaptation of Jonson's *Epicoene, WormsEye ReView* (co-author), and for radio, *Now You See Me.* He is at present working on a play set during the Interregnum for the Gateway Theatre, Chester. He is actively involved in developing cultural policy in Birmingham, and regular reviewer/contributor to *Plays and Players* and *Tribune.*

Plague of Innocence

Noël Greig

Plague of Innocence was first produced and performed by the Sheffield Crucible Theatre-in-Education Company in February 1988. The director of the play was Phil Clark. The acting company was: Fiona Bruce, Paul James, Dave Warburton, Michelle Warsama and Gill Waugh. Designed by Nettie Scriven, music by John Tamms. Company manager was Phil Green.

One

The sun is going down on England,
land of a dead Empire
where the sun never set.
But now the Empire's gone,
along with Scotland
Ireland, Wales,
out of the iron grip
of England.
And now a lonely little land says,
Goodbye
to the day.
To the year.
To the century.
Two thousand's creeping up,
out of the east,
out of the mists.
Twenty-first chance to get it right.

But not here yet,
not quite yet:
clock creeps towards midnight,
three seconds to go,
brief moments before the chimes
and the world holds its breath,
hearts beat in hope,
in fear, in love, in hate,
all feelings mingled
in a timeless world,
sliding us out of one age
into
another.

A drowning people.

Waiting for the new dawn.

Two

New Dawn,
capital N
capital D.
When did that first crop up in
the national vocabulary?
Seemed like New Dawn had been here
for ever.
National Party, New Dawn.

State Party, New Dawn.
Party of unification.
No opposition.

When did that happen?

But here it is in the corner of the room
on the PTV
(that's what used to be
the telly, the gogglebox,
the nightly choice of channels,
but not now,
now it's only the official view,
the Patriotic Teleview).

And here's the Primo of England
proclaiming:
New England,
reborn
in the New Dawn
of a new century.
Rejoice.

Well, who dared not?
Rejoicing was official.
And then the silence,
born of those last three seconds
beating on the brink of a new age.

Three

And someone says,
It's only a dream,
a sick joke.
But no one listens,
no one dares.
Hardly dare listen to your own thoughts
these days.
So they stay silent
as the clock ticks,
as the seconds slide into the future
and their eyes glaze over.

Soon sleep will come,
sliding in from the sea
to the sad chalky cliffs,
exhausted fields,
stunned cities,
stained arteries of concrete,

rising moorlands,
bleached bones of rock and crag.
Sleep,
to the people,
the chalky, exhausted, stunned and stained
people.

The dreaming people.

Four

In the heart of England,
a village:
deserted place of low stone walls,
doors off their hinges,
windows wide to the windy skies.
Name of Eyam,
place not far from Sheffield,
but could be a million miles from anywhere
these days.
These days of sealed-off cities,
soldiers in the streets
and the crumbling places,
deserted places in between the cities,
in the wilderness, the wildness.
Places no one goes to.
Places like Eyam.

But here in Eyam
this night at the end of the year,
four people,
crouched and dreaming,
clutched in the cold heart of England.

In the corner of a hill,
two men:
Gerald,
Winston.

In the corner of a stone wall:
Spider.

In a corner by a grave:
Sarah.

And someway off, a fifth,
gazing up at the stars,
her eyes splintered with the light of the night:
they stare but do not see,

and a trickle down her cheek
could be a tear
but it is not,
it is red.
This was Julie,
who went to Eyam that night,
never to reach it
but to lie on its edge
and dream forever.

But in their separate places
four living hearts spin out the last few seconds
of a dying year.

In dreams.

Five

Sarah. Spider. Winston. Gerald.
On a raft of dreaming,
floating them away from this night
back down the years that led them to
Eyam.

Past the daft dreams first,
the dreams like a merry-go-round,
like the dreams where Dad's dressed up
as Mickey Mouse, with a carving knife
and he's chasing the headmaster through a field
and I'm charging the whole school ten pence
per head
to come and get a look.
Or the dream where I'm stood in the high street,
everyone looking,
and I've only got my vest on.
Or the dreams you never tell,
where you're kissing your best friend
and you're liking it,
and you wake up
and you wish
you could tell.
Or the dreams where you're flying and free.
Or the dreams where you're frightened and falling.
Or the dreams of the dead and you're crying:
for Mam and Dad
down the end of the tunnel
and you can't reach them,
for Granddad

and you're on his shoulders,
but he's got blood coming out of his mouth.

Then the dreams of a big house,
everyone I ever knew in it,
but the top room's not built,
just a flight of stairs, up and up,
then a gap to the sky
and we're all climbing the stairs
to the gap
and I'm shouting
Don't
Don't
but no one listens,
feet up the dusty treads,
to the gap,
then the last tread,
feet at the brink,
Don't . . .

Falling . . .

Screaming . . .

Six

The Primo of England is not dreaming.
The Primo of England sits in a car,
sliding through the night with its
bright accompaniment of motorcycle
escort, its army-armoured vehicles,
and the silence dissected by the
helicoptered blades, the searchlights
seeking out the signs of life
that might betray a threat
to the Primo.

But there's no threat to this metal parade
from south to north:
the countryside's a wide tangle,
dead trees, dead towns,
places where no one's left
to dream.

And the Primo passes on
to Eyam,
the Primo has a purpose
in Eyam,

this night
at the end of the century.

Seven

Spider had heard the rumours.
Spider: sixteen, short and cropped,
kitted out in red and purple scraps.
Spider: name she'd chosen for herself.
Why not? Did everything else for herself,
out there in the ragged hills
with the other kids.

Kidgangs,
all out in the hills,
runaways from nowt to nowt,
'cept ruins and rich pickings
from the dead dumps:
rusty cans full of goodstuff,
bottles of hardstuff.

She'd heard the rumours:

Primo men sniffing round this way . . .

What for?

Primo coming here maybe . . .

Why's that?

Dunno. But big build-up of Primo men
round Eyam . . .

Why Eyam?

Dunno. But big build up of gun-gang blokes, too.

Eight

Winston had heard the rumours.
Winston: late-twenties, bit of a beanpole,
sort of chap'd make you say,
Don't hang around on't street,
else dog'll take you for a lamp-post.

Winston told Gerald
earlier that night,
Heard what they said back there?
Primo's men round Eyam.

Gerald: fortyish, going to pot a bit,
type of chap'd say,
It's the beer,
I'll take up jogging,
be slim and sexy this time next year
(but he never did).

Gerald angry at Winston:
Eyam?
Then why the hell head there?
Demanding that they run
another way.

For they are on the run.
Two men,
thin uniforms
(not really uniforms,
uniforms are smart,
uniforms are dignified,
even a copper's uniform with its saggy serge bum,
that's a uniform,
not these)
thin cotton, dirty green,
number printed on the sleeve,
bright red patch above the heart,
three letters in black:
HIV.

Run towards Eyam?
Gerald wasn't having any of it.

Winston knows why,
remembers good advice from friends
back in the days before the Primo:
Remember, when the cops are out to get you,
the safest place to be
is right outside the cop-shop!
Sound of dogs in the valley.
And they run,
legging it across the moors,
tearing their flesh on the limestone bones.
To Eyam.

Nine

Sarah had heard the rumours.
Sarah: mid-forties, spare in body,
ebony-polished face,
eyes of rising anger

as she'd sat at home that day
waiting for the new age,
watching the Primo on the screen . . .

England has risen again
in this New Dawn we have been waiting for
tomorrow.
And the name of Eyam is on the Primo's lips,
Eyam, a place in the heart of the land.

(But why Eyam?
What could England do for Eyam?
What could England do for itself?
Once England had a world to organise;
now it had shrunk to a stained tablecloth,
a rat-run on the edge of Europe,
a bitter, shrivelled apple.)

The Primo knew:
We still have in Eyam
an example
of our great tradition
of self-sacrifice.
And on to the PTV
Insistently, Compulsorily,
The Story Of Eyam.

Sarah spat at the screen,
hoping they'd not invented a spit-detector.

Ten

Julie knew Eyam:
had been there many times,
in the times when people packed sandwiches
and cans of coke and picnicked in the
green and pleasant places.
She'd taken the Attercliffe district kids
in the beat-up old van from the club,
piled them in, then up and over the hills
to the little stone village with its
tourist knick-knacks, backpack walkers,
earnest teachers with their school parties,
all telling each other the old story,
the story of Eyam.

Julie with her maps and books,
pointing out the houses where . . .

How long ago Miss?

Back in the sixteen hundreds,
when they had the plague . . .

What sort of plague Miss?

Bubonic plague,
it came with fleas from rats,
it came to Eyam . . .

Curious children
standing on the graves
of the long-dead,
asking:
Will the plague be down there still?

Ring-a-ring-a-roses . . .

You've got it!

She's got it!

Will I get AIDS, Miss?

Julie, urgent:
It's not a plague this time . . .

It's what the Primo calls it . . .

(How can a teacher teach
the truth of the matter,
when the heart of the matter
is screened with lies?)

Eleven

Liar, said Sarah,
watching the spittle drip down the Primo's glass face.
Liar.

Twelve

But the Primo did not hear.
The Primo was talking of history,
of a village once
in the green places of Derbyshire,
when an old plague came
and the people started dying
and Mompesson spoke out.

Mompesson: man of the cloth, man of the church,
preacher from the pulpit
(back in the days when the pulpit,
like the PTV,
spoke to all the people).
Mompesson, speaking Sunday-sermon wisdom,
saying to the people of Eyam:
The plague has visited
and some have died here,
and more will do so.
We have all been touched by plague,
we are all potential carriers.

And panic spreads in Eyam . . .

Run from it,
Run from the plague . . .

But Mompesson says, No.
The right, the good, the godly way
is not to run, to spread the plague.
The right, the good, the godly way
is to stay,
to draw a line round Eyam.
To cut ourselves off,
to sacrifice ourselves
and do it willingly
for God, for England.

Thirteen

And they did
and they died,
and centuries later
the school parties,
and Julie with her mob of girls from the club,
saying:
AIDS is not like that . . .

Fourteen

The Primo never used the words
HIV and AIDS.
The word the Primo used was:
Plague,
and used the history of Eyam and its dead

to demonstrate
how this is the English spirit at its best,
let us learn from this,
let us follow their example,
let us see that all potential carriers remain
contained,
cut off.

And the great choir sang:
Good Mompesson, Man of God,
Said that the hand of death
Had touched us all,
So let us freely, willingly,
Make sacrifices for our liberty.

Fifteen

And so Sarah said,
Liar.
She knew.
She was a nurse.
Spat again, saying:
That's for me Mam, she came here all that time back,
shivering down the gangplank
to do your dirty work.
Sarah thought of the man on the poster
(man with a big cigar and the name of
Winston) saying:
Come to England,
in England there is liberty
and work.
Then Sarah laughs;
remembers her son,
how she'd called him the same.
Winston.
But that was before she'd known the real England.
Before England had shown its real face.

Face on the screen,
face with a scream beneath the bland remarks,
voice that barks beneath the softness,
voice that's forced all the bitternes of a
dead land
into the word
Plague.

This is England on the brink
of it's twenty-first chance to get it right.

Sixteen

> And on this night
> at the end of the year, the century,
> at the edge of Eyam,
> lay Julie, drifting into dreaming.
>
> While Spider holds her, talks to her,
> anything to hold the mind, stop the drift:
> Choclet . . . Gun-gangs . . .
>
> Gun-gangs. . . ?
>
> Blokes with guns,
> the ones against the Primo,
> they live out here like the kidgangs,
> they kill the Primo's men
> they make their battles.
> Big battle at Eyam tonight,
> I'll get some choclet,
> there's always choclet in their pockets
> when they're dead
> after a battle.
>
> Julie looks at a stub of a girl,
> tries to remember . . .
> a child . . .
> who cried . . .
>
> Spider never cries.
>
> But once . . .
> nine years back . . .
> not called Spider then . . .
>
> Always called Spider.
>
> Crying . . .
>
> Never.
>
> For Cath . . . and Margaret . . .

Seventeen

> Sarah had helped with the birth
> (Best midwife in Yorkshire,
> some women had told her)
> and some years later,
> Cath and Margaret at the door:
> You'll look out for her, eh?
> If anything should happen?

(Cath knew: she came from one of those places,
one of those other places
where people disappeared
and now, here in England, things
could . . .
did . . .)
Well, we've heard the rumours.

Sarah (at that time still believing
in the best of England) saying, Yes, yes . . .
(Not thinking of a time when Cath, Margaret . . .
What. . . ?
Went. . . ?
Ran off. . . ?
Vanished. . . ?)

Where's my mumses?

No reply from Sarah when it happened.
Sarah as silent as the official response:
Whereabouts unknown.

Then sometime later, Spider too:
slipped off some night,
out into the dark, aged seven,
just a note: Gone to look for the mumses.
Spider off to the kidgangs
and the shattered countryside.

But still looking,
still hoping to find two women
whose faces were fading from memory.

But this was a time of forgetting.
Forgetting was safer.

Eighteen

Like Winston now,
trying to forget he'd ever danced all night at
the discotheque, ever played the classical
guitar, ever studied for exams.
Why bother now?
Just an HIV now,
a number on a tatty uniform,
running for his life.

But he did remember Sarah,
his Mam, with her cool black hands
when he'd scuffed himself at games

(Do they still have games at school?
Do they still have school?)

And then the day when Sarah's cool
was turned to heat and hurting:
Gay? So what's that, eh? You telling me
my son is. . . ? What you been doing?

Been doing nothing, Mam. What you think I've
been doing?

Sarah not saying.

Why not saying?

Just doesn't want her son to die.

Done nothing to die of, Mam.

Being . . .
She hated to use that word. It tasted like
vinegar in her mouth . . .
Being . . .
Gay.

That's not a death sentence, Mam.

Well . . . what you do.

Do what? Say it!

Another word she was afraid to say . . .

Sex? You mean sex?

It wasn't a banned word,
she knew the word was allowed.

Mam, I've never had sex. Not yet. But I will.

She wanted him to live.

Sex and death, Mam, they're not the same, they're different
words. Different things.

But all the same, her head, her heart
hurt,
thinking of the sex she didn't want
to think about.

And Mam, Gay is not just sex. Gay is what I am.
Not a fad, a fashion, a phase. It's in my bones, my
being. It's the whole thing I am, it's all the
parts of me.

Nineteen

Sarah looked an inward look,
like she was dreaming:
of the time perhaps when she'd be going to
Eyam
on a frosty, brightstar night coming up to a
new age.
Going to Eyam with a vaccine wrapped gently
in an old scarf
(Vaccine: substance used for innoculation
against disease).
Sarah going to save lives.
Lives the Primo said
could not be saved.

Primo on the PTV,
Personal Message to the nation:
There is no vaccine against HIV.
No vaccine means
quarantine.
And the great choir sang:
Mompesson.

And compulsory testing began.
All citizens to report to . . .
etcetera.
And identity cards were issued:
All citizens required to . . .
etcetera.

When was that?

Twenty

Back in the days of picnics, perhaps?
Picnics in Eyam with the Attercliffe kids
(little Spider amongst them, though not called
Spider then)
and the dancing on the graves
and the questions:
Will I, will I Miss?

Not from graves
or touching
or sneezing . . .

Atishoo, atishoo, we all fall down!

And then the first decree:
For the protection of Family Life,
For Real Families,
For Legitimate Families.
And the great choir sang:
A family is a man and a woman and their offspring,
bonded together by God and the State,
to promote any other
as proper
or acceptable
is now
not allowed.

And Spider saying at the club
(little seven-year-old,
who did not know God personally,
did not know what the State was):
But my family's my Mumses.

And Julie saying,
Yes, that's right, Cath and Margaret,
they're your family . . .
And then the letter:
Unfit person to be responsible for young people,
license to work withdrawn.

Why you got to leave the club, Miss?

How do you tell a seven-year-old that,
somewhere in London, someone had said,
You cannot speak of certain forms of
love; as far as we're concerned, certain forms of
love are invisible,
banned,
illegal,
illegitimate.

She knew it was a lie.
She'd told the truth.
She lost her job.

Twenty-One

Gerald suggested a course of action.
Gerald: good old pal from university,
Julie felt comfortable with him,
said once:
You're like a big old, cosy old sofa.
(Gerald wasn't sure he liked being called a
sofa

But he was a bit well-padded these days
It was the beer.)

We'll get married.

Julie wasn't out to get married.
(But then the interview for a new job:
Single woman? Tricky, that . . . Says here you lost
your last one through promoting . . .)

And so a new word floated down
from Whitehall,
entered the hearts and minds of
the English:
Promoter.
Definition:
To encourage the growth of,
development of . . .

Julie had not promoted anything, encouraged
anyone: she'd simply said
that if two people loved each other . . .

But love was becoming a dangerous word,
love was being replaced by new words:
Promoter.
Potential.
And single women, on their own
(or not on their own,
women together with each other,
Cath and Margaret . . .)
were left exposed.

Julie agreed with Gerald,
she'd best hide
in a marriage,
a pretend marriage.
A man,
a woman,
all pretence.
But a marriage smiled on
by the State.
Perhaps they'd be safer now.
For a while.

Twenty-Two

And all the while
the decrees,
more and more,

floating down from the sky
like snow, like sleet.

Potential.

Then that day, some years later,
Gerald at the door,
bags in hand:
I'm a Potential now.
I'm an HIV
(and it wasn't to do with sex,
Gerald never had sex,
it was to do with something he had
said).
Then the waiting van
to the train,
to the destination decided for him.

Twenty-Three

When and how did HIV
stop being something specific?

When it all began,
HIV was a virus, a medical term,
something you got,
something that could
(but not necessarily)
lead to AIDS.
HIV. Something transmitted
from body to body
(sexual intercourse in all its great variety),
from blood to blood
(hypodermics in all their uses and abuses),
from adult to child
(a new contamination of nature's gifts).

Once there were carriers of HIV.

Once there were particular groups at risk,
potential victims of HIV.

So how
and when
did
victim
become
villain?

How did
Potential carrier of HIV

become
Potential enemy.
Of the family.
Of the State.
Of the Primo?

Potential.
A word for anyone
who didn't fit.

NO!
Said the government
(that was when there was
a government,
just before there was
the Primo),
NO!
The tests are medically based.

But who had access to the results?

Not Sarah,
working now in the isolation wing
of a local hospital,
caring for young men not unlike Winston.

Not Winston,
working now in the isolated group
of local activists.

Not Gerald, not Julie,
isolated in a pretend
marriage.

Twenty-Four

But there it was:
Compulsory testing.
Results:
Classified information.

And the disappearances began.
First in the hospitals,
in the prisons,
workplace, school, homeplace.

And the popular phrases
seeped into the language like
a leaky sewer . . .

You're nothing but an HIV . . .
Stop talking like an HIV . . .
There's an HIV if ever there was . . .
Who's a naughty little HIV then . . .

Then:
Restricted movement for all potential carriers,
Compulsory testing for all potential carriers,
and a whole new category of person:
Potentials.

All Potentials to report to . . .
All Potentials to declare that . . .
All Potentials to prepare to . . .

Root them out.

Like the trees.

Twenty-Five

No trees now.
Eyam coming up in the night.
Gerald, breath rasping,
Winston, feet bleeding.

Gerald had known these parts in his
youth,
Going for a ramble,
Keeping the tracks open.
But no more trees, not now,
just chemicals leaked into the body of
England,
that was a plague, a real one.
(A by-product,
said the Ministry,
An unfortunate by-product of progress,
sad
but
inevitable.)

Twenty-Six

Nothing is inevitable,
Gerald had said one day in class . . .

Winston, eager pupil, eyes and ears attentive to
favourite teacher . . .

The only thing that is inevitable is
death,
and even then most deaths happen too
soon, too early, too
painfully . . .

Like how Sir?

Like through starvation, war, disease, like . . .

Like AIDS, Sir?

(Dangerous ground for Gerald now,
standing on a land-mine now,
one foot on the government demand for:
The teaching of diseases within curriculum-designed
lessons on sex,
the other foot on the government decree that:
No promotion of homosexuality is acceptable).
Yes.
Like AIDS.
And it can be avoided . . .

Snigger at the back,
Yeah, if you keep clear of the queers!

Gays!

Silence in the class.
Winston holding his breath.

Gerald had said it.
Not a very shocking word, but was it too
positive?
Had he overstepped the mark? Should he have said,
Yes, queers, perverts, sinners?
Was that the correct reply in the mind of
that someone,
that minister, official, adviser,
who'd woken up one day and suggested:
It is best not to be positive
about people who are bound
inevitably
to be
antibody
positive?

All right,
(Gerald sweating, were the rumours of microphones
in the classroom true?)
All right,

you want to know?
Well, Gay
and HIV are two separate things.
One is a medical condition of the body.
The other is something perfectly . . .
(Dare he?)

Rows of faces, waiting for him to say . . .

Natural.
Nothing to do with disease.

But they get it, Queers get it!

And so do others.

But how do *they* get it?

Well . . .
(Why should a teacher be frightened of telling
the truth, what sort of
education is that?)
Well . . .
Here's how you don't get it, you don't get it by
a handshake, a sneeze, a cough, a kiss . . .

Anger in the faces at the desks,
why was he afraid to say?

Anxious Winston, willing the truth out of him.

Anger in Gerald's voice, forcing the words
out,
Blood.
Semen.

How? How? How?
Demand to know,
How blood?
How spunk?

(But how to speak of acts between two
people, when certain of those
acts, certain of those
people were being wiped off the
map, forbidden?
Deep breath . . .)
Like when two men who
love
each
other . . .

Winston hearing those words for the first time
ever:
Two men who love each other.
Winston saying in his heart,
Thank you, thank you, thank you.

(Julie saying later,
Well done!

Gerald not sure, he wasn't cut out to be
a rebel, he'd rather be a cosy sofa and keep
his nose clean, head down.)

And, for example
(he said the next day, when the subject,
inevitably, came up again),
for example, in Africa it's generally found in
the heterosexual population,
not Gays, and evidence suggests it
came to us from
Africa.

Winston leaping to his feet, no thanks in
his eyes now, anger in his eyes now:
You about to say . . .

Say what, Winston?

Winston was used to the taunts,
the jeers,
(not the ones about queers, those were to come when
he'd come out)
the phrases his mother had borne with a shrug,
but not him:
Blame the Blacks, eh?
Something new to load on the Blacks,
you saying that? You saying let the Gays off the
hook and hang the Blacks on it?

No.

Then what?

I'm saying no one's to blame.
Except those who refuse to help.
Don't blame the starving of the world, blame
the hoarders of food.
Don't blame the dead of the wars, blame
the starters of the wars.
Don't blame the victims of disease, blame
the governments, the gutter press, the preachers of
hate, the teachers of hate, blame the ones who turn

victims
into villains.

There were microphones in the classroom.

There were tears in Winston's eyes.

Gerald was in trouble up to his neck.

Winston was in love with Gerald.

Twenty-Seven

Sarah knew now, accepted it now.
Knew something else too,
knew that those isolated in the
hospital wing, the ones with the
virus (HIV), the ones with immune
deficiency (AIDS), were not condemned
inevitably
to death.

A young man,
Person With AIDS, saying
I'm living with AIDS. Saying,
I watch football, I'm a United supporter,
I like mashed bananas,
I do crossword puzzles,
I read detective novels,
I sometimes write poetry and I think
I'm a potentially good writer.
I also have AIDS.
So what?
Well, so something, but
there's more to me than that.
I'm living with poetry and mashed bananas and
crossword puzzles and paperback thrillers.
And AIDS. I'm living with that, too,
that's all.

And Sarah knew. There were vaccines,
she'd heard.
Vaccines for the privileged.

Twenty-Eight

I know Mam, I know.
Winston, at the university,
publishing pamphlets, spreading hope and

knowledge,
(both things soon banned)
and always the message:
Never,
absolutely never,
accept second-class humanity.

Then the official form:
To Be Filled Out By Every Household,
Accurately, Truthfully
(New Dawn, Society of Total Truth)

Sarah and Winston, staring at the document,
at the demands:
Box C, Sexuality. All members of the household,
Hetero, Bi-, or Homo (either gender),
practising, abstinent, regular, infrequent, to
declare etcetera, all information withheld will be
regarded with the utmost
etcetera, etcetera . . .

And so filled in.
No choice
(New Dawn, Society of No Choice).

When it began, it crept up slowly, like a
snake in the grass, searching the shopping
precincts with its cold, glass eyes,
seeking its programmed information in
plastic identities:
to get into the match, the club, the cinema,
more and more devices, to watch, to
listen.
A smooth snake. Armed with the evidence of
filled-in forms.
Some said,
There's machines now that'll tell a lie in
a print-out, where a tiny hesitation on your part
tells them your very secrets.
(New Dawn, Society of No Secrets).

So Winston gone.

To the place where Gerald had gone.

To the Gladelands.

Twenty-Nine

Gladelands,
said the Primo,

Happy lands to the north
where the plague carriers can
live,
separate,
apart.

And the choir sang
of Mompesson,
of Eyam,
of sacrifice.

Thirty

It's the Gladelands!
Spider at Sarah's door one night
(one of her visits, irregular but constant
over the years; slipping in from the kidgang
countryside with news and choclet).
Spider describing the places that start near
Eyam . . .

(Place where Winston might be . . .)

Gun-gang blokes had told her:
Big stretch of land to the north,
Gladelands they call it,
keep clear of the watch-towers,
keep clear of Eyam,
that's the gate in.

So she'd gone. Stood at the edge of
Eyam, looked out over the desolation where
sheep once grazed. Stood one spring day,
with its watery-melon sun . . .

Don't come this way, kid
(man in a tattered uniform).

Why not?

Bad place to be, best go back . . .

Why?

Primo men with guns after me . . .

What for?

No time to tell, but give us some news, give us
some scraps, are things beginning to change, is there any
hope?

She didn't know, just wanted to know if two
women were . . .

He couldn't help, too many people in the Gladelands
now,
Still, if she'd some food, perhaps . . .
(desperate look of the starving,
hopeful look of the hunted).

Bar of choclet (very precious).

Still not able to help.
Then off, a near-skeleton, torn by thorn
and bramble.

Spider stands near the humming wire,
imagining somewhere behind there,
the two women (faces faded now) she'd called
her Mumses,
once upon a time.
Tells Sarah now,
They're there.

Winston, too. Here's food, in case . . .
And here, here's medicine, it's
precious, it's vaccine, it's for . . .
there's more, I know where to get it.

Spider takes it now, Sheffield to
Eyam,
weekly food and vaccine
to the men and women of the Gladelands
in return for scraps of information:
Two women, Cath and Margaret,
a man called Winston,
you seen them. . . ?

Thirty-One

Have you seen the vaccine?

Sarah, now put to work in the private wings,
places where the rich come to be . . .
(yes, a cure but not for the
poor, a cure for the Primo's friends,
who were not ill, officially,
of course).
So she filched it for the ones the Primo
did not need.

What vaccine?

But they knew, they all
knew, even when the Primo said,
There is no vaccine.
(New Dawn, Society of Official Ignorance.)

Don't let's die of it, Mam,
said Winston
the day before the men came,
when the van came.
Said,
It's only ignorance that kills.

And she remembered Marlene and
laughed. Marlene, all those years back at
school, the girl with the ruddy face and freckles,
propped up by a radiator
with a bag of sherbet, saying how
a baby can happen from a toilet seat.
Sarah had believed it for a year,
afraid to sit down when she went, just
hovering there, terrified. Nearly killed her,
that did.

Mother and son laugh, imagine the day
when the Primo will say,
A baby can happen from a toilet seat.

Only ignorance kills, Mam
not love.

Thirty-Two

You loved me?
Gerald, blushing.

Winston, laughing.
Yes. There's lots fall for their teachers . . .

But not . . .

What?

A crush . . .

I was fourteen, I knew I was
Gay . . .

How? When did it. . . ?

When I was seven or something.

Seven?

I reckon.

You were having sex at seven?

I said Gay, I never said
sex . . .

Yes, but . . .

When did you know you were straight?

Well, I . . .

Didn't think about it?

Well, no . . .

Didn't have to have sex to know it?

Well, no . . .

Well then damn you, don't doubt
me. And don't go thinking I've still got
the hots for you . . .

I didn't . . .

You're safe with me, I'm not out to tamper with
your precious masculinity.

Gerald had done his best at school, he'd tried
to tell the truth, he'd
lost his job . . .

Winston wasn't having that, he'd friends who'd
lost life,
lost dignity in death,
lost all right to be human, to
speak out, to
help each other.

In the midst of that great silence,
just the adverts on the telly, soft-focus,
full spread in the papers, advising all the
pretty boys and girls
(all white, all heterosexual)
to be safe.
Promiscuity promised to the chosen ones, if
they did it safely.
Then they'd not get what the queers
got.

Then nothing.
No advertising,
just the compulsory testing.
The Test.
Results classified.
No appeal.
And the Gladelands.

HIV: anyone who did anything to
displease the State, to
displease the Primo.

That's what happens,
when you deny some people their
desires;
do that and the next on
the list will be
you.

So here they were, at the edge of the
Gladelands, overlooking
Eyam.
Putting their arms around each other,
both teacher, both pupil.
Warding off the cold with the only warmth
to hand.
Warmth of the flesh.

An arrestable offence.

Like dreaming.

Thirty-Three

Tell us your dreams last night.

Julie had got the summons:
October to December,
surnames A to D will report for
dream-detection, State-search centre,
local area Chesterfield, 9 a.m.

Name and occupation?

(No occupation,
that's what she wished to say,
I have no work.
But the phrase 'No work' does not exist
in the New Dawn. New Dawn turns its eyes
and ears away from the jobless, they don't
exist).

Long-term trainee.

Tell us your dream last night. If
you lie, the screen will indicate the dream
was wrong.

(Danger. She wants to murder her
dream, last night's dream of desire, of

forbidden pleasures,
pictures of the body of
England, of her own
body, free
from the Primo,
free, to love and to say, free
to imagine
freedom.

Why are you hesitating?

Once, she'd read of a child trapped beneath a
car, and the mother running, running to the
vehicle, and with a scream, lifting it
bodily,
freeing the child,
saving the child . . .

Well?

So she screams inside herself
and lifts the dream she'd had,
throws it into the vacant space
at the back of her mind
and lies . . .

Well?

I dreamed . . .

Yes?

I dreamed of white lace . . .

And . . .

The Queen was sitting on the end of my bed . . .

Ah.

Eating cucumber sandwiches.

And she was in white lace?

She was in turquoise, with a
tiara. The white was my wedding-dress. She'd
worn it at her coronation. She was lending it to
me, for . . .

For. . . ?

My wedding.

So you dreamed of your wedding?

Yes . . . (why was she sweating?).

You're sweating.

It's hot in here.

When people lie, they sweat.

I'm not lying.

That was your dream?

Look at the screen . . . (relief, not a flicker, she'd
controlled her heart, she'd
lied successfully).

Good. It's good to dream of
the Queen. But not so good to sweat
so much. You've had the Test?

Yes.

A sure sign is night sweat. We'll put you in
for another Test . . .

But I . . .

No buts, unless you've something to be
afraid of?

No.

Goodbye Julie. And
remember . . .

Yes?

Don't ever try to cheat the machine.

Thirty-Four

Then Spider didn't come again.
Sarah alone again,
New Year's Eve, facing the
PTV,
spitting, thinking:
What can one woman do?
not too young,
not the approved shade of angel blonde.

Then, a story her mother told her.
Her mother: big and strong from the warm islands,
come as a muckgrubber for that other
Winston, the Winston with the fat
cigar, the one who'd given her son a
name, the one who'd stolen her mother's
life.

Her mother, telling a tale:
of a woman somewhere,
America perhaps, a place called Alabama,
yes,

saying, No, no she would not stand in a bus
when a white man wanted her seat.
That's all she did, just refused to stand.
And something happened, something like a
fire of hope and anger, stored up for ages in the
people's hearts,
sweeping the land, set loose by that one
woman,
refusing, sitting on a bus
in a place called Alabama.

In a place called Sheffield, Sarah
sits. Thinks,
Tonight I'll walk to Eyam, take the
vaccine myself.
It's only a small thing, but it's something I
can do.
And she wraps a batch of bottles in her mother's
old, worn scarf.
Goes out of her door.
Goes out of Sheffield.
Goes into history
To Eyam.

Thirty-Five

Winston and Gerald on the very edge
of Eyam now. Sound of motorbikes
down the valleys now, sight of the sweeping
searchlights, sweep of the 'copter blades
cutting the night. Now there's nowhere left
to run.

But maybe . . .

Yes?

There's something left to hope for . . .

What?

Believe in magic?

Oh yes, there'd been magic happening in
England for some time. Thought
magic'd away, dreams
magic'd away, words, phrases, all
magic'd away, people
magic'd away, magic'd into
things, into
Promoters, Potentials, HIV's.

So why not something magic now in
Eyam?
Something new in the world, some new thought
in the world.

Thirty-Six

Door goes,
windows shatter,
HIV arrest.

Julie screaming, You don't get HIV from
dreams . . .

Who says?

HIV comes from blood and cum . . .

Where did you get that crap, that crap's been banned.

Where are my Test results?

Classified. Well? There's the van.

Thirty-Seven

Sarah at Eyam now, crouched by a grave,
thinking of a woman in Alabama, in a
bus, saying,
No.
Down below, a village crawling with khaki.
She whispers,
No.

Primo not there to hear,
Primo in car,
Primo stealing up on Eyam
like a thief in the night.

Thirty-Eight

In a train, windows painted over, more
whispers:

Where they taking us?

Somewhere nice, they said . . .

Somewhere quiet . . .

Somewhere clean . . .

Julie's face twists, the word comes out like
spit . . .

That's right, those
Gladelands . . .

Government word for disaster area, nice clean
word for a dirty place for us to
die . . .

Ssh . . .

We're a bunch of trouble-makers, being
dumped in a radioactive . . .

Not so loud . . .

Why shutup now? No one gives a toss what Potentials do
or say . . .

You never know . . .

At least we can use words again.
Words.
We're being sent to a concentration camp . . .

Glass shattering, falling,
wheels grinding, falling,
guns in the night, falling,
screams . . . falling, falling, falling . . .

Thirty-Nine

Choclet!
Spider's rifling pockets, bodies spilled out
on a green bank,
wrecked train down a slope, blood and
wrecked limbs in the mud.
Choclet!
Another body, body with a face she . . .

What's your name?

Spider.

Not then. Then it was . . .

Gun-gang blokes, plunging down the bank out
of the pitchnight:
Best stay here, girlies, safest here with the
dead'uns . . .
Big battle in Eyam tonight, girlies, we'll make
meat puddings out've Primo's men tonight . . .

You stay put, girlies . . .
Then gone again.

What was it? My name?

But Julie had begun her drift, downwards,
inwards . . .

So Spider talked gun-gangs, choclet,
anything . . .

To the final dreaming . . .

And Spider
(forever Spider, now)
walks on,
to Eyam.

Forty

And so four people, in their separate places,
wait:
Winston,
Gerald,
Sarah,
Spider.

It is three seconds to midnight.

And down in the village streets, a car
slides in like a shark, a figure
alights. The Primo of England has arrived
in Eyam.

But no one in England knows,
they are asleep,
all dreaming.
Even the men in the uniforms, the
men with the guns, the
men with the cameras,
they too could be sleeping, each with the same
milky look of the dreamer.

Only the Primo, with the razor
smile, seems
waking
in this New Dawn.

For dawn arrives at
midnight,
suddenly,
leaping up like a devil from hell

out of Eyam,
out of the arc lamps,
into the sky,
a brighter dawn than ever seen,
an artificial dawn made for
the cameras, made for
the PTV tomorrow, made while
England sleeps.

And the Primo speaks
to the cameras,
Of Mompesson,
of past and present plague,
of quarantine,
of blood and soil and
sacrifice . . .

(Take care:
When they start to speak of
blood, of
soil, beware.
It's your blood they're after,
your body they plan to put
in the soil.)

And it seems as if England has but
one voice now, voice of
the Primo
promising:
Perfection.

And the microphones offer up the words
to the hills:
Perfection.

And in their sleeping dreams, four
people touch themselves, touch
their own bodies, touch
those things that lie behind
the Primo's words . . .

The clean body of the nation,
The uncorrupted body of the State,
The pure body,
The uncontaminated . . .

Body,
whispers Sarah,
My body they mocked for its colour.

Winston's body, not allowed
to show its love.

Spider's body, longing for the love of
two women who know her name.

Gerald's body, hunted down for the thoughts
in his head.

These are their dreams.

And down in the Eyam streets, the perfect lines
of men, guns at the ready, protecting
the Primo.

From what?
Who was going to contradict now?
Who was left to say, No?
When the only person saying
anything
is
the Primo.

The Primo will ferret out, from every
corner, from every heart
the plague, the whisper
of plague, the very thought
of plague, the plague that is anyone
who says,
No,
to the Primo.

But in the corner of the hill, the wall, the
grave,
four people dream, and in their dreams they
know,
they understand the barricade,
the final barricade they have against the words,
the guns.
The last,
the lonely,
the only
barricade:

The body.

The Primo is afraid of the body.

The Primo and all the Primos ever were or
will be, all terrified
of the body.

When there is nothing left to challenge with,
when they think we are defeated,
what do we do?
Do we go willingly into the gas chambers, the

charnels of the past, the Gladelands of
the future?
Do we go willingly, because our
bodies, our
minds, our
sex, our
desires
do not fit well with their
idea of
perfection?
Have we gone already, when we accept their
judgements?
When we mock each other
and ourselves
for lacking, for
imperfection?

(These are only dreams, remember, these
four asleep on the edge of Eyam lie
utterly defenceless . . .

But . . .

But . . .

History can change on a
But . . .

Dreams have changed history.)

And down in the village
the hair on a soldier's neck
bristles.
It passes down the line.
Danger, they're trained to sniff it out, to
snuff it out with a gun . . .

For over the brow of the hill,
out of the Gladelands, towards
Eyam,
a thousand, thousand bodies, walking
together,
naked,
holding each other,
advancing,
towards the guns.

And with them (perhaps) others,
rising from the ground, the anonymous dead
from a past plague, saying:
We believed Mompesson, believed we had to
sacrifice ourselves, and so

we stayed, contained,
cut off, cast out.

And Mompesson, saying:
But that was long ago, we did not
know, we were innocent in our
ignorance, we did not have your
knowledge.
But you, you
know, you have the
means and do not use them.

And all saying:
Your ignorance is not
innocent. Yours is the
ignorance of those
who use their science to
destroy the body
of the world
and refuse your science
to those who are in need of help
and healing.

And the Primo is silent.

Silent the soldiers.

As the naked and
the dead
advance
down a hill, saying:
There is no right or wrong,
good or bad,
in the human body.
Asking: Why do you fear it, contort it, distort it, beat it, rape
it, mock it, abuse it, condemn it, hide it, hide from it?
Saying:
There is no plague,
there never was,
there are seemingly incurable
afflictions
and when they come our way,
we cure them if we can,
and if we cannot, then we
care for the bodies of the
dying, but we do not
condemn. Once we condemn, then
we condemn ourselves,
to the Gladelands and the guns,
to the Primos and the preachers.

There are only two plagues:
The plague of Ignorance and
The plague of Innocence.
Choose!

And in the arcing light, the unthinking guns
raise themselves in all their phallic
wonder, ready to penetrate
flesh.

Except one.

And a soldier remembers,
what it was like, once,
to be touched
without fear,
to touch
without loathing
and he lowers his gun,
for a moment.

And a plague of innocence
descends
on England.

For a moment.

End.

Plague of Innocence

Although *Plague of Innocence* has, over the last six years, been performed by a wide range of theatre companies both here and abroad, it was first produced in the specific context of Theatre-in-Education. The Crucible Theatre in Sheffield commissioned me to write a play for secondary-school pupils in the city, which would embrace the subject of HIV/AIDS. The actors, director, designer and myself did not wish to create a piece of work that would be viewed as an 'AIDS play', knowing that this would re-inforce in our audiences the perception of HIV/AIDS (and people with HIV/AIDS) as 'nothing to do with us'. Of course, such matters as disease, loss, death and prejudice could not be shied away from, but we knew we wished to create a story-world which would also explore desires, dreams and imagination. I was interested too in the history of social attitudes towards disease, epidemic and plague, and the ways in which these are constructed and manipulated by authority. (Nor was this a purely academic interest, given that we were – this was 1987 – being beaten about the head with the 'Gay Plague' hysteria.) It became clear that I wanted to create a parallel world, one which would have its roots in our own past, present and future but which was as far away from a factual documentary or slice-of-life as possible. When the director said 'Why not set it in the last three seconds of the century?', I at once decided that the whole piece would be a dream: events that had not happened and never would, but which contained shadows and resonances of what was happening.

The final piece, as I re-read it now, certainly reminds me of the terrible times we lived through in the eighties: the jingoism of the Falklands, the real fear of nuclear annihilation, police battalions attacking mining communities, the catastrophe of AIDS. No wonder I set the story in a dystopian world. One reviewer (in a Gay publication) dismissed the play as the 'typical hysterical product of Left-wing paranoia', and I suppose I can only say that sometimes there might be a justified basis for feeling paranoid. Even so, when I handed my first draft in, I did wonder about certain aspects of it: for some reason or other I had come up with the notion that (within the story) certain people who adopted different ways of living were classed as 'promoters' and consequently deprived of their civil rights. Where that image came from, I don't know. Yet a few weeks later it was clear that someone else had already conceived of the idea: it was called Clause 28, and I then decided that my imagination was not quite as lurid as I had thought. As it turned out, the play provided exactly the sort of open-ended, non-naturalistic narrative which enabled its audiences to express their own fears, desires, uncertainties and dreams. I didn't envisage the play being produced beyond the context of its original commission. But – perhaps because of the 'myth-world' of the narrative – it reached beyond its setting of Sheffield and Eyam, beyond a dystopian England, and has held meaning for audiences all over the world.

Style of the Play

A common reaction to this sort of text is, 'But that's not a play'. Certainly it doesn't have the usual signposts which let us know how it is to be staged; no stage directions, no indication of who says what, etc. What I would say is, first of all, don't worry about that, just read it as a long, dramatic poem. After all, there is a strong tradition of presenting the great classical epics on the stage, and they pose the same (interesting) problems. On the most basic level, *Plague of Innocence* could be staged with one actor on a bare platform, assuming all the parts and all the narrative. To my mind, this is the most exciting style of performance, since it takes us to the very heart of the actor's skill: the act of transformation, without any of the usual props and disguises. It is the very essence of theatre, the invitation to inhabit two realities simultaneously, and I would say that *Plague of Innocence* has always worked most effectively on stage when it has allowed the actors to create the world of the play entirely with their own physical and vocal skills unencumbered by elaborate settings or costume.

Regarding how a company of actors decides 'who says what', here are some suggested ground rules. There are five major characters around whom the story is woven. It is clear from the text which lines of dialogue belong to whom (even though character names do not appear in the margins). Beyond this, one obvious and immediate choice would be for the actor playing the character to also take the lines of narrative which apply directly to that character. For example, the actor playing Sarah would then take the whole of the following speech:

And then the day when Sarah's cool
was turned to heat and hurting:
Gay? So what's that, eh? You telling me
my son is. . . ? What you been doing?

It would be a mistake to assume that the first part (actor as narrator) and the second part (actor as character) are necessarily delivered in totally distinct styles – 'neutral' and 'full character'. It becomes much more interesting when the actor uses the narrative lines to build towards the dialogue lines, rather like a diver on a diving-board. The actor 'runs along' the narrative line, building momentum, transforming herself from narrator to character through the line.

Conversely, if the first part of the speech were given to the actor playing the son, a very different interpretation would result: the actor would use the lines (as narrator) to give us an insight into the son's feelings on that day. Whatever choices are made (and there are many more) it is clear that narrative is never delivered in 'neutral', but is always fully invested with emotional and intellectual attitude.

Most productions of the play have utilised choric-speaking (in one, the Primo was not played by one actor, but spoken by all of them; this very cleverly emphasised the iconic aspect of the Primo, and did not invite the audience to identify him/her as a particular contemporary political figure). Also, because it does not demand 'character-specific' costumes, the actors can 'become' different characters solely through their physical and vocal skills, switching from one to the other in the space of a line.

Apart from a great personal liking for this style of theatre, in that it fully liberates the actor's skill of transformation, there is another reason why I have used it fairly frequently. For those of us who write for theatre and who do not have access to large-scale budgets, and generally work for the shrinking number of small companies who are hard-pressed to afford even four actors, it is a way of working on a large scale. If anything, the starving of theatre at its roots has contained the message that only the big companies can do big work. When I wrote *Plague of Innocence* for young people in Sheffield, I was determined that our small company should bring to their school hall a large-scale piece of live theatre, performed in a style that emphasised to the full its 'liveness'. Since then, that style has enabled it to be performed by sizes of cast that have varied enormously – large youth-theatre ensembles as well as smaller casts of professional actors.

Noël Greig
Sheffield, 1994

Noël Greig has worked in theatre since 1966, as an actor, director and writer. For many years he was closely associated with Gay Sweatshop and his plays for that company include: *The Dear Love of Comrades*, *Poppies* and (with Drew Griffiths) *As Time Goes By*. He also writes regularly for companies performing to children and young adults. His play about Sir Roger Casement, *Raising Roger*, was commissioned by the Royal National Theatre. He works regularly in Canada and Singapore.

Beautiful Thing

Jonathan Harvey

Characters

Jamie, *Nearly 16, a plain looking lad*
Leah, *Jamie's neighbour, 16. Attractive in a rough way*
Sandra, *Jamie's mother, 35*
Ste, *Another neighbour, also 16. Attractive in a scally way*
Tony, *Sandra's young man, 27. Middle class trying to rough up*

All the characters in the play except Tony have broad South East London accents. Also heard, but not seen, is Ste's dad Ronnie, who is Irish. This part can be doubled by the actor playing Tony. Tony speaks with an irritating middle-class, trying to have street-cred, accent.

The play is set in Thamesmead, south east London, May 1993.

Setting

The play is set on the landing walkway in front of three flats in a low-rise block in Thamesmead. This walkway is referred to in the script sometimes as balcony, landing or walkway. Ste's flat is on the left, facing us. Quite run-down. A clothes horse with dry washing hanging on it stands outside. Ste changes these clothes during Scene Four. There is a window with frosted glass in, beside the front door which is Ste's bathroom. This is also a feature of Scene One. Sandra's flat sits in the middle, a rose between two thorns. Her door has recently been painted and there is a hanging basket next to it. Either side, on the ground, are two tubs, also of flowers. On her bathroom window hangs a net curtain which rises in the middle. Leah's flat is to the right of Sandra's facing us. It should be pretty nondescript. A child's rusty tricycle sits outside.

Also onstage we can see Jamie's bedroom, represented by a single bed and a bedside light. This could be located to the side of the flats. A 'Hello' magazine lies on the floor, along with a small Body Shop bottle.

When actors enter they either enter from a flat or from the right side of the flats, along the walkway. This should give the impression that Ste's flat is at the end of a row.

Beautiful Thing was first performed at the Bush Theatre on 28 July 1993, with the following cast:

Jamie	Mark Letheren
Leah	Sophie Stanton
Sandra	Patricia Kerrigan
Ste	Johnny Lee Miller
Tony	Philip Glenister

Directed by Hettie Macdonald
Designed by Robin Don
Lighting by Johanna Town
Sound by Paul Bull

The play was revived and toured in 1994, ending with a run at the Donmar Warehouse, London. Sandra was played by Amelda Brown, Ste by Shaun Dingwall and Tony and Ronnie by Richard Bonneville. All other credits remain the same.
In October 1994, the play opened in the West End at the Duke of York's Theatre, London.

Act One

Scene One

'It's getting better' by Mama Cass blares out before the lights come up. As they do, the song fades. We find **Jamie** *and* **Leah** *sitting on their respective doorsteps in the sun.* **Jamie** *is wearing school uniform,* **Leah** *is not. Their front doors are open.* **Leah** *is smoking,* **Jamie** *has a can of coke. They are both looking out in front of them, up at the sky . . .*

Jamie   Richard of York gained battle in vain.

Leah *tuts.*

Jamie   Richard of York gained battle in vain.

Leah *tuts.*

Jamie   Oright oright!

Leah   If you don't shut up I'm gonna get a brick and smash it right in your face.

Sandra *comes to the doorway of her and Jamie's flat. She is holding a black bin bag full of rubbish, which she is taking out to the chute. She kicks* **Jamie** *out of the way and walks down the walkway and off.*

Jamie   What you thinkin?

Leah *tuts.*

Jamie   Eh?

Leah   Bout that brick.

Jamie   Nah go on.

Leah   Jamie!

Jamie (tuts)   Oright. (*Pause.*) Hot init?

Sandra *comes back empty handed. She doesn't stop, but goes straight back into her flat, passing them an Exocet glance as she does.*

Leah   Oright Sandra?

Sandra   Slag.

Jamie *shifts and she disappears inside.*

Leah   Who's Richard of York?

Jamie   Dunno. Gained battle in vain though dinn'e?

Leah   He would, bloody toff.

Sandra *comes out with another bin bag. This time she stops.*

Sandra You know what they'll do, don't you? They'll put you into care. They'll say, 'She's an unfit mother, bang 'im into one o'them 'omes. Coz I mean, she can't even get him to do his PE.' That's what they'll do.

Sandra *exits with the bag.*

Leah She's such a liar.

Jamie I know.

Leah You're sixteen for Gawd's sake.

Jamie Fifteen.

Leah (*tuts*) Shut up.

Sandra *enters again, from the chute, empty handed.*

Sandra I was a brilliant netball player when I was at school. 'Watch out for the girl in the plaits' the other schools used to say. I could run as fast as anything.

Leah Did you have plaits?!

Sandra I'm talkina my son!

Leah Did you?

Sandra Yes! (*Exits to flat.*)

Jamie She's taking it out on the cupboard. Throwin' away everything I was saving for my kids. Books, toys. I don't want kids.

Leah Kids are cunts.

Jamie You're not looking.

Leah *tuts, then returns her gaze to the sky.* **Sandra** *comes to the door, brushing her hair.*

Sandra (*to* **Jamie**) Anyone been calling you names?

Jamie Like what?

Sandra I dunno.

Jamie No.

Sandra Stumpy? Anyone called you that?

Jamie No.

Sandra I told you it'd stop.

Jamie I know.

Sandra I told you you'd grow. You never take the blindest bit o' notice to me.

Jamie I do.

Sandra Oh yeah?

Jamie Yeah!

Sandra Well how comes every Wednesday afternoon without fail you're sittin' there?!

Jamie I've told you.

Sandra I'm gonna ring Miss Ellis.

Sandra *goes back in.*

Jamie Is your Mum like this?

Leah I hate my Mum.

Pause.

Jamie What d'you think?

Leah When?

Jamie When you're doing this?

Leah I sing. Helps me concentrate.

Jamie I can't hear ya.

Leah In me head you stupid git.

Jamie What d'you sing? What sort o' songs?

Sandra *(off)* I'm just a girl who can't say no!! (**Sandra** *laughs, off.*)

Leah You heard of Mama Cass?

Jamie Mighta done.

Leah It's by her innit?

Jamie What's it called?

Leah 'It's Getting Better'.

Jamie Oh.

Leah You see. Mama Cass, helps me concentrate.

Jamie Fair enough. (*Pause.*) Sing it.

Leah What?

Jamie Go on.

Leah No.

Jamie I won't laugh.

Pause. **Leah** *looks up at the sky, then sings. She drops her South London accent and adopts the American tones of Mama Cass. She has quite a good voice.*

Leah *(sings)* I don't feel all turned on and starry eyed.
I just feel a sweet contentment deep inside.
Holding you at night
Just seems kind of natural and right.
And it's not hard to see
That it isn't haff of what it's going to be.

Jamie Haff?

Leah   Coz it's getting better
Growing stronger
Warm and wilder
Getting better every day
Better every day.

During the song **Sandra** *has come to the door. She watches* **Leah** *with a quizzical look.* **Leah** *stops.*

Sandra   Keep goin'. Might persuade him to go back to school.

Leah   Libs!

Sandra   It's not natural.

Jamie   What aint?

Sandra   For a girl of her age to be into Mama Cass.

Leah   She's got a really beautiful voice!

Sandra   Whassamatter with Madonna?

Leah   She's a slag!

Sandra   Hypocrite! (*Goes back in.*)

Jamie   Take no notice.

Leah   Fat chance.

Enter **Ste**, *in school uniform and carrying schoolbag.*

Jamie   Oright Ste?!

Leah   Ste! oright?

Ste   Yous two been bunkin' off together have you?

Leah   Not together, no.

Jamie   We've been watching rainbows.

Leah   No we haven't. We haven't. I didn't even know there was a rainbow in the sky. I hate rainbows.

Sandra *comes out with another bin bag.*

Sandra   Hello Ste.

Ste   Oright Mrs Gangel?

Sandra   Well it's nice to see someone can stay at school for the full day.

Ste   We done football today.

Sandra   It's the wrong season for football, innit?

Ste   Student teacher.

Sandra (*to* **Jamie**)   Is that the problem?

Jamie   No.

Leah   You get all dirty playing football don't you?

Ste   Yeah.

Jamie Muddy.

Sandra Nothing wrong with a bit o' mud.

Leah Did you win Ste?

Ste As always.

Leah Ah.

Sandra Hippopotamuses have baths in mud.

Jamie Takes one to know one.

Sandra (*cuffs him round the earhole*) You're just scared of a bit o' rain! That's all! Fifteen minutes o' bloody rain and you come running home! And look at it now! I'm bloody roastin'!

Jamie I hate games.

Leah Well, that's the difference between you and me Jamie, see, coz I love games.

Jamie Well, why don't you go and bloody try it?!

Sandra Yeah, put your money where your mouth is Madam!

Ste See I'm gonna use me sport when I'm older. Fancy workin' at the Sports Centre. So I gotta put the hours in, you know.

Sandra I know Ste, I know. And it's a bloody good centre actually, coz I go to Step Classes there. (*To* **Jamie**.) You don't!

Ste Swimming's my favourite sport.

Leah Yeah?

Ste Yeah.

Sandra (*to* **Jamie**) You can swim.

Leah I bet you look blindin' in your trunks Ste.

Sandra The pair o' you, you wanna get down them Step Classes, get a bit o' life into ya!

Leah You're not my Mother!

Sandra Thank God for that!

Sandra *exits with bin bag in direction of the chute.*

Ste Anyway, gotta get in.

Leah Stay out here Ste.

Ste I'm doin' the tea.

Leah Stick it on then come out here.

Ste Bubble and Squeak, Leah. You can't leave Bubble and Squeak. Gotta watch it, like a hawk.

Leah Don't that make you fart. Bubble and Squeak?

Jamie (*to* **Leah**) Only if you've got a fat arse.

Ste 'Ere Jamie, you wanna do football you know. It's all right. People'll talk to you then.

Leah What you having for afters Ste? (*Looks at* **Jamie**.) Spotted Dick?

Jamie (*to* **Ste**) I don't like it.

Ste You joined in in juniors.

Jamie Juniors is different.

Ste How is it?

Jamie I dunno it just is.

Leah People talked to you in juniors.

Jamie What would you know? You aint been a' school in six months!

Leah I'm psychic!

Jamie Psychotic!

Ste She's only tryina help.

Leah Tell him Ste!

Jamie Yeah well I don't need fuckin' 'elp.

Enter **Sandra**, *empty handed.*

Sandra Language Jamie! An' anyway Leah, you couldn't go back to school if you wanted.

Jamie Yeah, you're excluded.

Leah Aint my fault.

Sandra Whose fault is it then?

Leah The system. Me Mum said.

Ste Oh I'm goin' in.

Jamie See you Ste.

Ste Yeah. Later Jay.

Ste *lets himself into his flat.*

Sandra Face facts Leah, no bugger wants you.

Leah That bloke from the telly wants me.

Sandra Shut up.

Leah He does so there! He's doin' a documentary called 'Victims of the System'.

Sandra He's already made it Leah. Your mother told me. He said he couldn't have you on it (**Jamie** *joins in.*) coz you were such a cow.

Leah He was a pervert anyway.

Sandra (*to* **Jamie**) I want you inside. She's a bad influence.

Leah (*to* **Jamie**) She's a bad influence.

Sandra Jamie!

Jamie I'm staying out here!

Sandra Right. I'm ringing your teacher.

Jamie (*tuts*) Leave Miss Ellis alone, she must hate you.

Sandra Shift your arse.

Jamie *shifts and* **Sandra** *goes indoors.*

Jamie (*tuts*) I wish I was on home tuition.

Leah I wish I was at school.

Jamie You only wanna go coz Ste goes.

Leah I don't.

Jamie D'you fancy him?

Leah *tuts.*

Jamie Everyone fancies Ste.

Leah No they don't.

Jamie Even Señorita Pilar de Moreno.

Leah Do what?

Jamie The new Spanish teacher. She run her fingers through his hair today and said untold things in fuckin' Dego talk.

Leah I shoulda been Spanish.

Jamie You shoulda been somin'.

Leah When we used to watch that 'Digame' programme with Miss Seale, I thought, 'That's me. Siestas, mini-faldas, discotecas'.

They adopt the husky Spanish tones of the programmes they have seen.

Jamie Me llamo Marcus, y me gusta ir al cine.

Leah Me gusta los platanos, me gusta los discotecas, y la musica pop.

Jamie Tengo diezinueve años.

Leah Mama Cass done a song about a Spanish garden. 'Ere!

Jamie What?

Leah There's someone in Ste's bathroom.

Jamie Yeah?

Leah *gets the rusty old trike.*

Jamie What you doin'?

Leah You hold it steady while I get up.

Jamie Leah!

Leah He's just won a game of football, he's covered in mud. Said so hisself. Well what d'you do when you're covered in mud? Have a bath. Hold it. Steady Jay.

He holds the tricycle steady while she climbs up and attempts to peer through the window and into **Ste**'s *bathroom.*

Jamie Can you see anythin'?

Leah Yeah.

Ronnie (*off*) What the fuck?!

Leah Ooh sorry mate!

Laughing her head off, and trying to get down from the tricycle, she goes flying.

Ronnie (*off*) Y'dirty slot!

Leah It's his Dad! Takin' a dump!

Ronnie (*off*) Y'dirty slot!

Jamie Oh no!

Sandra *comes out, dressed for work. She is buttoning up a light jacket as she speaks.*

Sandra Miss Ellis has gone home. Secretary says I can speak to her in the morning. Now. There's a cheese salad in the fridge.

Jamie I aint hungry.

Sandra I can always throw it down the chute with the rest of your crap Jamie Gangel.

Jamie Salad's fine.

Sandra It's good for ya. There was a phone in on 'Richard and Judy' this mornin' about the bonus of a well planned diet.

Jamie I bet you rang in an' all. You can't keep off that bloody phone.

Leah (*to* **Sandra**) D'you fancy that Richard Madeley Sandra?

Sandra Oooh no!

Jamie She fancies the copper in 'Crimewatch'.

Sandra Don't you knock 'im!

Jamie She phones in saying she recognises the photofits off the incident desk, only she don't, she just does it coz she thinks she'll get through to the copper.

Jamie *and* **Leah** *laugh.*

Sandra Oh you can laugh. I've only done it the once, don't exaggerate. And if you must know Jamie, I only did it coz it looked like your Dad.

Leah What?

Sandra The bloke who done the post office in Plumstead. I'm convinced.

Leah *laughs even more,* **Jamie** *is subdued.*

Sandra And for your information Jamie love, I've gone off that copper.

Leah My Mum fancies Bill Beaumont off 'Question of Sport'.

Sandra He's cuddly.

Leah That's not the word I'd use.

Sandra Well I don't know as many foul words as you. Now. The salad with the beetroot's for Tony.

Jamie Tony?

Sandra He'll be round in a bit.

Jamie But you're goin' work.

Sandra He's comina see you.

Jamie Me?

Leah This your new man Sandra?

Sandra So you're not on your own.

Jamie I don't need a baby sitter.

Sandra I know.

Leah I wouldn't mind meetin' him as it goes.

Sandra Eh! Hands off!

Leah I'm not into sloppy seconds, anymore.

Sandra What about the blokes we see knocking at your door? Very sloppy. (*To* **Jamie**.) And I shall be checking your homework when I get in, so be warned.

Leah Oh and just when he was thinkin' of having a sex orgy.

Sandra My son's got taste love. See you Jay.

Jamie Yeah.

Sandra *exits. A toilet flushes in* **Ste**'s *flat.*

Leah (*sings*) Sing for your supper and you'll get breakfast
Dine with wine of choice,
If romance is in your voice.
I heard from a wise canary
Trillin' makes a fella willin'
So little swallow, swallow now.

Now is the time to sing for your luncheon and you'll get dinner
Dine with wine of your choice . . .
(*Spoken.*) Fancy liking that bloke off Crimewatch. He's ancient.

Jamie   She's ancient.

Leah   D'you reckon it was your Dad what done the Post Office in Plumstead?

Jamie   How should I know?

Leah   I hate old people.

Jamie   You like Mama Cass.

Leah   It's allowed if they're dead. Oh I dunno what to do.

Jamie   Watch your rainbow.

Leah   It's gone now. (*Pause.*) I dunno whether to go the park.

Jamie   Don't look at me.

Leah   I'll go in.

Jamie   You do that.

Leah   I will.

Jamie   Give us all a break.

Leah   You and your mother. Two peas in a fuckin' pod mate I'm tellin' ya.

Jamie   See you slagbag.

Leah *wallops him one.*

Leah   You asked for that!

Jamie   I know.

Leah *goes indoors.* **Jamie** *sits there. Presently Mama Cass' 'Better Every Day' comes blaring out of* **Leah** *'s flat.* **Jamie** *winces. Shortly* **Ste** *'s front door comes flying open and* **Ste** *pops his head out. A dog starts to bark somewhere.*

Ste   Me Dad's tryina get some kip!

Jamie   Knock her up Ste, go on. Go on Ste, knock her up.

Ste *goes to* **Leah** *'s front door and hammers it with his fist. It opens slowly and* **Leah** *appears, hairbrush in hand like a microphone, singing to the song.*

Ste   Turn it down Leah, me ole man's tryina get some kip in there.

Jamie   Go on Ste, tell 'er.

Leah *sings louder, raunchier, and waves two fingers in the air.*

Ste   Don't mess me about Leah.

Leah   That's my idol!

Ste   I couldn't give a shit who it is.

Leah   You could learn a lot from 'er!

Ste   Leah!

Leah *sings even louder.*

Ste   Leah, I'm warning you!

Leah   Do I look scared?

Ste   Turn it down or I'll fuckin' brain ya!

Leah   Go back to your Bubble an' Squeak!

Ste   Not until you do that!

Leah   Oh yeah? Gonna make me?

Jamie   Leah . . .

Leah   You can shut up an' all.

Jamie   You know what his Dad's like.

Ste (*to* **Jamie**)   Oh don't start.

Jamie   Who's startin'?

Leah   I like this bit.

Ste   Leah he'll kill you if he don't get his kip.

Leah   God it's only on volume six.

Jamie   You know what happened the last time.

Ste (*to* **Jamie**)   Shut up!

At this point **Tony** *enters. He carries a plastic bag.*

Leah   Your Dad might scare you Ste, but he don't scare me.

Ste   I'll fuckin' scare you in a minute.

Tony   Afternoon all!

Jamie (*tuts*)   Oright?

Ste (*nods*)   Afternoon.

Leah   Evening.

Tony   Okay Jamie?

Jamie   S'pose.

Ste   Leah!

Tony (*to* **Leah**, *recognising the music*)   Mamas and Papas?

Leah (*tuts*)   Mama Cass, you thick git.

Leah *swings round and goes back in. The door slams. The music gets turned down.* **Ste** *looks at* **Tony**.

Ste   I owe you one mate.

Jamie   Me Mum ain' in.

Tony   Yeah. Just bumped into her. In the parking lot.

Ste   You got wheels?

Tony   Four.

Ste   Let's have a look?

They look over the edge of the balcony.

Jamie   Which one is it?

Tony   Volkswagen Camper. Gravy brown. Left hand drive. Picked it up at an auction. Four hundred notes.

Ste (*not impressed*)   See you Jay.

Jamie   Mm.

Ste *makes his way back to his door.*

Tony (*to* **Jamie**)   Close your eyes.

Jamie   What?

Ste *stops on his step to watch.*

Tony   Close your eyes Jamie coz I got something.

Jamie *closing them reluctantly, tuts.*

Tony *gets a brand new football out of the plastic bag. He slips it into* **Jamie***'s hands. He opens his eyes.*

Jamie   Oh.

Ste   Say thank you.

Jamie   Oh, thanks Tony.

Ste   Thassa good one.

Ste *goes indoors.*

Tony   Your Mum told me straight. You know. Problems. Been there. Mm. Walking through the park, game going on, my heart, you know, races. Scared Jamie. Scared of the ball coming, you know, near me. Hey, we can fight this one together. Fancy a knockabout?

Jamie   Not really.

Tony   No, me neither. But some time, yeah?

Jamie   Yeah.

Tony (*looking at his watch*)   You watch 'Grange Hill'?

Jamie   No.

Tony   Oh. Great.

Jamie   You can.

Tony   Oh. What you gonna do?

Jamie (*sighs*)   Homework.

Tony Bit of a problem at the moment. New kid in the class. Think they're gonna follow a bullying storyline, you know? Don't quote me.

Jamie Don't worry, I won't.

Tony Great weather.

Jamie Blindin' weather.

Tony D'you mind if I go in? Only, I think, you know, something wrong with my retinas. Keep having to squint.

Jamie You wanna get a pair o'sunglasses.

Tony Shades, great.

Jamie *takes the football in.* **Tony** *follows him.*

Scene Two

Some sort of row is going on in **Ste**'s *flat. This is heard quite distantly throughout the scene.* **Tony** *sits on the step of* **Sandra**'s *flat later that night. It's still quite warm and he is topless. His shirt lies on the ground before him. He is smoking a joint. The door of the flat is ajar, and a faint murmur of a television can be heard.* **Jamie** *comes out holding a plate of salad.*

Jamie Aren't you gonna eat this.

Tony Sure. (**Jamie** *passes him the salad and he looks at it.*) Your mother, she's . . . she's amazing. She's, you know, something else. You joining me?

Jamie *comes out on the walkway.*

Jamie I done me maths homework.

Tony Yeah?

Jamie Pythagoras theorem. Wasn't Pythagoras a cunt?

Tony Yeah.

Jamie You're supposed to tell me off if I swear.

Tony Right.

Jamie I hate beetroot.

Tony How d'you spell 'offensive vegetable', right?

Jamie Where did you meet my Mum?

Tony Planet earth.

Jamie Where?

Tony   Oh, you know, out and about, here and there. What's a place? It's somewhere where, you know, shit happens.

Jamie   Yeah, but where?

Tony   Gateways.

Jamie   You aint the first. She's not a slag or nothin', but you aint the first.

Tony   I'm the fourth, right? (*Chuckles, annoyed at* **Jamie***'s choice of word.*) Slag?!

Jamie   There was Colin the barber, Alfie the long distance driver, and Richard the barman.

Tony   I just, you know, took a shine to her. She's got . . . charisma.

Jamie   She turn you on?

Tony   (*gives a neurotic, what-sort-of-a-question-is-this? look to his left, then up at* **Jamie**) Sure.

Jamie   She's thirty-five!

Tony   What's age? Age is just . . . just number. You know?

Pause.

Jamie   Mum said you was a painter.

Tony   Right.

Jamie   I know why she chose you. She wants the lounge doing. Only put the paper up last year and she already hates it. Bloke what selled it her said it got velvet in it, but it aint, it's imitation velvet. She feels gutted. Like that, my Mum, goes off things fast. (**Tony** *laughs.*) What's so funny? She might go off you. You won't be laughing then will ya?

Tony (*short pause*)   Jamie, how old are you?

Jamie   Fifteen. How old are you?

Tony   Twenty-seven. Not old enough to be your Dad, right?

Jamie   What?

Tony   You know. (*Pause.*) Sure.

Jamie   What?

Tony   It's just shit isn't it?

Jamie   What?

Tony   The whole concept. Yeah. Anyway. I think we should, like, move towards getting away from that. Right?

Jamie   Is that a spliff?

Pause. **Tony** *doesn't know how to reply.*

Jamie   Give us some.

He passes him the joint. **Jamie** *has a big drag on it.*

Jamie (*looks out to Canary Wharf*) When I was ten, me Mum met this bloke called Richard. He was a barman like her. I used to . . . pretend he was my Dad. Didn't realise he was only about eighteen. I used to tell people . . . and that.

Pause.

And then one night. I went in the kitchen for a glass of water. And there's me Mum, sat on the floor, tears pouring down her face. Two black eyes. I never saw Richard again.

Pause.

I used to sit on his knee. He used to put his arm round me when we walked down the street and that. Called me trouble. And then . . . it's weird innit? When somin' can just stop like that.

Tony That's cool.

Jamie Just . . .

Tony Hey . . .

Jamie What?

Tony Your Mum's gonna be all right.

Jamie But things do don't they? They just stop happening. Don't they? Feelings and that. The way . . . the way you feel.

Tony Some carry on.

Jamie She stopped crying. That's good init.

Tony Good. You're sensitive. (**Jamie** *shrugs his shoulder and passes back the joint.*) I'm sensitive. Sometimes I just. Kind of. Cry. You ever done that?

Jamie Yeah.

Tony Yeah it's called release. Famous people cry. Gazza.

Jamie Anne Diamond.

Tony Thatcher. (*Spits on floor.*)

Jamie Princess Di.

Tony Princess Di.

Sandra *enters from work.*

Sandra This little Princess is fuckin' knackered. 'Scuse language. Has he been behaving hisself?

Tony *stubs the joint out with his foot.*

Tony Sandra! You look great.

Sandra Oh Tony!

Tony What?

Sandra You haven't eaten your little cheese salad.

Tony Think I've got an ulcer. Or a gallstone. Right off my food.

Sandra My feet. Someone's sticking swords in my feet.

Tony   I get that, it's got a name.

Jamie   It's them heels.

Sandra   It's your bedtime Jamie.

Jamie   Aren't you gonna check me homework?

Sandra (*sitting on step, taking shoes off*)   Ooh sod that I'm knackered. All I fancy now is a cup o'tea and me bloody bed. Cor.

Jamie   I had maths and art.

Tony   Painting by numbers.

Sandra *sniggers, rubbing her weary feet.*

Jamie   Well. Night.

Tony   Night kid.

Sandra   Night Jay. Oi! (*Taps her cheek. He bends to kiss her.*)

Jamie   Night then.

Sandra   Sweet dreams.

Jamie *goes in.* **Sandra** *inspects her legs.*

Sandra   Look at that. Varicose veins. Never work in a bar.

Tony *gets on the floor and kisses her legs.*

Tony I stink o' the pub. All booze an' fags. Oh don't. I like it. Tony!

She hits him with a shoe.

Tony   He's a good kid.

Sandra   I've heard his mother aint that bad either.

Tony   I'll have to meet her, she sounds like quite a gal.

Sandra   The name's Gangel. That's Angel, with a G in front.

Tony (*puts his hand on her stomach*)   And that's magical.

Sandra   Oh don't. I had some scampi fries. I feel a bit queazy.

Tony   Working tomorrow?

Sandra   Mm, I'm practically running that place.

Tony   I'll come and keep an eye on him.

Sandra   (*tuts*)   You don't have to.

Tony   I know. I'm an individual. (*Leans over to kiss her.*)

Sandra   You can say that again.

They have a kiss. **Sandra** *still has her shoes in her hand, and runs the heels down his back. Mid-kiss,* **Ste**'s *door flies open and* **Ste** *runs out in a bit of a state.*

Sandra *and* **Tony** *keep kissing, till* **Sandra** *spots* **Ste**, *then breaks away.*

Sandra Ste!! (*Laughs.*)

Ste All right?

Sandra What's the matter with you eh?

Ste Can I stay over Mrs Gangel?

Sandra You know my name Ste!

Ste Can I?

Sandra Is it your Dad again?

Ste Our Trevor.

Sandra You'll be top to tail with Jamie I'm afraid.

Ste I'd rather that than be in there.

Sandra (*to* **Tony**) Inn'e a lovely lad eh Tony?

Tony Great.

Sandra (*to* **Ste**) Well you get yourself in then Ste. Go on, you get yourself to bed.

Ste Thanks Mrs Gangel.

Sandra Ere Ste.

Ste What?

Sandra D'you wanna little cheese salad?

Ste Can I?

Sandra D'you mind beetroot?

Ste No.

Sandra Go on, take it, good for you salad. Go on!

Ste Thanks.

Sandra *passes* **Ste** *the salad. He steps over them and into her flat.*

Sandra (*calls after him*) Mind you don't get crumbs in the bed! (*Laughs to* **Tony**.) Don't want stains on my sheets! (*Laughs.*)

Tony What sort?

Sandra What sort d'you think? (*Laughs.*) Beetroot! (*Laughs.*)

Tony *tries to kiss her again. She's having none of it.*

Sandra His bloody family. Wait up. I gotta do somin'.

Sandra *goes to* **Ste**'s *door and bangs on it. We hear* **Ste**'s *Dad,* **Ronnie**, *shout from inside.*

Sandra Ronnie? Trevor? It's me, Sandra! (*To* **Tony**.) You go in love.

Tony *gets up and goes indoors.* **Sandra** *opens the letter box and calls through.*

Sandra   Your little Steven's round at our place tonight. I've every mind to report you! Ronnie? Ronnie are you listening to me? This is Sandra here! I am NOT happy!

Ronnie (*off*)   Ah fuck off y'arl nacker!

Sandra   This has got to stop!

She lets the letter box drop. She goes to go indoors. She stops at her plants and picks off a few dead leaves.

Sandra   You look parched love.

She goes indoors.

Scene Three

Jamie *sits up in his bed wearing a pair of reading glasses.* **Ste** *stands by the bed, holding the plate of salad.* **Jamie** *has a magazine out in front of him, his mother's 'Hello'.*

Ste   You don't mind?

Jamie   No.

Ste   You sure?

Jamie   Course.

Ste   I could sleep on the floor.

Jamie   You hate the floor.

Ste   And you don't mind?

Jamie   No. I don't.

Ste   Great.

Ste *lays the salad on the bed and sits on the bed to undress. During the following he begins to undress for bed.*

Jamie   Haven't you eaten?

Ste   No. It's not yours is it?

Jamie   No. Do you want the light off?

Ste   Do you?

Jamie   Don't care.

Ste   D'you mind it on?

Jamie   No.

Ste   Coz o'the salad.

Jamie   Fine.

Ste *is taking his shirt off now. Then his trousers follow.*

Jamie Mum went really mad at me today. This games business. She threw a load of me old stuff out I was hangin' on to.

Ste Yeah?

Jamie Yeah.

Pause. **Ste** *now has his boxer shorts on.*

Jamie D'you want another T-shirt?

Ste Nah I'm all right Jay.

Jamie Are you sure?

Ste Sure.

Jamie Well, if you do.

Ste Cheers. I'm getting in now.

Jamie Right.

Ste *gets into bed. His head the opposite end to* **Jamie**. **Jamie** *passes him a pillow.*

Jamie Have this.

Ste Cheers.

Ste *puts the pillow behind him and sits up. He makes a start on the salad.*

Ste D'you mind me eating this?

Jamie Nah. I was gonna read anyway.

Ste What you readin' then?

Jamie Er . . . it's me Mum's. (*Holds magazine up.*)

Ste Oh yeah? I've seen that in the shop. (*Notices it's called 'Hello'.*) Hello!

Jamie Hello!

They have a bit of a giggle about this.

Jamie 'Ere, d'you wanna fork?

Ste Nah, eat it with me fingers.

Jamie Want some bread?

Ste This is great.

Jamie Right. (*Pause.*) I'm gonna read now.

Ste Okay.

Silence. **Jamie** *casually reads the magazine,* **Ste** *munches on the salad.*

Ste Cor I'm starving.

Jamie Can't have you goin' hungry can we?

Ste What bit you reading?

Jamie It's about Sally from Coronation Street.

Ste What, the blonde one?

Jamie   Yeah.

Ste   What's it say then?

Jamie (*reads*)   Although Sally spends her working week filming in Manchester, she likes nothing better than to spend her weekends at her London penthouse flat. Weekends are busy for Sally, juggling a hectic social life with time for that special man in her life. Her partner is another actor, but she is coy about revealing his name. Saturdays are spent shopping and eating out, and Sundays are set aside for catching up with old friends or taking long strolls on Hampstead Heath which her flat overlooks.

Pause.

Ste   That's north of the river, innit?

Jamie   Mm.

Ste   So she's called Sally? In real life as well as on the telly?

Jamie   Yeah, I hate that name.

Ste   It's not her fault I s'pose.

Jamie   I blame the parents.

Ste   Mm. D'you always wear glasses when you read?

Jamie   Supposed to.

Ste   You don't in school.

Jamie   Hardly fetching is it?

Ste   Nah, looks all right.

Jamie   Yeah?

Ste   Yeah, I'm telling ya.

Jamie   How's your salad?

Ste   Bang on food.

Jamie   Good for your sports.

Ste   That's right. Good for your spots an' all.

Jamie   You haven't got any spots.

Ste   Yours are clearing up.

Jamie   Tar.

Ste   D'you fancy that Sally?

Jamie   Not really. Do you?

Ste   Nah. Haven't given it much thought.

Jamie   D'you fancy her next door?

Ste   Fancy Leah?

Jamie   She fancies you.

Ste   Don't.

Jamie I'm only saying.

Ste Jamie.

Jamie What time should I set the alarm for?

Ste Quarter-to-eight.

Jamie Right. (*He gets alarm clock off the floor. Whilst setting it.*) If you wanna bath in the morning I can put the water on.

Ste Nah, I'll get home.

Jamie Right.

Ste Jamie?

Jamie What?

Ste Will your Mum mind if I leave this beetroot?

Jamie No.

Ste Only she asked if I liked it.

Jamie Leave it if you don't wannit.

Ste She won't mind?

Jamie No. She's not a very good cook my Mum.

Ste She is.

Jamie Hmm, that's a matter of opinion.

Ste *puts the plate on the floor and starts to settle down in the bed.*

Jamie You goin' sleep?

Ste Yeah I'm knackered.

Jamie I'll turn the light off.

Jamie *puts the magazine on the floor and turns off the bedside lamp. He settles down. Silence.*

Jamie Ste?

Ste Mm?

Jamie You all right?

Ste Yeah.

Jamie Right. (*Pause.*) Ste?

Ste What?

Jamie I thought you were making the tea tonight?

Ste I burnt it.

Jamie Oh.

Ste Mm.

Jamie What was it?

Ste Bubble and Squeak.

Jamie   Oh yeah. (*Pause.*) Ste?

Ste   What?

Jamie   Night.

Ste   Night Jamie.

Silence.

In the blackout 'California Earthquake' by Mama Cass plays, leading us into the next scene.

Scene Four

A few days later and it's still hot. Out on the walkway **Leah** *is sunning herself in swimming costume and baggy T-shirt, lying on a towel. She is reading a geography text book.* **Tony** *sits doing a newspaper crossword in one of two white patio chairs outside* **Sandra**'s *flat.* **Leah**'s *and* **Sandra**'s *doors are open.*

'California Earthquake' floats out from **Leah**'s *flat.*

Leah   D'you think I'm tall for my age?

Tony   Come again?

Leah   I said 'D'you think I'm tall . . . for my age?'

Tony   Depends how old you are. If you were three, yeah. Forty-eight, no. Yeah? (*Pause.* **Leah** *returns to her book.*) Revising?

Leah   I am tall.

Tony (*in reference to her book*)   Any good?

Leah (*reads chapter headings from book*)   The rock formations of Wooky Hole. Sedimentary Discharge of the Gaping Gill. A day in the life of Jean: A girl who lives on the San Andreas fault. Bully for her. 'It's scary' says Jean 'but you learn to live with it.' Silly bitch.

Tony   Oh but think about it. Living on the edge of a big slit of earth that could open up, and like, swallow you whole.

Leah   No, you should just look where you're going. Or move house. No use moaning about it and going in books.

Tony   Right.

Leah (*looking at book*)   She don't look very tall does she? They wanna write it next to her picture. 'Jean's a bloody midget'.

Tony   You know why you're so tall, don't you? Coz you're mature.

Leah   Wassat?

Tony   Grown up.

Leah   You wanna tell her that.

Tony   Who?

Leah   Your bird.

Tony   Sandra?

Leah She talks to me like I got cunt written on my forehead.

Tony You shouldn't use words like bird.

Leah (*pause*) You wanna watch yourself.

Tony Why?

Leah She's got a reputation.

Tony Yeah?

Leah I'm saying nothing. (*Pause.*) But I wouldn't tell anyone round here you were seeing her. If they read the crap I do, they'd say Sandra was the San Andreas Fault and the Gaping Gill rolled into one. The way she walks she couldn't stop a bull in an alleyway. (*Laughs.*)

Tony I'll tell her that.

Leah (*still laughing*) She already knows!

Jamie *comes out and goes and knocks on* **Ste***'s door during the last line.*

Leah He aint back yet.

Jamie In'e?

Jamie *makes to go back in but* **Sandra** *comes to the door. She's wearing summery gear. In one hand she holds an unlit cigarette. In the other, the end of a green garden hose.*

Sandra (*holding cigarette up*) Anyone got a match?

Leah Yeah, my arse your face.

Jamie Your arse aint that nice love.

Sandra Pump me up Jay.

Jamie *goes in. Soon we hear him manually pumping water inside the flat. Water splashes out of the hose.*

Sandra I like getting pumped up. D'ya know what I mean?

Leah (*to* **Tony**) What did I tell you?

Tony (*to* **Leah**) Hey remember feminism, yeah? Sisters together, sisters strong!

Leah My sister lives in Crayford. I aint seen her in six months.

Sandra (*holding the hose between her legs like a man having a wee*) 'Ere Tony, you when you've had ten too many.

Leah (*as* **Tony** *laughs*) You're funny.

Sandra *turns and squirts* **Leah** *with water.* **Leah** *jumps up.*

Leah Oh bloody 'ell!

Sandra Oh sorry Leah, didn't see you there!

Leah Grow up!

Ste *comes in from school.*

Ste (*to* **Leah**) Oright?

Leah Do I look it?

Sandra   Had a wash today Ste? (*Laughs.* **Ste** *makes a dash for his flat and she squirts water at him.*) You have now. Okay Jamie.

Ste *lets himself into his flat.*

Leah   You've soaked me Sandra!

Sandra   Oh stop moaning, you're young intya?

The water goes off. **Jamie** *comes to the door.*

Jamie   Was that Ste then?

Sandra   Yeah. Little surprise for us in the fridge Jay, go and get 'em.

Jamie *goes in.* **Ste** *comes out to take the drying off the clothes horse.*

Tony   Yo Ste! Blinding day for drying.

Ste   Blinding yeah.

Leah   Blinding. (*She applies suntan lotion to her legs.*)

Tony (*to* **Leah**)   What factor's that?

Leah   Four.

Sandra   S'probably nicked. Youth of today.

Leah (*tuts*)   Shut up is it nicked!

Tony (*to* **Leah**)   Could I use that after you?

Leah   What, borrow it?

Tony   Aha.

Leah   No.

Jamie (*coming out with arms full of lager cans*)   Who wants a lager? Get pissed!

Leah   Go on then.

Tony (*to* **Jamie**)   Great specs.

Jamie   Want a lager Ste?

Ste   Er . . .

Sandra   Go on Ste, it's just what you need on a day like this.

Ste   Stick it there I'll be out in a sec. (*Takes drying in.*)

Sandra (*to* **Jamie**)   Give Tony one please. (**To Tony.**) It's genital, bar work.

Jamie   Genetical mother.

Sandra   That an' all you humourless git. Crack one open for me while you're at it Tony. I fancy somin' wet dribbling down the back o'me gullet. What d'you say?

Tony   I say ditto, right?

Sandra   You say whatever you want Tony. Better in than out, d'you know what I mean?

Leah (*lager*)   This is beautiful.

Sandra (*shouts like a barmaid*)   Can I have your glasses gentlemen please! Drink up now, let's be having you! (*Own voice.*) Born to brewery, it's in me water. (**Ste** *comes out with a new pile of drying.*) See that? That's women's lib that is.

Leah   There's no women in his flat to lib.

Jamie   You're gonna get smoke all over Ste's clothes now.

Ste   Don't matter, s'only me Dad's.

Sandra   You okay today Ste?

Ste   Yeah.

Jamie   Mum!

Tony   Jamie!

Leah   I went to have a look at a new school today. Up in Greenwich. Might have a space for me next month. There's only twenny kids in the whole school.

Ste   There'll be twenny two if you go. You and Mama Cass. (*Laughter.*)

Sandra   Is it residential?

Leah   No.

Sandra   Shame. Coulda given you an 'and packing.

Leah   That's a cuss.

Sandra   And I could've packed that fat bitch an'er music an'all.

Jamie   You shouldn't speak ill of the dead.

Sandra   Aw I know. Shame how she died. (*Giggles.*) Oh shouldn't laugh.

Leah   How did she die?

Sandra   Tell her Tony.

Tony   Bread and margarine. Not the typical ingredients of a Molotov Cocktail.

Ste   Do what?

Sandra   What you on about Tony? She died choking on a sandwich.

Ste   No!

Leah   Did she?

Sandra (*to* **Jamie**)   Now you know why I tell you not to gobble your chips down.

Leah   What sort o'sandwich?

Sandra   I dunno.

Tony   Wasn't she heavily into the drugs scene?

Leah   Was she?

Ste   They all are them pop stars int they? Bloody headcases the lot of 'em.

Sandra   Oswald Moseley eat your heart out.

Leah   No Ste. East 17 aint into drugs, and they're all pop stars.

Sandra   Yeah but Leah, what you gotta remember is, East 17 are healthy lads. Mama Cass was obese.

Jamie   So?

Sandra   So she was probably very unhappy, and prone to, you know, dabbling.

Jamie   She mighta been happy being fat!

Leah   Yeah!

Jamie   Just coz she's different to you, doesn't make her a weirdo!

Sandra   Well answer me this then Jamie. If she was so happy being fat, why was it she died choking on a sandwich, eh? Why wasn't it a walloping great fry-up or somin'?

Tony   You got a point there.

Jamie   Bollocks.

Ste   Mighta been a bacon and egg sandwich.

Jamie/Leah   Yeah.

Sandra   No! No. It's all coming back to me now, it was chicken . . .

Tony   Or beef or something . . .

Sandra   Yeah, it was definitely somin' low in cholesterol.

Sandra *takes the hose indoors.*

Leah   She's full o'shit.

Tony (*to* **Leah**)   Hey watch it.

Leah   Shut up!

Jamie   My Mother's the fountain of all knowledge. You should know that by now.

Sandra *hears this as she re-enters with her Vileda Supermop. She continues mopping up the water that has splashed on the walkway.*

Sandra (*to* **Jamie**, *entering*)   Yeah well when you can keep up with the questions on Bob's Full House, you get back to me. All right?

Jamie   Bob's Full House? I'm more of a Mastermind man.

Leah   Liar!

Tony   Remember University Challenge? (*Beat.*) Crap show.

Sandra (*accentuating her mop movements in time with her speech*)   'If You Sprinkle When You Tinkle, Please Be Sweet And Wipe The Seat'. (*Chuckles.*) Got that on the door of the Gents loo at work. (*To* **Jamie**.) You could learn a lot from that.

Jamie   And you could learn a lot from keeping your mouth shut.

Sandra (*to* **Ste**)   Ooooh I bet you don't speak like that to your ole man eh Ste?

Ste   I don't speak. Full stop.

Sandra   Oh yeah. No offence Ste, d'you know what I mean?

Jamie   Mum!

Leah It's disgustin' init? When men dribble. You wanna use a cloth Jamie.

Sandra (*to* **Leah**)   First decent thing you've said all day girl.

Jamie Shut up.

Tony Men of the cloth (*Sniggers.*)

Jamie (*tuts*) Oh shut up!

Sandra Oi! Manners!

Jamie Me Mother never taught me none!

Sandra Er, she taught you please and thank you and respect God's creatures, so keep your trap shut.

Jamie Shut up.

Sandra Shut up? Shut up? You're killing the art o'conversation you are.

Jamie What conversation? No one gets a word in edgeways with you around.

Sandra Inn'e a wit eh? Inn'e a laugh? Eh? Makes me die he does.

Jamie That IS the intention.

Sandra And that from the same boy who used to send me Valentines.

Jamie Oh don't start.

Sandra I've started so I'll finish! (*Laughs.*) He wouldn't leave my side when I took him to nursery you know. Kept getting phone calls. 'Mrs Gangel, he won't settle without ya. Pines for you he does. Pines for you at the drop of an 'at.'

Jamie No I never.

Sandra They thought you was being abused you was such a quiet bugger. Huh, they should see you now. They'd get a right shock. Had me down as a bad Mother coz you told them you slept in a drawer.

Jamie I did!

Sandra Only coz I couldn't afford a cot! If they could see me now, they'd think I was bleedin' marvellous. Show me another woman on this estate who can say she goes with an artist, and I'll show you a bloody liar.

Tony Great music.

Leah Artist?

Sandra (*poses*)   Quick Tony! Paint me picture, I feel gorgeous!

Ste Are you an artist Tony?

Sandra Come on Tony, get your brush out and give us a few strokes.

Leah Are you Tony?

Tony Mm.

Ste And you paint pictures and that?

Tony Sometimes.

Ste   Blindin'!

Leah   He's a dark horse.

Tony   I used to work in a factory actually, six months.

Sandra   Ignore 'im, he's an artist.

Tony   I'm not an intellectual, right?

Jamie   I thought you was a painter and decorator.

Tony   I could be . . .

Jamie   Well what you doin' with her then?

Sandra   I'm artistic!

Leah   How are you artistic?

Jamie   Yeah!

Sandra   I got good colour sense. Tony said so. You've seen my lounge diner.

Jamie   Hardly makes you Van Gogh though does it?

Ste   I'm going in.

Sandra   You do that Ste. I'm just about to chop me ear off.

Jamie   Stay out here Ste.

Ste   Nah, I'm going boxing with me Dad later.

Sandra   Can't get enough of it eh? (*Laughs.*)

Leah   That's a cuss!

Ste (*to* **Sandra**)   Spectating.

Sandra   Oh you kids today, there's no life in ya.

Ste *goes in,* **Sandra** *carries on with no break.*

Ste   See ya.

Sandra   When I was your age we made our own fun.

Leah   What? Set fire to dinosaurs and watch 'em burn?

Sandra (*laughs uproariously*)   Cheeky cow!

Jamie (*to* **Sandra**)   Oh why can't you just shut up?

Sandra   What?

Jamie   That's bang out of order what you said to Ste.

Sandra   Oh we all know his Dad leathers him, I'm only having a laugh.

Jamie   What 'bout when that bloke o'yours beat you up? Weren't laughing then were ya?

Tony   I think now's the time to change the subject.

Jamie   Well change it then.

Tony   Did anyone see that documentary last week? About . . .

Sandra   No Tony. He's a clever bastard. And don't we just know it eh? (*To* **Jamie**.) Just remember you, I give you them brains so think on.

Jamie (*making to go indoors*)   I always thought you'd had a lobotomy.

Sandra (*laughs*)   What did you say?

Jamie   Explain it to her someone. (*Exits.*)

Tony   Lobotomy, it's when . . .

Sandra   I know what it means Tony. (*To door.*) Cheeky little barstool! (*She goes to the door and calls through.*) You're not too old to be taken over my knee young man! D'you hear me?

Jamie (*off*)   I hear you, the whole o'bloody Thamesmead can hear you!

Sandra   Get a life! Get a sense o'humour!

Jamie (*comes to door*)   Well maybe if you say something funny for once in your life, I'll start laughing.

Sandra   I AM funny!

Jamie   Funny in the head.

Sandra   You spotty little wimp, how dare you say that to me?

Tony   Sandra . . .

Sandra (*to* **Jamie**)   Look at you, butter wouldn't melt. I've got your number Jamie, and if anyone needs help it's you. You're fuckin' weird.

Tony   Hey, cool it guys . . .

Leah   I'm goin' indoors.

Sandra   You do that lady!

Leah (*gathering her stuff up*)   I'm gonna go somewhere where I can get some peace and bloody quiet.

Sandra   Try Uranus.

Tony   Sandra.

Sandra   You! In!

Tony *and* **Leah** *both disappear inside.*

Sandra   I work all the hours God sends to keep you in insults. If this was my pub I'd have you barred.

Jamie   Well go on then. Bar me. Kick me out. (*Sniggers.*) You wouldn't dare. I'm all you've got. Me and your fucking plants. Coz he aint gonna be around much longer.

Sandra   What would you know? You don't know nothing!

Jamie You've got my number? Well I've got yours, Sandra. So. Why don't you try and be a little more like a mother to me?

Sandra Oh yeah, pull that one on me. I'm a terrible mother who don't know her arse from her elbow. Well listen to me Jamie and listen good. I never had a Mum so sometimes I'm gonna make mistakes.

Jamie I'm not surprised she abandoned ya.

Sandra You cheeky little bastard.

She slaps him across the face. He slaps her back. She lays into him, fists flying. He holds his hands up to his face, protecting himself. She's not giving up so he hits back. They fight like cat and dog, knocking Ste's washing over in the process. Finally **Sandra** *is sitting on* **Jamie***'s chest, a fierce look in her eyes. This dissolves to tears. She weakens her grip.* **Jamie** *pushes her off. He goes and sits in one of the patio chairs.*

Jamie Am I like my Dad?

Sandra No. You're like me.

Jamie How am I weird?

Sandra Oh give it a rest Jamie. Christ.

Jamie You said it.

Sandra You're all right. Okay, so you got me for a mother, but who said life was easy? You are. You're all right.

Sandra *gets up and goes indoors.* **Jamie** *starts to cry. The door to* **Ste***'s flat opens and* **Ste** *stands on the step.*

Ste D'you wanna come the boxing?

Jamie Shut up.

Ste Got a spare ticket.

Jamie Leave me alone.

Ste You all right?

Jamie Apparently.

Ste *sheepishly goes back indoors.* **Jamie** *wipes his face.*

Scene Five

That night **Jamie** *and* **Ste** *sit up in* **Jamie***'s bed, sharing a bottle of lemonade,* **Ste** *opposite* **Jamie***.* **Sandra** *calls off.*

Sandra *(off)* Jamie?! D'you wanna watch 'The Sound of Music'?!

Jamie *to* **Ste**, *tuts*.

Sandra (*off*)   It's on Sky Jamie!

Jamie   Who does she think I am?

Sandra (*off*)   D'you want me to tape it?

Jamie (*calls*)   Yeah!

Sandra (*off*)   Okay!

Jamie (*to* **Ste**)   Anything for a quiet life.

Ste   I wish I had a Mum.

Jamie   What happened Ste?

Ste   Come in from the boxin', this ole mate o'me Dad's turns up. Pissed. Kept goin' on about West Ham drawin'. Irish like me Dad. 'Fucking draw' he kept saying, 'Fucking draw!' And me Dad starts joining in, and our Vinnie, and our Trevor. Going on and on about it.

Jamie   So why?

Ste   I never joined in.

Jamie   You're okay here.

Ste   They don't even ask where I've been.

Sandra (*off*)   D'you want some toast lads?

Jamie (*calls*)   We're goin' asleep.

Sandra (*off*)   Oh. Sorry lads.

Jamie (*to* **Ste**)   Can I see?

Pause. **Ste** *turns his back on* **Jamie** *and lifts up his T-shirt.*

Sandra (*off*)   Jamie? Sorry love. Who played the Baroness?

Jamie   Eleanor Parker.

Sandra (*off*)   Oh that's it, I wanna show off to Tony. Sorry lads. Won't happen again.

Ste   Have I got any on me back?

Jamie   Couple.

Ste   Never looked.

Ste *pulls his T-shirt down. He takes a swig of lemonade.* **Jamie** *gets a small 'Body Shop' bottle from the floor.*

Jamie   I got this stuff. It's me Mum's. It's from the Body Shop. Peppermint foot lotion. It soothes your feet. I use it coz I like the smell. (*Pause.*) Lie down and I'll rub it into your back. If you want.

Slowly **Ste** *lies down.* **Jamie** *pulls* **Ste**'s *T-shirt up.* **Ste** *lifts his head up, he holds the lemonade bottle out in front of him.* **Jamie** *pours a little lotion onto* **Ste**'s *back.*

Jamie Cold init?

Ste Yeah.

Jamie *slowly massages it into* **Ste**'s *back.*

Ste They think I'm a wimp.

Jamie My Mum thinks I am an' all.

Ste But I aint.

Jamie Neither am I.

Ste A wimp wouldn'a come round here. I done somin'. Wimps don't do nothin'. (*Pause.*) I'm gonna work at the Sports Centre. Do me shifts in the fitness pool, do me shifts in the leisure pool. I know I can do it.

Jamie Swimming's your favourite.

Ste You're on your own when you're swimming. You can't think about nothing else. Just the strokes, and where you are in the pool. Up and down. Up and down. (*Pause.*) I'm gonna stink of mint.

Jamie Peppermint.

Ste Peppermint.

Pause.

Jamie Have you ever kissed anyone? And stuck your tongue in?

Ste Looking like this?

Jamie You ain' ugly.

Ste They've made me ugly.

Jamie I don't think you're ugly.

Jamie *rests his head in the small of* **Ste**'s *back. They stay like this for a while.*

Ste Carry on doin' me back.

Jamie Dunnit hurt?

Ste Only a little bit.

Jamie Turn over I'll do your front.

Ste I can't. (*Pause.*) I'm too sore. I'd make too much noise and then your Mum'd come in.

Jamie She's watching telly.

Ste No Jay.

Jamie I won't hurt you.

Ste I think we better get to sleep.

Jamie *pulls the T-shirt down.*

Ste Turn the light off.

Jamie   No.

Ste   Please.

Jamie   I don't wanna.

Ste *gets under the covers.*

Jamie   Can I come up that end with you?

Ste   No.

Jamie   Please.

Ste   You stay where you are.

Ste *gets the pillow and moves round to lie next to* **Jamie**, *head to head.*

Ste   Satisfied?

Jamie   Mm. Night. (*Leans over and kisses* **Ste** *once on the lips.*)

Ste   D'you think I'm queer?

Jamie   Don't matter what I think.

Jamie *switches off the bedside light.*

Jamie   Can I touch you?

Ste   I'm a bit sore.

Jamie   Yeah.

In the darkness, 'Sixteen Going on Seventeen' from 'The Sound Of Music' plays.

Act Two

Scene One

A week later, mid-afternoon. It is still hot. **Jamie** *is sitting on the step of his flat, with the front door open. He is cleaning his glasses.* **Ste** *comes on from the street. They both wear school uniform.*

Jamie   Hiya.

Ste   Oright?

Jamie   Bunkin' off?

Ste   No, I'm at school, what's it look like?

Jamie   Not like you.

Ste   It's only Sports Day.

Jamie   Not like you to miss a race.

Ste   First time for everything.

Jamie   You're in the relay team.

Ste   Yeah well . . . don't wanna put . . . put strain on me ankle. It's . . . injured in training.

Jamie   Oh.

Ste   S'not the end of the world.

Jamie   I was gonna stay and watch you, then Miss Penrose said you'd pulled out so I came back here. Told me Mum it wan't compulsory. Sports Day.

Ste   Thassa big word init?

Jamie   Compulsory? I know.

Ste   I been down Tavy Bridge.

Jamie   Get anything?

Ste   Nah, skint.

Jamie   I aint seen ya. Where you been hiding?

Ste   Nowhere.

Jamie   Knocked for you a few times.

Ste   I aint been hiding.

Jamie   Thought you mighta come round.

Ste I aint been hiding, all right? It's hot, bloody heat wave Jamie, and you expect me to be indoors?

Jamie No, it's just, you know, just a bit weird.

Ste I was out. All right? What's weird about that? I wan' hiding. I was just, you know, out.

Jamie Been worried about ya.

Ste Don't be.

Jamie Well I was.

Ste Well don't be!

Jamie Have they. . . ?

Ste No.

Jamie What?

Ste Nothing's happened. Yeah? I'm all right. I'm pucker. Everything . . . everything's pucker.

Jamie You aint running coz you're black and blue. That's why init? I know. I've seen. That's why you aint in the relay team.

Ste Give it a rest Jamie.

Jamie Oh things getting better then are they? Life a bowl o'cherries in the end flat? Daddy laid off the fist work? Or haven't you burnt the tea lately?

Ste I said leave it out.

Jamie You're scared.

Ste I aint scared o'nothin'!

Jamie Yeah?

Ste Yeah! Last week, right. I went Woolwich. Comin' out of a shop and there's this geezer in the gutter, pissed out of his skull, lying there. And everyone was just walking past him. I had to step over him. (*Pause.*) And it was my old man. (*Pause.*) Got me thinking on the bus. Why be scared of a bloke who's dead to the world?

Jamie When he knocks ten different types o'shite outa ya.

Ste He's an embarrassment. Nothing more, nothing less. Why be scared o'that?

Jamie Scared o'being called queer?

Ste (*pause*) Are you?

Jamie (*pause*) Dunno. Maybe. Maybe not.

Ste And are you?

Jamie Queer?

Ste Gay.

Jamie   I'm very happy. (*Pause.*) I'm happy when I'm with you. (*Pause.*) There, I've said it now haven't I? Go on, piss yourself.

Ste   No.

Jamie   Why not? Don't you think it's funny?

Ste   I don't wanna.

Jamie   I think it's hilarious.

Ste Yeah?

Jamie   Too right.

Ste   Well why aren't you laughin' then?

Jamie (*pause*)   D'you wanna come round tonight? (*Pause.*) 'No Jamie, I don't!'

Ste   I got a tongue in me head!

Jamie   Well say somin' then.

Ste   Can't.

Jamie   Well say no then.

Ste   Let's do somin'.

Jamie   What?

Ste   Let's go the park and have a kick-about.

Jamie   Football?

Ste   Yeah, go and get your new ball.

Jamie   What?

Ste   Come on Jamie, I can't hang around here all day it does me head in.

Jamie *disappears inside. He returns quickly with the football* **Tony** *bought him earlier. He stands in the doorway holding it.*

Ste   Come on then, on the head son!

Ste *angles to do a header,* **Jamie** *keeps the ball.*

Jamie   I can't.

Ste   Jay . . .

Jamie   I'm crap.

Ste   That's coz you never try.

Jamie   I hate football.

Ste Just kick it. (**Jamie** *tuts and kicks the ball to* **Ste**.) No you're doing it wrong. Like this. (*Kicks it back to* **Jamie**, *demonstrating a proper kick*. **Jamie** *kicks it back again*.) Yeah that's more like it. Keep your foot like this, it's all in the angle.

They kick the ball between them.

Jamie Are you gonna come round then?

Ste I don't know.

Jamie Go on. Come round.

Ste Jamie.

Jamie (*they carry on kicking as they speak*) Is this how Gary Lineker started d'you think?

Ste What? Like you?

Jamie Yeah?

Ste If I remember rightly Jamie, whenever we had football in juniors, you ran up and down the field playing 'Cagney and Lacey'.

Jamie Shut up.

Ste You used to row with Neil Robinson over who was gonna play the blonde.

Jamie You mean Cagney, Chris Cagney. (*Adopts an American accent, in imitation of Chris Cagney*.) My name's Christine Cagney and . . . and I'm an alcoholic.

Ste You never went near the ball.

Jamie Gary Lineker was just the same!

Ste Yeah?

Jamie Yeah.

Ste Which one was he then?

Jamie Lacey, the fat one.

Ste (*laughs*) He aint fat.

Jamie I know.

Ste He's pucker.

Jamie I know, he's all right inn'e? (*Giggles, keeps the ball and reverts to his Cagney impersonation*.) I dunno Marybeth . . . I . . . I just don't seem to be able to find the right kinda guy. They take one look at me, a cop in a pink fluffy jumper, and just . . . back off.

Ste Oh Christine Cagney, you make me heart bleed!

They have a bit of a laugh, **Jamie** *kicks the ball over and they carry on. Just then,* **Leah** *pops her head out of her door.*

Leah Oi!! You got any lead piping? (*The lads laugh.*)

Ste No!

Leah Jamie?

Jamie No!

Leah   Well, any sort o'piping?

Ste   No, why?

Leah   Oh have a look round your flat Ste. Your Trevor has all sorts knockin' about in there. Please Steven, it's really important.

Jamie   What d'you need lead piping for?

Leah   An experiment. Ste?!

Ste (*going in*)   I'm telling ya now, he won't have any.

Leah   Cheers Ste. (**Ste** *goes in, she comes out.*) Are you sure you haven't got any pipes?

Jamie   Positive.

Leah   Go and ask your Mum.

Jamie   What's this experiment? (**Leah** *taps her nose.*) Oh oright.

Jamie *goes indoors.* **Leah** *fidgets for a bit, then her gaze comes to rest on* **Sandra**'s *hanging basket. She moves towards it and headbutts it.*

Leah   Ow!! (*Sings a note.*) La-a!! (*She headbutts it again then sings a note.*) La-aa!!

Sandra *rushes out.*

Sandra   Get off o'there you little cow. I won that basket in the South East Thames Barmaid of the Year Award. Look it's engraved. Sandra Gangel, 1985. You know that coz me picture was in the New Shopper.

Leah (tuts)   Sorry.

Ste (*coming out empty handed*)   Can't see none.

Leah   You sure?

Sandra   What on earth do you want lead piping for?

Leah   Mind your own business.

Sandra   You're bloody warped you are, don't you know lead's poisonous?

Leah   Look who's talking.

Sandra   Yeah and I talk sense, which is more than you do Madam.

Leah   I talk plenty o'sense!

Jamie *comes out at this point with the garden hose.*

Sandra   You wouldn't know sense if it came up to you, slapped you round the face and said 'I'm sense'.

Leah   Oh stand on your head and let your arse do the talking.

Jamie   Will this do?

Leah   Blinding.

Jamie   D'you want me to turn it on?

Sandra   I'm having no water fights Missis!

Leah   No don't turn it on. Just hit me over the head with it.

Jamie Eh?

Ste What?

Leah I'll look away. Yous keep talkin. Then as a surprise, hit me over the head with the hose.

Sandra It won't be a surprise then will it you thick git!

Leah Don't tell me when you're gonna do it!

Jamie I don't understand this, d'you want me to hit you hard?

Leah Yeah. Ste you do it, you're stronger than him.

Ste No!!

Sandra I'll do it!

Jamie I'll do it!

Leah Talk!

Leah *turns away, her back to the three of them.*

Ste What d'you want us to talk about?

Leah Anything, just talk will ya?

Jamie The weather?

Leah You aint talking. Oh here read this. (*She gets a cassette cover out of her pocket.*) Read that. The underlined bit. (*Passes it to* **Ste**. **Jamie** *hovers with hose as* **Leah** *turns her back again.*)

Sandra Steven?

Ste (*reads*) Cass Elliot followed them there, but the group initially resisted her repeated requests to join them, arguing that her range wasn't high enough for Phillips' new styled compositions.

As **Ste** *reads,* **Jamie** *approaches* **Leah** *slowly, from behind, hose in hand.* **Sandra** *stops him by grabbing his arm and takes control of the hose.* **Jamie** *steps back.* **Sandra** *now approaches* **Leah** *slowly.*

However a lead pipe struck Cass on the head during a bout of interior decorating and having recovered from the resultant concussion, she discovered that her voice had changed.

Leah (*bewitched*) She discovered that her voice had changed.

Sandra *pulls the hose over* **Leah**'s *head and pulls it round her neck, strangling her.*

Sandra So!! I'm a slapper am I? I'm the Gaping Gill and the San Andreas Fault rolled into one?! You twisted little bitch! How dare you say all that to my fella? You venomous little cow, what are ya?

She releases the pressure of the hose and pushes **Leah** *to the ground.* **Leah** *chokes and coughs.* **Sandra** *slaps her round the head briskly.*

Sandra I dunno what that home tutor teaches you Leah, but it certainly aint respect!

Leah (*sings a note*) La-aa!!

Ste Should I phone an ambulance?

Sandra Call a vet, have it put down.

Leah (*another note*)   La-aa!!

Sandra   You could never turn Tony's mind against me Leah, d'you hear me? Coz he sees you for the interfering little slapper that you are.

Leah (*tearful*)   I wanted it to change.

Sandra   Yeah well some things never change.

Leah   I wanted it to change!

Sandra   The leopard never changes its spots, and the slapper never changes her knickers! Be told!

Sandra, *brandishing the hose, goes inside as* **Jamie** *steps aside for her.*

Jamie   My Mum aint a slag!

Ste   You shouldn't have said that to Tony!

Leah   Don't you start. (*Still crawling round, coughing.*)

Ste   Come on Jamie, let's go the park.

Leah (*grabs football*)   I'm coming!

Jamie   There's enough dog crap in that park as it is without you adding to it an' all.

Leah   Let me come!

Jamie   No way!

Ste   Grow up Leah!

Leah   Let me come or I'll spread it round where you slept every night last week.

Jamie   What?

Ste   Dunno what you're talkin' about.

Leah   Let me come.

Jamie   He slept on the couch.

Leah   Not what I heard. Top to tail your Mum said. Very nice.

Ste   Give us the ball.

Jamie   Take no notice Ste.

Leah   I'm seeing your Trevor later for a drink.

Ste   Give it to me!

Leah   You know how alcohol loosens the tongue!

Ste   Leah!

Leah   Try it.

Ste   I don't like hitting girls.

Leah   Hit me then, go on, hit me you stupid queer. (*She throws the ball at* **Ste** *and gets up.*) He already knows! You know what these flats are like, walls are paper thin. Why d'you think he's twatting the face offa you eh? He knows!

Ste   There's nothing to know!

Leah   Top to tail?

Jamie   You know fuck all.

Leah   Oh really?

Jamie   Yes really.

Leah   I know this much. I've been sticking up for you. For the pair o'ya. Told him I knew you'd slept on the couch. Told him I'd been in and seen. (*Pause, while this registers.*) You think I'm such a loser don't ya? You think you can say what you like to me coz at the end of the day I'll still be at the bottom of the slag-heap. Just coz I was kicked outa school. Just coz . . . you think it's all just gonna wash over me!

Jamie   Leah.

Leah   All I wanted was a bloody kick-about, in the park. I was only bored for Christ's sake! (*Changes tack.*) I goes 'You shouldn't say things like that about Jamie and Ste. About your own brother. They're just mates.'

Ste   Nothing happened.

Leah   I was only thinking of you.

Jamie   Nothing's happened.

Leah (*to* **Ste**)   When was the last time your Trevor hit you?

Jamie   What's it to you?

Leah   When? I bet it was Thursday.

Ste   So?

Leah   That's when I told him. That's when I lied.

Jamie (*pause*)   Let's all go the park. You can come with us Leah.

Leah (*shakes her head*)   It's all right. I int after sympathy

Leah *goes into her flat.* **Jamie** *kicks the ball to* **Ste**, *half-heartedly.* **Ste** *kicks it straight at him.*

Ste   Come round tonight?! Come round tonight?! How the fuck can I come round tonight?!

Jamie   I thought you wanted to go the park?

Ste   Oh and play 'Cagney and Lacey'?

Jamie   Have a knock-about.

Ste   You don't like football!

Jamie   I don't feel confident with it.

Ste   Yeah well neither do I son, neither do I!

Ste *makes to go in his door. From* **Leah**'s *flat comes the sound of 'I Can Dream Can't I?' by Mama Cass.*

Jamie   Ste!

Ste   What now?

Jamie   (*pause. He walks over to* **Ste** *with the ball*)   You may as well have this.

Ste   (*knocks it out of* **Jamie***'s hands*)   You wanna feel confident? You go and practise! Go and kick it against a wall. Go on! Let's see how good you get. Go and kick it against a brick bloody wall!

Ste *goes in and slams the door.* **Jamie**, *left on his own, bounces the ball on the ground, over and over again. As the lights dim, 'I Can Dream' gets louder, linking to the next scene.*

Scene Two

The next morning, about eight o'clock. **Sandra** *comes out in her dressing gown with a clipboard and biro. She is working out the staff rota for work. She obviously wants to get out of the house. She stands there filling in the rota chart.* **Jamie** *comes out, off to school, without his reading glasses. He hands his mother a cup of tea.*

Jamie   From Tony with love. Says it's nectar from the Gods for a very special angel.

Sandra   Has he put sugar in it?

Jamie   Dunno. See ya.

Sandra   (*takes a swig*)   He hasn't. (*As* **Jamie** *goes.*) Oi!

She taps the side of her cheek for a goodbye kiss. **Jamie** *comes back and kisses her. As he does,* **Ste** *comes out of his flat to go to school. But seeing* **Jamie**, *he goes back inside.*

Jamie *tuts.*

Sandra   What's his problem?

Jamie   He's in love, that's all.

Sandra   No!

Jamie   Mm. See ya.

Sandra   Yeah. Tatafilata. B.Y.E.

Jamie *exits.* **Tony** *comes to the door with his own tea. He's wearing* **Sandra***'s spare dressing gown.*

Tony   Did you get my message?

Sandra   Very nice. Shame about the sugar though.

Tony   Oh. I'll . . .

Sandra   No. It's all right . . .

Tony   Need a hand?

Sandra   No I'm all right.

Tony   (*moving to her*)   Come on. Two brains, get the job done quicker.

Sandra   No Tony, it's all right.

Tony   I thought we could go to Greenwich, the park. Legs astride the Meridian as they say.

Sandra   Who?

Tony What?

Sandra Who says that?

Tony Oh, you know, folk. (*Northern.*) There's nowt so queer as folk.

Sandra Mm, well I got too many things to sort out in there. (*Indicates flat.*) You go if you want.

Tony (*looking over her shoulder at chart*) Sharon can do Thursday lunch. Stick Warren up there, gives you the night off.

Sandra Tony . . .

Tony You need a window in your diary.

Sandra Listen, I'm not seventeen and doing a Friday night at the Bargepole for pin money any more. This is my living, and I'm bloody good at it.

Tony Sure. You're right. I'll do some hoovering. Or whatever.

Sandra I thought you wanted to go to the park?

Tony No problem.

Sandra Oh it's a lovely day. Take your sketch pad and doodle.

Tony You're addicted to that pub, addict!

Sandra Hey, don't knock it, there's money in booze!

Tony Is that all you want from life? Big bucks?

Sandra Oh Tony I'm not talking about swanning off to Monaco and bonking Grace Kelly's widower. I'm talking about having enough handbag to get a decent pair o'shoes that don't let the rain in.

Tony I can get you shoes.

Sandra No, it's all right.

Tony I can make you shoes.

Tony Get your sketch pad and go the park. Draw a few trees for me.

Tony All my gear's at the studio.

Sandra Right. (*Gets a fiver out of her dressing gown pocket.*) Here's a fiver. Buy a sketch pad.

Tony You can't afford that.

Sandra It was a good night for tips last night, go on.

Tony I'm not a charity.

Sandra And I'm not Minister for the Arts.

Tony I wish you were. You'd be knockout. (*Takes the money.*) I'll get dressed.

Sandra Good idea.

Tony (*goes to the door, turns to* **Sandra**.) Hey and Sandra . . .

Sandra What?

Tony (*winks and clicks his teeth, very Hollywood schmaltz*) Thanks.

Sandra *cringes.* **Tony** *goes in. She gets on with her rota.* **Ste** *comes out.*

Ste Oright?

Sandra Well hello there Casanova.

Ste What?

Sandra A little bird tells me you're in love.

Ste No.

Sandra Oooh, four letter word, love. Don't look so worried. Jamie's told me all about it.

Ste What?

Sandra Yeah well about time too. You deserve a bit o'luck. You're all right you are.

Ste What?!

Sandra I'm jealous. Twenny years younger, coulda bin me!

Ste Oh yeah?

Sandra Come on, what's she like?

Ste Sandra . . .

Sandra Well what's her name then?

Ste No . . .

Sandra Short for Nolene is it? Very 'Home and Away'! Well I hope it works out for ya Stevie. 'Ere, buy Nolene a present wi'that. (*Gets another fiver out of her pocket.*) Sign of affection a present.

Ste No I couldn't.

Sandra Go on I don't need it. Get her some flowers!

Ste No Sandra, really . . .

Sandra (*chucks the money onto the walkway*) Well I'm not picking it up. (*She goes to her door.*) Is she like me? (*Does a little wiggle and laughs.*)

Ste I can't take your money Sandra.

Sandra Don't look a gift horse up his wotsit. D'you know what I mean?

Sandra *goes indoors.* **Ste** *stares at the fiver, struggling for a bit. Then he grabs the fiver and runs.*

Scene Three

Jamie's *bedroom that night.* **Jamie** *sits fully clothed on the bed.* **Ste** *stands beside him holding a plastic bag.*

Jamie You wasn't in school.

Ste I'm aware of that.

Jamie I musta really pissed you off.

Ste No.

Jamie If you want, I could write you an absence note.

Ste I went up Woolwich, had a ride on the ferry. Got you this. (*He hands* **Jamie** *the bag.* **Jamie** *unwraps a shaggy hat.*) Had a bit o' money like.

Jamie Is this for me?

Ste I'll have it if you don't wannit.

Jamie No I'm having it.

Ste You like it, yeah?

Jamie Yeah I do.

Ste Well put it on then. (**Jamie** *puts the hat on.* **Ste** *sits on the bed.*) It just don't feel right, I'm sorry Jay. Here. Your Mum and Tony the other side o' that wall, my ole man and Trevor that side. I've got an aunty in Gravesend. She's dead old. Thought we could go and stay there one night coz she's deaf. But that wouldn't feel right either.

Jamie Look what I got. (*Moves his pillow and pulls out a copy of 'Gay Times', hands it to* **Ste**.)

Ste (*flicks through then reads a bit*) Dear Brian, can you transmit the HIV virus via frottage? What's that?

Jamie (*tuts*) Yoghurt. It's French.

Ste Cor, thick git! (*Reads some more.*) Dear Brian, I am twenty-three, black and gay. The problem is that although I'm happy being with a man and have a strong desire to live with a lover, I get that horrible feeling that people are going to talk about me behind my back, and that they won't accept me as I am. Also, my family don't know. Unhappy, North London.

Jamie Get over that river mate, I'll make you happy! (**Ste** *whacks him on the head with the magazine.*) See Ste, you're not the only one in the world.

Ste I know, there's whatsisname out of Erasure.

Jamie Find page ninety-two.

Ste What? (*Leafs through.*)

Jamie Column four, ten down from the top.

Ste (*reads*) The Gloucester Pub. King William Walk. Opposite Greenwich Park Gates.

Jamie One-eighty bus'll take us right to it.

Ste So?

Jamie So d'you fancy it?

Ste I dunno. Someone might see us.

Jamie We'll go in disguise. Wear sunglasses.

Ste Bagsy your hat.

Jamie Are you gonna come then?

Ste I think I can squeeze you in somewhere.

*As **Jamie** says the next speech, he gets up off the bed and runs his fingers over the hat, very much the temptress.*

Jamie   I've never had a hat for a present before. It's a nice hat. You gave it to me. And now, I'm gonna give you somin' to say thank you that you'll never forget.

Ste   Jay?!

Jamie   On your back!!

Ste   (*lying back*)   What you doin' Jamie?

Jamie   Close your eyes.

*Ste closes his eyes then opens them again. **Jamie** coughs a reproach. **Ste** shuts them. **Jamie** whips out a pad and pen from under the bed. Writes.*

Jamie   Dear Miss Ellis. Sorry Steven wasn't in school today, only he was feeling a little queer. Lot's o'love, Ste's Dad!

They collapse laughing.

Scene Four

*Jamie's bedroom. The early hours of the morning, a few nights later. Complete blackness. **Jamie** is in bed. **Sandra** comes in, in the dark.*

Sandra   Jamie? You awake? Jamie I know you are.

Jamie   What?

Sandra   Where've you been please?

Jamie   Nowhere.

Sandra   Oh yeah? It's half-one in the morning actually. (*Pause.*) Where did you go?

Jamie   Out.

Sandra   Jamie! (*She bends and switches on his bedside light. **Jamie** doesn't move, lying with his back to her.*) You went the Gloucester din't ya? Look at me. (**Jamie** *rolls over.*)

Jamie   Only went for a drink.

Sandra   That's where gay people go. They go there and they go Macmillans in Deptford.

Jamie   It's not just gay people who go. Other people go.

Sandra   People like you?

Jamie   Yeah?

Sandra   It's no time for lying Jamie.

Jamie   It's not a lie.

Sandra   I had a phone call tonight.

Jamie   Oh you're lucky.

Sandra   From your tutor.

Jamie   Miss Ellis?

Sandra   She's worried about ya.

Jamie   God, coz I bunk off games does it mean I'm gay?

Sandra   No. Coz someone hit you.

Jamie   Everyone gets hit.

Sandra   And called you queer. And it aint the first time. She's worried about what it's doing to ya.

Jamie   I'm all right.

Sandra   Are you Jamie? Coz I'm not sure you are. I mean, what am I supposed to think? When you're . . . you're going out drinking and coming home at half-one. Getting hit, getting moody, I don't think you are.

Jamie   Well I am so go back to bed!

Sandra   Er, I'll go when I'm good and ready if you don't mind.

Jamie   I'm tired.

Sandra   You're pissed.

Jamie   No I'm not.

Sandra   Pissed from a bloody gay bar!

Jamie   How d'you know it's gay anyway?

Sandra   Coz it's got a bloody great big pink neon arse outside of it. Jamie, I'm in the business, I get to know these things!

Jamie   You been spying on me?

Sandra   No. Someone at work seen you go in . . .

Jamie   Don't mean I'm gay . . .

Sandra   Going in with another boy, so who was that?

Jamie   (*beat*)   Ste.

Sandra   Ste? Right.

Jamie   Still don't mean I'm gay. They wanna mind their own business.

Sandra   That's what I said.

Jamie   Well then, what you goin' on at me for?

Sandra   Because sometimes Jamie, I can put two and two together and make bloody four, I'm not stupid you know.

Jamie   I never said you were!

Sandra   So I think I deserve an explanation.

Jamie   I went for a drink. Big deal. Everyone in my class goes drinking.

Sandra   Yeah but they don't all go the bloody Gloucester though do they!

Jamie   Some of 'em take drugs, at least I'm not doing that!

Sandra   I bloody hope you're not!

Jamie   Ah well thanks a lot. Thanks a bundle. Go back to bed!

Sandra   I can't sleep Jamie!

Jamie   Well don't take it out on me.

Sandra   Jamie. Will you just talk to me?!

Jamie   I'm knackered.

Sandra   Please Jamie. Talk to me.

Jamie   What about?

Sandra (*sitting on bed*)   I'm your mother.

Pause.

Jamie   Some things are hard to say.

Sandra   I know. I know that, Jamie . . .

Jamie (*crying now*)   I'm not weird if that's what you're thinking!

Sandra   I know you're not love.

Jamie   You think I'm too young. You think it's just a phase. You think I'm . . . I'm gonna catch AIDS and . . . and everything!

Sandra   You know a lot about me don't ya? Jesus you wanna get on that Mastermind. Specialised subject – Your Mother. Don't cry. I'm not gonna put you out like an empty bottle in the morning. Jesus, I thought you knew me well enough to know that. Why couldn't you talk to me eh? Going behind my back like that, getting up to allsorts. There's me going to bed of a night feeling sorry for ya, coz you had to share a bed with Ste. And . . . and all the time you were . . . you were doing a seventy minus one . . .

Jamie   What?

Sandra   Think about it.

Jamie *tuts.*

Sandra   Do you talk to him?

Jamie   Me and him's the same.

Sandra   He's sixteen years of age Jamie. What pearls of wisdom can he throw your way? He aint seen life. He's never even had a holiday.

Jamie   It's difficult init.

Sandra   Am I that much of a monster?

Jamie   No!

Sandra   Don't get me wrong. I like the lad. Always have. All I'm saying is he's young.

Jamie   He's good to me.

Sandra   Is he?

Jamie   Yeah.

Sandra *is bottling up the tears. She can't bring herself to cry in front of* **Jamie**. *She gets up quickly and runs out of the room. She comes on to the walkway and starts to cry.* **Jamie** *bawls.* **Tony** *comes into* **Jamie***'s room.*

Tony   What's up?

Jamie   Go away.

Tony   What have you done now?

Jamie   Nothing!

Tony   Then why's she so upset?

Jamie   I'm a queer! A bender! A pufter! A knobshiner! Brownhatter! Shirtflaplifter!

Tony   I get the picture.

Jamie   Leave me alone.

Tony   And she knows this.

Jamie   No, I thought I'd tell you first.

Tony   This is . . . it's . . . it's okay. Night kidder.

Jamie   Yeah.

Tony *leaves the room and comes out onto the walkway where* **Sandra** *stands crying. It is dark on the walkway, except for a thin shaft of light which creeps across from* **Sandra***'s open door.*

Tony   There's no need to cry.

Sandra   Oh isn't there?!

Tony   It's okay, I know. It's natural. (*Pause.*) You like tomatoes. I like beetroot.

Sandra   Shut up.

Tony   Hey I'm not saying it's easy, yeah? No way. (*Tries to cuddle her.*)

Sandra (*wriggling free*)   Off of me.

Tony   I know. That's cool.

Sandra *gets some fags out of her pocket and a lighter. She lights up, her hands shaking. She wipes her face as she speaks.*

Sandra   He was . . . he was the most beautiful baby in Bermondsey you know. Pushed him round. In his little frilly hat. In a big blue pram called Queen o'the Road. Oh fuckin'ell.

Tony   None of that's changed.

Sandra   State o'me.

Tony   Just let it out Sandra.

Sandra   Shut up.

Tony   You're fighting it hon.

Sandra   Fighting? I've been fighting all me life. Kids pickin' on 'im – I was there. Council saying bollocks to benefit, I was there. When I had three pee in me purse and an empty fridge I went robbin' for that boy. And you say I'm fighting. You! What have you ever had to fight for in your life?!

Tony   Come here.

Sandra   I'm all right.

Tony   Sandra . . .

Sandra   Go back to bed Tony.

Tony   You need support.

Sandra   I wanna be on me own.

Tony   No.

Sandra   Yes.

Tony   If you're sure.

Sandra   I'm sure.

Tony   Well . . . I'll be waiting.

Tony *submits. He's ready to go back in when* **Leah***'s door swings open and* **Leah** *steps out, her door swinging shut behind her. She holds an egg whisk to her chest. She steps forward. When she speaks she does so in a deep South American drawl. She is tripping on acid.* **Tony** *is waylaid by her.*

Leah   (*to* **Tony**)   Not so fast! This is my big speech.

Sandra   Oh for crying out loud.

Tony   Huh?

Leah   I've never won anything in my life before. Certainly not Slimmer of the Year.

Leah *clears her throat.* **Sandra** *and* **Tony** *look to each other, then to* **Leah***.*

Leah   Thank you to all members of the Academy. This means so much. I'd like to thank my manager, the wonderful Ted Bow-Locks. And my band, they're all here . . . (*Waves to* **Tony***.*) Hi guys! I'd like to thank Jesus Christ for coming to earth. I'd like to thank the President for being great . . . but most of all I'd like to thank one very special person . . .

Sandra   What the . . .

Leah   The woman from whom all energy flows. This award is as much hers as mine. The woman who gives me so much . . . inspiration. Let's hear it for . . . Mama San!

Sandra   Leah?

Leah   People say to me, they say . . .

Sandra   Leah are you drunk?

Leah   'Where do you get your energy from?'

Sandra   Leah it's half-one in the morning.

Tony   Has she taken something?

Leah   And I say 'Hey! Mama San!'

Sandra (*to* **Leah**)   Is your mother in?

Leah   Mama San! Git down honey! Your vibes are shootin' right through of me!

Sandra   Is she working nights?

Leah   Don't let the light leave you Mama San.

Sandra (*goes to* **Leah***'s door and bangs on it*)   Rose?! (*To* **Leah**.) Get your keys out. Hurry up.

Tony (*to* **Leah**)   Have you taken, like, a trip, you know?

Sandra (*tuts. Calls through to her flat*)   Jamie?! Leah, have you got your key please?!

Tony   Don't shout at her!

Leah   You're giving me bad vibes Mama!

Tony   She's on something.

Sandra   Jamie!!

Leah (*to* **Tony**)   You're an old, old man. And I don't like old men.

Tony   That's cool. That's no problem.

Sandra   It is a problem actually Tony. Don't pander to her.

Tony   I'm not pandering to her.

Leah   Panda? Where's the panda.

Jamie *comes to the door.*

Jamie   What now?

Leah (*spies an imaginary panda*)   Oh there he is! Hello!

Sandra   Jamie does she take anything?

Jamie   What like?

Tony   Look we're not talking aspirin here, right?

Jamie   Drugs?

Sandra   Jesus.

Jamie   Dunno.

Sandra   Get her key off her Tony.

Leah *is caught up in looking closely at* **Sandra***'s hanging basket.*

Tony   We mustn't touch her.

Sandra   Get her away from my special basket Tony! You're being too easy on her!

Tony   No, we'll freak her out!

Sandra   She's freaking me out Tony!

Jamie   What you taken Leah?

Sandra   I've never seen anything so ridiculous in all me life. (*Grabs* **Leah**.) Leah! Give us your bloody key!

Leah *whimpers and fights for breath.* **Tony** *grabs* **Sandra***'s arm.*

Tony   Sandra!

Sandra   Er, body language Tony! (*Struggles with him.*)

Jamie   Look at her!

Leah (*slipping to floor*)   I'm dead. Dead and buried. (*Flops to floor.*)

Tony   Look what you've done now.

Sandra   I don't believe you just did that Tony.

Jamie   What's she doing?

Sandra   I'll have a nice bruise in the morning thanks to you.

Tony   Christ, er, I saw a video about Woodstock once. What do we do?

Sandra   I've got a nice suggestion, but there's children present.

Tony   We can't leave her there all night!

Sandra/Jamie   Why not?!

Ste *comes out of his flat in his bed gear, the light from his flat brightening the walkway.*

Ste   What's the noise?

Sandra   Oh let's make a party of it shall we?

Jamie   You don't know anything that's good for drug addicts do ya?

Ste   What?

Tony   She's not a drug addict!

Sandra   And my name's Wincey Willis! (*To* **Ste**.) Tony thinks she's taken acid. And Tony knows these sorts o'things coz he's that way inclined hisself I wouldn't wonder.

Ste   Orange juice. (*Everyone looks to* **Ste**.) Me brother says if you have a bad trip on acid, drink orange juice.

Jamie   'Ere, it might be that Ecstasy! Everyone takes that round here.

Tony   It's not Ecstasy.

Sandra   Oh really?

Tony   No, the symptoms are all wrong.

Jamie   Have you got any orange?

Sandra   No.

Ste   We have.

Tony   Will you get it?

Ste   Yeah. (*Exits.*)

Sandra (*to* **Tony**)   Proper little Doctor Dolittle intya?

Tony I don't need this right now Sandra.

Sandra Oh and I do? I'm telling ya, I'll be glad to get outa this bloody place.

Tony Can we just keep the noise down?

Jamie What d'you mean Mum?

Sandra Oh and I suppose you like standing out on the landing at two in the morning? Surrounded by drug experts and the like.

Tony Oh loosen up Sandra.

Sandra Oh you can shut up Tony if you don't mind.

Tony (*to* **Jamie**) Your Mother's tired.

Sandra I said shut up, didn't I?

Ste *comes out with a carton of fresh orange. He hands it to* **Tony**. **Tony** *leans over* **Leah**. *The others watch, fascinated.*

Tony Leah? (*Pause.*) Leah? (*Still no response.*) Mama Cass?

Leah (*immediately lifts her head. Conspiratorially*) I know they're all talking about me. I know it. But what do you expect? This is the price of fame. Ask any of the greats, they'll tell you: Betty, Joan, Marilyn.

Tony (*holding carton out*) I've got a beautiful drink here. And if you drink it, you'll have the time of your life.

Leah Really?

Tony It's the best.

Leah You see the problem is . . . you have seventeen heads. And my Mother made me swear that I'd never take a drink off a guy with seventeen heads.

Sandra (*to* **Jamie**) I'm sorry, this is knocking me sick now.

Tony Right. Ste, you try.

Ste No.

Jamie Go on Ste, give it a try.

Ste (*steps forward. To* **Jamie**) Wish me luck.

Jamie At a boy Ste.

Sandra *watches this exchange with interest.* **Tony** *hands* **Ste** *the drink.* **Sandra** *stares at* **Jamie**, *then round to* **Leah**.

Leah Mm. Pretty boy.

Ste (*to* **Leah**)   Right . . . see this right . . . you know if you drink it, you'll feel better. D'you know what I mean?

Leah (*giggles to* **Tony**)   Is he a fan or something?

Tony   Yes.

Leah   Mmh!

Tony (*to* **Ste**)   Call her Mama Cass!

Jamie (*laughs*)   Gutted!

Ste   No.

Tony (*grabs carton*)   Mama Cass?

Leah (*takes carton and drinks some*)   Why Sir! Your juice tastes mighty fine to me!

Tony   Have some more.

They all watch as **Leah** *drinks. As she does,* **Sandra** *speaks.*

Sandra   There's a pub up in Rotherhithe. The Anchor. The brewery want me to be temporary licensee. (*They all, bar* **Leah***, look to* **Sandra***.*) It's got a little beer garden, and a piano. And you can watch the boats go up and down on the Thames. And it's got a nice little flat above it. Room for a family.

Leah (*to* **Tony**)   Are you in the band?

Tony   No.

Leah   Yes you are.

Tony   Yes. I am.

Jamie   Why didn't you tell me?

Leah   You know, you're very good.

Sandra   You were out.

Tony   Cheers.

Leah   You're a very beautiful person.

Jamie   But . . .

Leah   Am I a beautiful person?

Tony   Yes. You're immensely beautiful.

Jamie   You coulda told me before.

Sandra   Snap! Tony, how long's this gonna take?

Ste   Ten hours.

Sandra   What?!

Jamie   Blimey!

Sandra   Ten hours?

Ste   I think so. I dunno. That's what I've been told. I don't do it. Respect meself too much.

Sandra   Her mother won't be back till breakfast.

Tony We'll have to take her inside.

Sandra Oh brilliant.

Jamie She's not getting in with me!

Sandra I hope you don't think I'm sitting up with her Tony, coz I'm telling you now . . .

Tony I'll sit up with her. It'll be all right. I'm good with kids.

Leah What's happening?

Tony Why don't you come into this nice house with me?

Leah Mama!

Tony Mama . . .

Leah Mm. I don't know.

Tony You'll love the wallpaper.

Sandra Oh thanks.

Tony Here. (*Holds out his hand so she can take it. The others stand aside so* **Tony** *can lead* **Leah** *in. She looks at them.*)

Leah Please . . . no autographs. (**Tony** *and* **Leah** *step inside.*)

Tony (*off*) Isn't it nice?

Leah (*off*) Groovy patterns, wow!

Sandra Right, the show's over. We can all get in now.

Jamie You played a blinder there Ste.

Sandra Jamie. I want you in.

Jamie I'm just talking to Ste.

Sandra You got school in the morning.

Jamie No I haven't. Tomorrow's Saturday.

Ste Time for my beauty sleep anyway.

Jamie Ste, she knows.

Sandra Who's she? The cat's mother?

Jamie Me Mum knows.

Pause. **Ste** *looks horrified. His lower lip starts to tremble.*

Ste You gonna tell my Dad? (*Cries.*)

Sandra No.

Ste Oh my God . . .

Sandra Oh don't you start, I said no, didn't I?

Jamie Ste it's all right. (*Attempts to put his arm around* **Ste**, *who shrugs him off.*)

Ste Jamie . . .

Sandra Jamie . . .

Jamie Ste . . .

Sandra Steven, stop crying please. I am not going to tell your Dad.

Ste (*to* **Jamie**) Why d'you have to go and grass?

Sandra Please Steven.

Jamie I never!

Ste Yeah well how come she knows?

Sandra Coz SHE never come down with the last shower! Jamie, get 'im an 'anky. There's a box of autumnal shades by my bed. (**Jamie** *goes inside.*) Jesus Ste will you stop crying? I don't believe in secrets. I like people to be straight up and honest. But I'm no fool. D'you think I want these flats to be infamous for child murder? No. So I won't be telling your Dad.

Ste He'd kill me!

Sandra Yes. I've just said that.

Ste No he would.

Sandra I think we've established that already actually Ste.

Ste They all would, all of 'em.

Sandra I'LL bloody kill you in a minute if you don't stop snivelling and shut up! You're a good lad. That's what counts. And . . . somewhere you'll find people what won't kill you.

Ste No I won't.

Sandra Well you've found the Gloucester.

Ste I hate it.

Sandra Yeah well somewhere else then, shut up.

Ste There aint nowhere else.

Sandra There is actually Steven, coz there's an island in the Mediterranean called 'Lesbian', and all its inhabitants are dykes. So I think you got your eye wiped there. (**Jamie** *comes out with a box of hankies.*) Now. Wipe 'em properly.

Jamie There.

Ste Tar. I'm sorry.

Jamie Don't be a dickhead.

Ste Fuck me.

Sandra Er, there'll be none o'that out here thank you. (*To* **Jamie**.) Are you gonna be long out here?

Jamie No.

Ste No Sandra.

Sandra Well . . .

Ste We won't Sandra. I'm going to bed. Honest Sandra.

Sandra That's me name Ste, don't wear it out. Night Steven. (*Goes in.*)

Ste Night.

Sandra *exits.*

Jamie What's Leah like eh?

Ste I know.

Jamie Jees!

Ste She's blinding your Mum.

Jamie She's all right.

Ste Init? Who else knows?

Jamie Only Tony. (*Pause.*) Give us a kiss.

Ste No!

Jamie Let's go the stairs, no one can see there.

Ste There's no such thing as just a kiss. I'll knock you up in the morning, yeah?

Jamie (*Christine Cagney*) Knock away Marybeth, knock away!

Ste See you Christine.

Ste *goes to his door.* **Jamie** *stays where he is and watches.* **Ste** *turns round.*

Ste What?

Jamie Watching.

Ste What?!

Jamie You!

Ste (*points to* **Jamie**'s *door and orders him to move*) Now!

Reluctantly **Jamie** *goes. Both doors close.*

Scene Five

The next evening, about seven-thirty. **Ste** *is out taking his drying back in.* **Leah**'s *door is open. She comes to the door and watches him quietly.*

Leah I wished I was the one that was going away. (*Pause.*) I wished. I hate it round here, don't you?

Ste S'all right.

Leah These flats. Them pubs.

Ste Done it all intya?

Leah   I gets up in the morning, bake me face in half a ton o'slap. Tong me hair wi'yesterday's lacquer . . . and that's it. Same every bleedin' day. Fuck all to look forward to except Mama Bloody Cass. Nothing ever happens. Nothing ever changes.

Ste   What about your new school?

Leah   Fell through.

Ste   D'you wanna come the Gloucester?

Leah   The what?

Ste   Gay pub.

Leah   I don't know any gay blokes.

Ste   Yes you do.

Leah (*smiles*)   Yeah.

Ste   Me and Jay are going in half-an-hour. Come on, plenty o'men.

Leah   Yeah and they all dance backwards and never get married.

Pause.

Sandra's *door opens, unseen by* **Leah**.

Leah   D'you think Jamie's Mum'd give me a job in her new pub?

Sandra *appears, dolled up to the nines. She looks gorgeous. She is carrying a full bag of rubbish to take to the chute.*

Sandra   Doubt it.

Ste   You look nice Sandra.

Sandra (*stopping*)   Cheers Ste.

Leah   Goin' out wi' your bloke?

Sandra   No. Girls from work.

Ste   Have a nice time.

Sandra   Thanks love. (**Ste** *goes in.* **Sandra** *puts her binbag down.*) No licensee in their right mind'd have you pulling pints Leah.

Leah   I can't help it. I'm a Gemini. I got a split personality.

Sandra   Bollocks, you know when you're being a little cow.

Leah   Everyone hates me.

Sandra   We despair of you. That's different. You can't wrap yourself up in a dead fat American git for the rest of your life you know.

Leah   I know.

Sandra   Well then. (*Picks up bin bag.*)

Leah   I gotta go in. Get ready. I'm going out wi' Ste and Jamie.

Sandra   The Gloucester?

Leah Yeah. I intend to find meself a nice dyke tonight Sandra, coz I'm tellin' ya, I'm through with men.

Sandra *chuckles.* **Leah** *goes in.* **Sandra** *turns to go to the chute. But* **Tony** *enters from the stairs. Leather jacket on, pretty swish. They stare at each other.*

Tony If I had a camera now . . .

Sandra (*beat*) What?

Tony Well . . . I'd take your picture.

Sandra I don't like having my picture took. Camera don't like me.

Tony My camera would love you.

Sandra No it wouldn't Tony.

Tony It would. It'd be like that . . . (*Blows a kiss. Laughs.*)

Sandra Tony, what you doing?

Tony Can't keep away from you Babes.

Sandra Tony I told you I was going out with the girls from work.

Tony Thought I could tag along.

Sandra Girls night out. You'd only be bored.

Tony I wanna celebrate too.

Sandra I know. But . . .

Tony They'd mind.

Sandra I mind.

Tony Right. Well how about one little kiss? Send me on my way. Something to think of till tomorrow. (*Goes to kiss her. She pushes him away.*)

Sandra You're drowning me Tony.

Tony Well. I'll ring you.

Sandra Tony . . .

Tony What's your next night off?

Sandra I dunno yet.

Tony Well you make the decisions.

Sandra I'm sorry Tony but . . . I think you better go.

Tony I'm not in a rush . . .

Sandra No. No. (*Beat.*) Put that down the chute for us will ya?

Tony stares at her. She turns to go in and freezes. **Tony** *waits a while longer, then picks up the bin bag and walks away.* **Sandra** *swings round, looking like she is going to call him back. Stops herself.* **Jamie** *comes out wearing a jumper. He has two glasses of wine. He hands one to* **Sandra**.

Jamie Mum? Have this. Get you in the mood.

Sandra Tar.

Jamie You're going Woolwich intya?

Sandra What? Yeah. Pub crawl then Stars Nightclub.

Jamie You'll pull dressed like that. (**Sandra** *sighs a laugh, looking at floor.*) Why don't you come with us? (*Beat.*) Ring the girls and tell them you'll see 'em later. (**Sandra** *shakes her head.*) You don't know how to enjoy yourself do ya?

Sandra Bloody cheek.

Jamie There's a male stripper on tonight as well.

Pause. **Sandra** *considers it.*

Sandra Give me five minutes!

Sandra *runs indoors.* **Jamie** *sits on the step, sipping his wine. From* **Leah**'s *flat 'Dream A Little Dream of Me' by Mama Cass comes floating across the balcony.* **Ste** *comes out, freshened up.*

Ste In't you gonna be hot in that jumper?

Jamie Well you bought it me.

Ste Yeah for up Rotherhithe. It's on the River. You'll freeze.

Jamie We're on the River here. (*Tuts.*) Anyone about?

Ste (*nods to his flat*) In there? (**Jamie** *nods.*) No.

Jamie (*beat*) Dance with me.

Tentatively they take each other's hands and start to slow dance to the music. They are lost in each other.

Leah *comes out, ready for the off. She stands on her doorstep and watches the lads. She hasn't got any pockets, so she holds her purse, fags, lighter and keys in her hand till the end of the scene. She takes a fag out and lights up.*

Sandra *comes out with her wine. She watches* **Jamie** *and* **Ste** *dancing and then looks to* **Leah**.

Sandra 'Ere Leah, gizza little drag o' that.

Leah *passes her the fag.* **Sandra** *takes a big drag.* **Leah** *goes indoors and turns the music up. She comes back out again.*

Leah Sandra.

Sandra What?

Leah Come on.

Sandra *and* **Leah** *start to slowdance as well. They chat intermittently.*

Sandra 'Ere Ste!

Ste What?

Sandra Imagine your Dad's face!

Pause.

'Ere Leah.

Leah What?

Sandra What's this dyke gonna be like?

Leah Oooh, big and butch!

Sandra What colour eyes?

Leah Green.

Sandra Yeah?

Leah Yeah.

Sandra Tall?

Leah I'll have to look up.

Sandra Nice.

Leah Yeah.

Sandra Yeah.

The music turns up of its own accord, blasting out. A glitterball spins above the stage, casting millions of dance hall lights. **Ste** *and* **Jamie** *are dancing.* **Leah** *and* **Sandra** *are dancing.*

The lights fade.

The End

Beautiful Thing

When *Beautiful Thing* was about to go on at the Bush I was called in to see a drama producer at the BBC. He sat me down and said how much he had enjoyed reading the play. Fair enough, I'd hardly have expected to be called in if he'd hated it. However I was quite taken aback by the reason he gave for enjoying it so much:

I just thought it was amazing. Here you have a woman who lives on a council estate and yet actually shops at the Body Shop.

That such a detail could make a play amazing I find incredible. That such a fact could in itself be amazing I found even more so. I took heart, maybe *Beautiful Thing* could lay some widely held misconceptions to rest.

I came to write the play during the summer holidays from my teaching job in 1992. I was 24 and desperate to get out of education. Writing for me was then a release, and I think it shows in the play. I started off by writing an argument between a son and his mother about him bunking off games at school. This was second nature to me. I hated football at primary school and used to look longingly at the girls' pitch where they played the much more enticing game of rounders. I'd pass the time avoiding the ball by playing Charlie's Angels with some other non-interested lads. Obviously, when using this detail in the play I updated it somewhat. Once I'd written the row I got bored and thought I'd introduce another character. I invented a next door neighbour who was a bit of a loudmouth and more than likely based on all the vocal girls I was teaching at the time. Leah may be a likeable character, but she'd be a bugger to teach. Bored again I invented love interests for the mother and the boy and girl. Compromising on character numbers in the hope of one day getting the play staged, I chose the same person, Ste, for the boy and girl to be interested in. Once I'd done this there was only one way the play could go.

I had no idea what was going to happen next. But each time I came to a crisis, either in the drama, or through me getting bored, I would have to make a decision about where to take the characters next. I think it is the factors that influence these decisions that make one writer different to the next. The decisions I make would certainly be different from Alan Bennett's, and his decisions would again be very different from Sarah Daniels'. I don't bandy these names around because I think I am as good as them, merely because I admire them.

When people ask if this is an autobiographical play, I would say that certain moments are, but where personal experience does play a major factor is in the decisions I took. I would hardly have Jamie run off at the end of the play to lead a fulfilling life in merchant banking, as I've never merchant banked. So I kept the characters always in a world which I know something about, and doing things I know about. Leah was the biggest problem. Where do you take a character that is obsessed with Mama Cass? Luck played a huge part in her journey, flicking through the Mama Cass tape cover I read about Cass Elliot's encounter with a lead pipe and the rest of her story in the play fell into place.

Growing up gay in Liverpool in the eighties, the only role models I had on TV and film were very middle or upper class ones. Two public schoolboys punting through Cambridge in cricket whites might have been exciting to watch, but it had very little to do with my personal experience. I suppose I wanted to redress this imbalance. I also wanted to redress the idea that if you are working class and gay that you end up getting kicked out onto the streets and sell your body for two Woodbines and a bar of Caramac. Yes, it happens, prejudice is not a middle class phenomenon, but neither is tolerance, understanding or the ability to embrace.

The age of consent is an issue close to my heart, and by choosing to make the boys in the play sixteen and under I hope I've done my bit to fight the status quo. I used to think I hadn't done enough, but when I watched the play on its opening night to a packed house of schoolkids, hen nights and binmen conventions at the West Yorkshire Playhouse, and I saw the audience embrace the characters and will things to work out well for them, I realised maybe I had done more than I'd previously given myself credit for. I think the character of Tony is an easy way into the play for many straight people. He's a bit of a laugh, he's trying his best, and once he's made you laugh you're more relaxed and ready to take the other characters on board. I wasn't aware of this at the time of writing, but I sat through the play enough times to recognise the more straitlaced members of the audience who would only relax after Tony's line 'You shouldn't use words like bird.' You could set a clock by their regular sighs of relief at this point. It was as if they were thinking, 'The writer knows there are people like us watching this play.' Well they were very misguided. I wasn't selling out to them in the character of Tony, I wrote him that way because I thought it was a bit of a laugh.

As a theatre writer you are always aware of limited resources, and none more so than when I was writing *Beautiful Thing*. I kept sets and cast to a minimum. It would have been very easy to write scenes between Ste and his Dad, but I prioritised and felt it was enough for Ste to talk about this. Some disagree, some want a bit more darkness, but I'm now glad about this decision to keep Ronnie off stage because the play becomes more of a celebration. I've just finished the screenplay for Channel Four and it has been a joy to write for Ste's Dad and Leah's Mum, and to see Jamie's teachers, but then I expect the screenplay to be a very different experience to seeing the play.

I think any writer writes from an obsession at the time of writing. It can be quite cringeworthy to then have to fight for those ideas and obsessions a few years down the line. Still, I'm not cringeing yet at the ideas in *Beautiful Thing*. I think it's very much a twenty-four year old writer's play, and can at times be twee and naive, but it still manages to move me and I think that theatre should move people. And two years down the line I still have great admiration for the music of Mama Cass, thank God I chose her and not the Nolan Sisters.

Jonathan Harvey comes from Liverpool and now lives in London. After studying Psychology and Education at Hull University he taught in London for three years. He has written nine stage plays: *The Cherry Blossom Tree* (Liverpool Playhouse, National Girobank Young Writer of the Year Award 1987), *Mohair* (Royal Court Young Writers Festival 1988/ International Festival of Young Playwrights, Sydney 1988) *Tripping and Falling* (Glasshouse Theatre Company), *Catch* (Spring Street Studio, Hull), *Lady Snogs The Blues* (Lincoln Theatre Festival), *Wildfire* (Royal Court Theatre Upstairs), *Beautiful Thing* (Bush/National tour/ Donmar Warehouse/Duke of York's Theatre, London/winner of the John Whiting Award 1994), *Babies* (Royal National Theatre Studio/Royal Court Theatre/George Devine Award 1993), and *Rupert Street Lonely Hearts Club* (for the RNT Studio). His television play *West End Girls* was shown on Carlton TV in 1993 and he is working on a second *Love Junkie* for the BBC. *Beautiful Thing* is currently being developed as a screenplay for Channel Four with Island World Productions.

Snow Orchid

Joe Pintauro

Characters

Filumena Lazarra, *Thirty-eight, a native of Sicily, she came to America as Rocco's bride when she was only sixteen. It turned out to be a loveless marriage.*
Rocco Lazarra, *Fifty-six. Born in Brooklyn, New York, he is Italo-American of Neopolitan extraction. A chauvinist and brute most of his life, he returns from a psychotic episode, hoping to bring order and beauty to the household he destroyed.*
Sebb (Sebbie, Sebastiano), *Twenty-one, their oldest son, an auto-mechanic who is secretly gay.*
Blaise (Blaze, Biaggio), *Sixteen. Too young and too American to fit into the family he desperately loves.*
Doogan, *Twenty-two, Sebbie's lover.*

Snow Orchid was selected by the Eugene O'Neil Conference, 1980 and was first produced in New York in 1981 at the Circle Rep. with the following cast:

Filumena	Olympia Dukakis
Rocco	Peter Boyle
Sebb	Robert Lu Pone
Blaise	Ben Siegler

Directed by Tony Giordano

The play was first produced in Britain by the London Gay Theatre Company at the Gate Theatre, London on 24 February 1993. The cast was as follows:

Filumena	Paola Dionisotti
Rocco	Roger Lloyd Pack
Sebb	Jude Law
Blaise	Jonathan Wrather
Doogan	Adam Magnani

Directed by Tim Luscombe
Designed by Rob Howell
Lighting designed by Johanna Town
Composer Jason Carr
Sound designed by Paul Arditti

The script published here accords with the staging of the play in London.

Set

This script accords with the staging of *Snow Orchid* in London in 1993. In that production, the stage was divided into two halves, downstage and upstage.

Downstage contained Filumena's bedroom stage right and Sebb's bedroom stage left. Both were minimally represented by shelves or a cupboard and a chair each. Also the downstage area (or a red box, as it became known, for that is what it was: a perspectived box with the front and back open) was the setting for the Rocco/Blaise 'fern room' scene. This is explained at the appropriate place in the script.

Upstage was a considerably more naturalistic representation of the main living room of the house, with a door upstage left which led to the front door of the house and the kitchen, and a door upstage right which led to the cellar and to where Rocco's old shrunken trousers were.

The back wall of the upstage area was mostly two disguised doors which opened at the moment when Filumena took a step outside the house: whereupon the entire set reverted and 'off' was 'on' and 'on' became 'off'. (See the end.) Fake snow was used for this moment.

Fibreoptics were used for the fern room scene. There was a window in the upstage part of the stage right wall of the red box and a 'St Sebastian dart board' on the downstage part of the stage left wall of the red box.

The floor of the red box was raked (and the ceiling and walls similarly angled in) so that some height was achieved between the back of the floor of the red box and the front of the floor of the upstage area. Two steps joined one to the other, and these two steps represented the stairs in the house. The living room upstage was 'downstairs' and the two bedrooms off stage were 'upstairs'.

The audience, in effect, saw through the house from front to back, through the fern room first, then through the red box (the bedroom spaces) to the back wall of the dining room, where two exit doors flanked the wall, a wall that in the end of the play springs open into infinite whiteness and snow.

Act One

Scene One

Church bells are heard. **Sebb** *and* **Blaise** *are heard off.*

Blaise It's quiet.

Sebb Where the hell am I gonna hide the box?

Blaise Hide it up in your room.

Sebb She might bump into me on the stairs.

Blaise She's probably locked in her room talkin' to Saint Anthony. (*His head appears around the door u/l, and he calls softly, teasing* **Sebb**.) Ma?

Sebb First your arms. Then your legs. (**Sebb** *and* **Blaise** *enter through the u/l door.* **Sebb** *is carrying a large rectangular gift-wrapped box.* **Filumena**, *in her bedroom, coughs.*)

Blaise She's havin' a cigarette. We got a minute of peace before Vesuvius erupts.

Sebb What you hafta waste a half-an-hour in Woolworth's for, huh, cauliflower-face?

Blaise Why'd you hafta go across the friggin' bridge into Manhattan for a lousy coat and dress? A new coat and dress ain't gonna get her to leave this house.

Sebb I told you to read that magazine article. There's a place in Denver that cures people a'scared to leave their house.

Blaise So a coat and dress is gonna fly her there?

Sebb I don't need you to help me with her.

Blaise What happened when her mother died in Italy and we hadda go get our passports? She turned into Niagara Falls on the subway . . .

Sebb Blaise, I'm warnin' you . . .

Blaise She gets the sweats when she has to answer to freakin' doorbell.

Sebb I'll take care of her.

Blaise You'd have to slip a dozen quaaludes in her macaroni to get her to New Jersey and he's talkin' about shippin' her to Colorado.

Sebb They should put your mouth on top of every ambulance.

Blaise She looked like a vampire on the passport.

Sebb She was in grief, you asshole.

Blaise She was in terror of the subways is what she was in. Did we get to Sicily? We didn't even get to Hoyt and Skimerhorn Street.

Filumena (*coming from her bedroom to the living room, running*) You sonofabitches the two of you.

Blaise (*overlapping into an imaginary microphone*)   Ladies and gentlemen, the hot lava has just entered the village of Pompeii destroying everything in its path . . .

Filumena   Where were you? You swore to me I wouldn't hafta be alone when that monster walks in.

Sebb   He kept me double parked for a half hour in fronta Woolworth's.

Blaise   Our father a monster. That's nice.

Filumena   And what you hafta go to Woolworth's for?

Blaise   A welcome home sign.

Filumena   A welcome home sign for a man who tried to commit suicide. (*She grabs the bag out of* **Blaise**'*s hand and rummages through it.*)

Blaise   So what, you're gone, you're gone. You come home. Welcome home.

Filumena   Party hats?

Sebb   Is that what I was wastin' gas for?

Filumena   He's not comin' home from the army you jerk, he's coming home from the crazy house. I'm sittin' here afraid to take a bath in case he walks in on me, and this kid comes home with party hats?

Blaise   So what if he sees your tits. He's your husband.

Filumena (*reaches to grab* **Blaise** *to slap him*)   Catch that kid. I'm gonna torture him.

Sebb   Lookit you gettin' all dressed up for the monster, Filumena.

Filumena   What're you crazy? I'm gettin' dressed for San Antonio.

Sebb   Saint Anthony?

Filumena   They're rollin' his statue in the streets.

Sebb   Saint Anthony ain't in December.

Blaise   They're passin' out his bread for Advent, stupid. Five dollars a loaf.

Sebb   He's got a big dong, eh, Filumena?

Blaise   Who? Saint Anthony?

Sebb   The ol' man, turkey. Like father like son . . .

Blaise   I think we get it from her.

Filumena   Shut up, trouble mouth. Wipe your greasy fingerprints off the light switches before your father sees them and go upstairs and close my window.

Blaise   Wait till he sees the oil bill. I'm tellin' him you keep your window open and turn the thermostat up so you could make believe you're back in Sicily.

Filumena   Do I spend your money?

Blaise   You ain't gonna either.

Sebb   He got his first paycheck today.

Filumena Oh yeah? You're gonna chip in here, big time. You're the one wanted to quit school . . . (*To* **Sebb**.) You come upstairs with me and help me get this dress on. I musta shrank the goddamn thing. (*To* **Blaise**.) Go for olives, you. He likes olives . . . and he hates the bread with the seeds. Get a loaf without the seeds. That Saint Anthony bread is full of seeds . . . five dollars . . . (**Filumena** *goes to her bedroom where she hears the Saint Anthony procession in the distance. She shuts the window against it and sits.*)

Blaise I hear you and Doogan split up, and he's movin' to Texas. I feel bad for you guys . . . You were a good couple.

Sebb C'mere . . . I jus' wanna shake your hand.

Blaise I was just bein' sadistic.

Sebb I ain't gonna do nothin' – c'mere a minute . . .

Blaise Ta ta . . . (*Exits u/l door.*)

Scene Two

Other room.

Filumena Some saint . . . right now you hadda make them pass out the bread . . . (*She bends to put on a black stocking. Her behind faces the doorway where* **Sebb** *is approaching silently.*)

Filumena . . . Who needs your bread? Who knows if they pick their noses those bakers or wipe their ass and not wash their hands? (*Then the other stocking.*) I shkeeve your bread. When I see you bakin' it with my own eyes, then I'll eat it.

Sebb What gorgeous cheeks. (*He gooses her.*)

Filumena Stop. You sonofabitch. (*She slaps him.*) Help me with this dress.

Sebb Stop sweatin'. You'll stink.

Filumena Where's my underarm. . . ?

Sebb Look at you, primpin' and powderin' like King Kong was comin' to pick ya off the cliff.

Filumena This powder ain't for your father.

Sebb Then why you gettin' dressed? Huh? You goin' to go to the sidewalk this year? Huh, Filumena?

Filumena Maybe I'll try to take the bread at the sidewalk. Why not?

Sebb Good. I'll help you down the stoop.

Filumena Leave me alone.

Sebb Liar. You forget the days he used to give us black eyes?

Filumena You're makin' me feel closed in.

Sebb Would the Jews wear perfume for Hitler?

Filumena Go look at Christ on the cross. You're supposed to forgive.

Sebb   Did you forget before Blaise was born . . . that shithole tenement over the Brooklyn Navy Yard where the three of us had ta sleep in one bed and he kicked us if we moved?

Blaise *enters the o/s area, preparing the table for dinner, etc.*

Filumena   Yeah, and you followed him around that tenement like a puppy. You cried when he went to work. All of a sudden he remembers the Brooklyn Navy Yard. . . . He never said boo to you. When was the last time he talked to you?

Sebb   I just don't like seein' him around my house using my bathroom. Eatin' in my kitchen.

Filumena   The kitchen's under his name with the rest of the house. You say 'hello' nice when he comes in and then you can forget him for the rest of your life. Now you work all day . . . and I'm the one who's got him. Twenty-four hours – Jesus! (*The procession is heard far away but nearer than before.*)

Man (*off*)   Pane! Sant Antonio!

Filumena   You hear? Saint Anthony's on Meeker Avenue. (*Shouting.*) Tell the little bastard to throw the rigatoni in the boilin' water . . . if it's boilin'.

Sebb (*calling*)   Blaise . . .

Blaise (*calling*)   The little bastard heard. Should I throw in salt, too?

Filumena   I salted it . . . I salted it. And he did turn on the gas under the sauce!

Sebb   Blaise?

Blaise   I did.

Filumena   Low.

Sebb   Low, Blaise.

Filumena   Tell him to lower it. I know that kid.

Blaise   I'm lowering it and I set the big table.

Filumena (*screams*)   Don't set the big table. What's that little trouble-maker up to? He knows your father eats alone in the kitchen . . . Hey, the lipstick, throw it away, Sebbie, please . . .

Sebb   I paid three bucks for this lipstick.

Filumena   So give it to Doogan.

Sebb   You know Ma, I warned you not to make cracks.

Filumena   Take a joke, undertaker-face. You're scared your father'll find out about Doogan? You're a car mechanic, not a dress designer. He'll never guess about you. Zip up the dress.

Sebb   Gorilla in a dress – (*With effort he yanks her dress down over her hips.*) Holy Christ . . .

Filumena   Oh! My tits are in my throat.

Sebb   Com'on . . . let's go down now and catch the bread. The people haven't seen you since we moved here.

Filumena I don't wanna see no people. I'm catchin' the bread from the window. Lemme alone. Hide my cigarettes.

Sebb I'll help you down the fuckin' stoop.

Filumena Catholic high school! How sweet your mouth turned out. Bedu Santu, where's my money now? You, Saint Anthony, the breadman, and Rocco all on the same fuckin' day. Hide these cigarettes.

Sebb You don't have to hide nothin'.

Filumena Put those cigarettes somewhere . . .

Sebb If he ever hits you, you call me, you hear?

Filumena Sure. So we can have a double murder. Brush my hair (*She hands him the brush.*)

Sebb How'm I gonna brush your hair if you don't sit?

Filumena This dress is too tight to sit.

Sebb (*tries brushing*) Ma, you gotta sit.

Filumena Okay. (*She sits.*) Oi! Gesu Greetsu. (*The dress rips.*) Chi Cazzu? Mannaggia la Madonna e tutti i Santi.

Sebb Holy Christ!

Filumena I exploded the dress. Looka me. This saint wants me to stay trapped in this room with him forever.

Sebb You wanna wear a new dress? Something terrific? Ma?

Filumena (*she cries silently*) It's no use. Sant Antonio, perche?

Male Voice (*off, selling bread*) Pane San Antonio. Pane San Antonio.

Filumena Brush! They're on the block. Brush! Please!

Sebb *brushes, roughly.*

Filumena Ouch!

Sebb I'm sorry.

Filumena No. I like it hard. Only you know how. It opens my sinuses. Mnnn.

Sebb Ma, a grey hair.

Filumena Pull it.

Sebb *pulls the hair.*

Filumena Throw it away. What's the big bird that swims on top of the water in English again?

Sebb A swan?

Filumena Si. La Cigna nivura. That's what they used to call me in Sicilia . . . the black swan 'cause I had my hair down here but I wore it like this. (*She demonstrates.*) Sixteen years old. And your father? A thirty-two year old man with white pants. An Amerigano. He was so crazy for me he went to my mother: I die if you don't give her to me. Well, an Italian from America, in white pants, Madonna . . . what connections he must have. Take her, my mother said. Who knew he was an electrician on vacation? Try to get him to fix a plug around here . . . and a Napulitano on top of it.

Sebb   Ma, when are ya gonna let it be American time on that clock?

Filumena   Never. That's my mother's clock from Sicilia; I know the time from the electric clock, six o'clock, but it's midnight in Sicily right now. The stars are out. I hold the clock and I can smell lemons from my bed. I hear the bells on the goats . . .

Sebb   Ma, them goats died twenty years ago.

Filumena (*she stares sadly out of her window*)   No. The goats are still alive, more than those skinny American trees outside that get hysterical soon as they smell the snow and tear all their hair out like crazy ladies. I hate snow . . .

Male Voice (*off, selling bread*)   Pane di Sant Antone. Pane di Sant Antone.

Filumena   Ooop, Madonna, they stopped in front of the house. Where's my money? (*She jumps up and opens the window, waving her twenty-dollar bill; but looking up, she discovers and points to seagulls, and takes it as a lucky sign.*) Hey, seagulls. See?

Man (*off, selling bread*)   Pane San Antonio.

Filumena (*looking down*)   Look. Look. Up here, stupido.

Man   No bread for the people who don't come to church. Father Sullivan said.

Filumena   Tell him to mind his business. There's a twenty-dollar bill. Throw me two loaves and get away from my door. We're expecting my husband.

Sebb   We'll go down and get your change, Ma . . . C'mon.

Filumena   Go 'way . . .

Man   Next Sunday, Signora Lazarra, you people come to church.

Filumena   Is that supposed to be Saint Anthony on your wagon? He looks like you stole some stiff from the back door of Pizella's Funeral Parlor.

Sebb   Ma.

Filumena   You wanna see the real Saint Anthony! What you think them seagulls are makin' a circle over this house for? 'Cause he's right here in my bedroom. This is my church.

Man   Catch your bread.

Filumena leans out, catches two loaves. Each loaf of bread has a purple Advent ribbon tied around it, and on the ribbon is pasted a paper reproduction of St Anthony's face.

Man (*sexily*)   Hey, lady, bend down for your change.

This brings **Sebb***'s head to the window.*

Sebb   She's my mother, money-hungry. Eat the change before I come down and shove it down your throat.

Filumena   Hey, you. Get inside.

Sebb *shuts window.*

Blaise (*running up stairs*)   Ma . . . Ma . . . did you see Saint Anthony?

Filumena   Grab him.

Sebb *teasingly grabs* **Blaise**. **Rocco** *enters the u/s area quietly, in coat and hat and with bags and belongings.*

Blaise   What I do?

Filumena   Take down those decorations . . . (*Slap.*) . . . and go to Scambati's and get Provolone cheese for grating.

Rocco *listens for signs of life in the house. He begins to hang up his orchid plants. These plants are attached to sphagnum moss and treebark: they are primeval looking, but unseen as yet, wrapped in dark green tissue.*

Blaise   When we gonna have an American dinner?

Filumena   Fuck America. Get Provolone.

Blaise   Jungle woman.

Filumena   Grab that housedress . . . hurry . . . that clown grates Provolone on his macaroni.

Sebb   What clown? Cheeks. (*Gooses her.*)

Filumena (*screams*)   Stop. The fat clown that sings in the opera.

Sebb   Pagliacci?

Filumena *becomes confused and winds up with one sleeve of the dress on, but the torn dress is not fully removed.*

Filumena   Get this . . . arm out.

Rocco *puts on a cassette.*

Filumena (*giggling to herself*)   Don't say Pagliacci to his face and make me laugh, you sonofabitch. Don't you do it.

Blaise   Do you think they made him wear a straitjacket?

Filumena   Don't you try to make me laugh in fronta him or I'll kill ya.

Sebb   Cheeks. (*Pinches her again.*)

Filumena *jerks away, pretending she's annoyed, but she enjoys it.*

Filumena   Stop! (*To* **Blaise**.) And you, you other sonofabitch, take down that welcome home!

They freeze as beautiful music sounds throughout the house. It is spatial, angelic music. **Sebb** *slowly makes his way down the stairs.*

Rocco (*startled*) Sebbie.

Sebb Pa. Gee. You look good. (*Stares at the changes in* **Rocco**, *sympathetically, then catches himself.*) How we sposta know who walked in here? What is that stuff playin'?

Rocco I thought it'd be a nice way . . . I wanted to surprise you that I was home. Thanks for the sign. Where's . . .

Filumena *and* **Blaise** *enter the u/s area.*

Rocco Filumena. Hey. Come' stai?

Filumena Rocco?

Rocco Yeah. She don't recognise me. Hey, I got thin, right?

Filumena Didn't they feed you? You look like you just got out of a concentration camp.

Rocco You look like you just got hit with an airplane. (*No reaction.*) So laugh at a joke. You go out while I was gone, Filumena?

Blaise Yeah, she stuck her head out the window.

Sebb *swings at* **Blaise**.

Blaise Lay off, beast.

Rocco Hey. Shut up. She'll go out when she feels like it. Right, Filumena? We'll get her out there. I learned a lot about that stuff. Whadya embarrassed to express yourself? . . . Somebody kiss me or somethin'.

Filumena Blaise, kiss your father.

Blaise Kiss him, Sebb. I gotta check the macaroni. (*Goes off to the kitchen.*)

Filumena And lower that music.

Rocco That's Zeff Gardner, that new guy.

Filumena (*she pretends to have heard of the composer*) Oh, yeah. (**Blaise**, offstage, turns off the music.)

Rocco You cut your hair, Filumena.

Filumena Uh, yeah.

Rocco I got a loaf of Saint Anthony bread . . . and wine . . . to go with the music. What're we eatin'?

Blaise (*re-entering*) Two minutes for the rigatoni.

Rocco Rigatoni? I'm so glad I'm home . . . Jesus . . .

Blaise *peeks into Rocco's blue drugstore bag.*

Blaise Pa, this says Prozac.

Rocco Get outta that bag. We gotta learn to respect people's privacy.

Filumena Then why'd you pull up the shades? (*She pulls them down again.*)

Rocco   I'm gone two years and you greet me with why'd I open the shades? They pass downers out like jelly beans where I come from.

Blaise   You just got these around the corner. It says Lorimer Drugs.

Rocco   What're you, a detective? Mind your business. Please. Hey. Welcome home, Rocco. This is it. Thank you for the sign.

Filumena   Thank you? Please? See what 'lectricity does for your brain?

Rocco   I didn't get no 'lectricity. I got . . . talkin' it out . . . I'll teach you how to talk and how to hear. This is all new . . .

Filumena   I'd rather have the 'lectricity.

Blaise   I set up your place in the kitchen, Pa, with a party hat.

Rocco   No, I wanna eat out here with all of you. Please.

Filumena *is attracted by Rocco's softness.*

Filumena   That's up to you. I don't care.

Blaise   A welcome home party.

Sebb   Count me out. I got an appointment.

Rocco   Cancel it, Sebb.

Sebb   Who does he think he's ordering around?

Filumena   He'll stay for dinner. C'mon Sebbie . . . for me.

Rocco   Once, Sebbie, once. Like a real family.

Sebb   Listen to him. You're the one never wanted anybody to eat with you. Now you wanna play Daddy?

Rocco   Daddy?

Filumena   Do it for me, I said.

Blaise   Yeah, do it . . . for someone else. (**Blaise** *exits to kitchen.*)

Sebb   I'm twenty-one years old, you. He's somethin' in my past. I gotta screw around this table 'cause they gave him a guilty conscience in some nut-house?

Rocco   It ain't for me, poison-face, that I wanna eat with you. It's for your own good. Okay, you little sonofabitch, so don't bust my hump ten minutes after I walk in the door of my own fuckin' house . . . (**Rocco** *stops short suddenly, hearing himself.*)

Sebb   What happened to 'please' and 'thank you'?

Rocco   Look, I'm sorry, okay. I'm scared, I'm nervous.

Filumena   We all sit down like he says for tonight . . . just tonight . . . 'cause tomorrow's a different story . . .

Sebb   Absolutely not. I gotta go to a wake.

Filumena   Hey, prima donna. Swallow your pride. And Rocco . . . give us a chance to get used to the 'please' and 'thank yous' 'cause you wasn't Jesus Christ last time we saw you.

Rocco   Sebb, will you put my tape back on? I want us to act like Americans. I wanna make a toast tonight. You'll see . . . Filumena. Honey, where's those pants of mine that you shrunk that time?

Filumena   In your drawer.

Rocco (*bottoming out a little*)   These are the clothes I was wearin' when I went in. I wanna throw them in the garbage, you hear? Same house, same smell, same door . . . (*He exits u/l.*)

Filumena   Filumena, honey?

Sebb   A toast?

Filumena   Twenty-two years he's a Neapolitan iceberg. All of a sudden he walks in, he's a radiator that wants kisses.

Blaise   Maybe he forgot who he is. Or maybe he got himself confused with some other guy . . . and Rocco went to that guy's house and that guy's the one we got.

Filumena   Smother this kid for me. Go for the olives, you little trouble-maker. Sebbie, you think he's got cancer?

Sebb   Who, Rocco? No such luck. (**Sebb** *puts in another of Rocco's cassettes and plays it.*)

Filumena   What is that? Crazy house music?

Sebb   I thought he was being punished by God, instead they made him think he was some kinda hero.

Filumena   What's he got there?

Sebb   This is the whole rain forest of Puerto Rico in here.

Blaise   Oh my God, this is like . . . 'Day of the Triffids'!

Filumena   Get the cheese.

Blaise   Don't pinch, okay, or I'll punch you in the mouth.

Filumena   See?

Sebb   Move your ass, pimples, before I stick my fingers up your nose.

Blaise   Poison-face . . . Rocco was pretty smart to come up with that. (*Exits.*)

Sebb *leaves to his bedroom to change his clothes. Filumena follows him.*

Sebb   Ma, don't be mad if I don't eat here tonight.

Filumena   Please.

Sebb   He makes me sick to my stomach. He had the right idea. He shoulda killed himself.

Filumena   Shut up. Maybe they taught him how to be good.

Sebb   I don't trust good men all of a sudden.

Filumena   So crucify me.

Sebb   Aggh, all that matters to you is that you get your rub-down tonight.

Filumena   Your filthy mouth drips. (*Slap.*) He disgusts me.

Sebb   Sure. I hope he chokes you in bed tonight. He's crazy as a ping pong ball.

Filumena Sebbie, Sebbie, looka me. You I love. Why do you think I put up with him for all these years?

Sebb Go love my brother. (**Blaise** *enters the u/s area.*) He's the one needs it.

Filumena That little brat don't know what we lived through with Rocco. He calmed down when Blaise was born. It was you and me sleepin' in the same bed with him, layin' awake while he snored, gettin' kicked, punched, ordered around.

Blaise has heard. He moves on to the steps with the cheese held behind his back.

Filumena Blaise don't need me. You I love. You I need. You, you bastard. Looka me.

Sebb I ain't eatin'.

Filumena Eat with us. Don't leave me, Sebbie, come on.

Blaise (**Blaise** *moves into* **Sebb***'s bedroom*) You forgot . . .

Filumena (*startled*) Jesus.

Blaise . . . to give me the money.

Sebb Cash your paycheck, cheapskate. Scambatti'll cash it.

Blaise Thanks, Filumena. Here's your cheese. (*He throws it at her.*) Next time go get it yourself. (**Blaise** *exits to kitchen.*)

Filumena Ooof. I got three husbands . . . and three loaves of Saint Anthony bread. Tonight the good luck's gonna hit this house like lightning.

Music rises through the house.

In the course of the music playing, **Rocco** *appears, looking good in clothes that fit.* **Blaise** *brings in the pasta.* **Filumena** *joins them at the table near* **Sebbie***. Music, soft at first, becomes crazy, paralleling the anxiety at table.*

Rocco (*opening the wine*) Listen to this. This is funny. I go into the liquor store. I tell the guy I want the most expensive wine. The guy goes down in the cellar and comes up with this dusty bottle. A hundred eighty-five bucks.

Filumena You paid what?

Rocco So I said no, I don't even have that much on me. And he felt sorry for me and gave me this one last bottle of somethin' . . .

Blaise How much?

Rocco Seven bucks.

Sebb Same old cheapskate.

Rocco No, that's not the point.

Blaise Put your party hats on, everybody. Be a sport, Pa. Put it on.

Filumena Might as well all go crazy.

Blaise C'mon Sebb. (*He puts a hat on* **Sebb***.*)

Filumena See. We're nice people. We have parties.

Blaise Ma, you look American. Don't she look American? You do.

Rocco   I want Sebb's glass.

Blaise, *enjoying the music, while mocking it:* '*Wheeee! Oooooohhhhh! Aaaaaaaaghhhh!*' – *whatever.*

Rocco   All right now, this is important. You hear?

Blaise   Don't I get no wine?

Rocco   Here . . .

Filumena   Half. Sebbie, don't make me look at you . . . Ooop. (*She breaks into laughter.*)

Rocco   Calm down. Now lemme toast . . .

Blaise *jumps up and raises his glass.*

Filumena   Son of Pagliacci. Sit. And hands off the macaroni. Rocco, hurry up. Toasty . . . toast and jelly.

Rocco   Okay.

Sebb   Spit it out, Hollywood.

Rocco   What's this 'Hollywood'?

Filumena   Hollywood?

Sebb   Hollywood came home skinny, with his hair combed over his ears. He forgot he's an electrician; he thinks he's Robert Redford.

Rocco   Okay, Sebbie, I give up; go take a walk if you wanna.

Sebb   Now I don't wanna. (*Drinks his glass of wine.*) Gimme some more wine. (*Fills wine glass again.*)

Rocco   First of all, I wasn't an electrician, Sebbie, okay? I was an electronics engineer.

Sebb   But they didn't pay you for that, did they? Ain't that what pissed you off so much? He went berserk in the plant.

Filumena   Blaise, turn off that goddamn music.

Rocco   You ever see my paycheck, Sebb?

Sebb   Didn't have to see your paycheck, not with all those snowmobiles under our Christmas tree each year, and a Stingray to drive to Harvard with.

Rocco   I give you fair warning, Sebbie, I'm a very different man than I was.

Sebb   If you're a different man, you should of gone to a different house, right, Rocco?

Filumena (*to* **Sebb**)   Son of a bitch.

Rocco   I came back to this house to clean up my shit.

Sebb   Your shit. Is that us, Rocco? Well, you're gonna need a big shovel.

Rocco   I got time.

Sebb   Oh, yeah? I heard your time was up.

Filumena   Close your mouth.

Sebb I thought you got retired. Hey. Tell Blaise about the night of your retirement party. What a blast!

Filumena Enough, you.

Sebb The kid's got a right to know.

Rocco You got any wedding plans, Sebbie?

Blaise Wedding plans? (*Giggle.*)

Filumena What's he talking about, wedding plans?

Rocco Guys his age already left home to start their own family, right Sebbie?

Filumena That's his business, Pagliacci, okay?! We start eating right now or I turn the whole goddamn table over on top of all of you.

Rocco You heard the boss . . . Lift your glasses.

Filumena Lift your glasses. Sebbie, lift your goddamned glass, do me the favour. Now talk, Rocco, spit it out.

Rocco Okay. I wanna toast my wife; I wanna promise her I'm gonna get her outta this house.

Filumena Oh, yeah. Tomorrow. Don't worry.

Rocco And I wanna toast my sons. I want more than anything for my sons to die a natural death.

Filumena (*sipping, then coughing into her wine*) You want them to die?

Sebb What the fuck?

Blaise (*has sipped, but not swallowed*) Hmmmmmmmmmmnn?

Filumena Spit out that wine. Spit it out.

Rocco No.

Filumena Spit . . .

Rocco You misunderstand. Sometimes a man is shy and he gets married anyway. He gets a family and insteada sayin', look, I'm scareda talk to ya, he just hits 'em. Ha. Like some ape. Man like that . . . thinks violent, like takin' his life . . . or wipin' out his whole family. Every one of ya. Clean you up or wipe you out. But . . .

Blaise Clean us up or wipe us out?

Rocco But I turned it on myself. Okay? Me, I took the dive, except . . . they stopped me . . . and showed me these statistics . . . that . . . that a man who commits . . . you know, suicide, his kids, they like follow his example. You should see these statistics. That's murderin' your sons, I said. No. I . . . gotta get home to save them boys . . . to . . . to . . . talk this over . . . because like there's a genetical tie-in to this stuff.

They stare. **Filumena** *breaks the ice.*

Filumena Okay, he's finished. Drink.

Sebb   Don't drink. You think your comin' home is saving my life? Rocco, I want you to know that nothing you can ever do can touch me, you hear? So go ahead and kill yourself, anytime you want.

Rocco   You're wrong, Sebbie. Because I'm your father, it . . .

Sebb   I don't want no father. I don't need no father. And neither does he.

Rocco   It's statistics. We gotta . . .

Sebb   We're Italian, okay? They're talkin' about other people. Don't you worry about us killin' ourselves. Now, Blaise, lift your glass. I wanna toast to the past, to the past of this family when there were no Prozacs to make our father such a good man.

Filumena   Shut up.

Sebb   Don't let him scare you, Ma. I know what he's tryin' here.

Filumena   Blaise, take the food inside.

Rocco   No.

Sebb   You know what's makin' him so cool? These pills (*He grabs the Prozacs.*) He's got a year's supply of heaven here. No wonder he came home a saint.

Filumena *grabs them from* **Sebb**.

Filumena   Gimmie.

Rocco *grabs them from her and opens the containers.*

Rocco   Should I dump 'em?

Blaise   Jeez.

Filumena   Please.

Rocco   We'll make it a fair battle, okay Sebbie?

Sebb   Sure. Go ahead.

Filumena   Blaise, grab the medicine. Grab . . .

Rocco *dumps all the Prozacs into the rigatoni.*

Blaise   He dumped 'em!

Filumena   In my sauce!

Blaise   He dumped 'em. The downers in the rigatoni. Madonna, what a mess!

Filumena   This son of a bitch! I can't believe you did this. Tutto ruinato.

Rocco   Gimme Sebbie's dish. (*He ladles it out.*) Here. Here Sebbie, get happy, eat my heaven.

Filumena   Leave him alone, you. He's got his own troubles, this kid.

Rocco   That's okay.

Filumena (*to* **Sebb**)   You got people waitin', go. (*To* **Blaise**.) Get your hands outta there.

Blaise   They didn't melt.

Filumena   Throw it all in the garbage.

Sebb Thanks for the wine, Rocco. It was real civilised you eatin' in the dining room.

Filumena Go upstairs, Sebbie. (*She places herself between* **Rocco** *and* **Sebb**. **Sebb** *goes to his room.*)

Filumena And you (*To* **Rocco**.) – take care of those things (*The orchids.*) you brought into this house.

Rocco I'll help you with these dishes. (*Lifts her dish.*)

Filumena You really want to give me heart failure? Gimme my dish.

Rocco Go take care of your prince.

Filumena Gimme my dish. (*They tug at the dish.*)

Rocco (*winning the tug of war*) Go, goddamnit. Go to him.

Filumena *slowly retreats to her room.* **Blaise** *goes towards the front door.*

Rocco Hey, hold it, you. There's that water mister down the cellar; Go dust it off and fill it up for me.

Blaise But Pa, I gotta . . .

Rocco You gotta what?

Blaise Gotta . . . uh . . .

Rocco Go do me the favor. I wanna show you something you can tell your teachers about that'll make their hair stand on end.

Blaise What teachers?

Rocco At Brooklyn Tech.

Blaise *reluctantly goes toward the cellar.* **Rocco** *clears dishes and goes into the kitchen as* **Sebb** *enters* **Filumena**'s *area in the red box area.* **Filumena** *is applying lipstick.* **Sebb** *carries the gift-wrapped box.*

Scene Three

Sebb Lipstick for Pagliacci after what he just did?

Filumena Mind your business. You . . . you don't have to make the peace. You just make the trouble. When his last pill wears off and I'm alone with him in this bed, where are you gonna be?

Sebb Still an' all, you put on lipstick for him.

Filumena I got chap lips. Okay?

Sebb He wants me to leave and start my family. Did you hear him?

Filumena Don't you dare . . . you hear? Don't you dare leave me stuck in this trap with no protection from them two.

Sebb   Ma, we gotta get outta here and we can't get outta here till you learn to walk out that front door. Now will ya open these? Move, for cryin' out loud.

Filumena   What is that?

Sebb   A gift. (*He tears the wrappers.*)

Filumena *continues to open the box.*

Filumena   Whose wake tonight?

Sebb   Mrs Doogan.

Filumena   Vinnie Doogan? Your boyfriend?

Sebb   His grandmother . . . and don't let me ever hear you say that word in front of me again, or I swear . . .

Filumena   What word did I say now?

Sebb   You're all itchin' for him to find out.

Filumena   Boyfriend. A boy you hang out with.   ·

Sebb   Shutup.

Filumena   Madonna! I don't know how I'm supposed to talk to you from one minute to the next. What's this? A black coat?

Sebb   With a fox collar. You know what a fox is?

Filumena   And a purple dress? These are Lent colors. What am I supposed to do with these? Die?

Sebb   You say you're ashamed to go in the streets 'cause you don't have good clothes . . .

Filumena   And I'm supposed to go to Scambatti's in funeral colors?

Sebb   Ma, I can't wait for you. This is it, Ma. You wanna leave with me?

Filumena   Shhh. Don't let him scare you. This is your house.

Sebb   You givin' me the deed? This is his house. This ain't my house, Ma. I'm splittin' . . . minavog . . .

Filumena   Don't you dare say that word.

Sebb   You ever hear of Colorado? There's a place where they cure people scared to leave their house.

Blaise *enters the u/s area with the water mister, rearranges furniture from dinner and waits for* **Rocco.**

Filumena   And where's Coloradu . . . gooma si giam?

Sebb   Colorado. It's in the middle of this country.

Filumena   In the middle, not the edge . . . take back your coat; save your money. At least here I sit by my window and smell the ocean. Sometimes I smell Sicilia . . . when there's a breeze.

Sebb   It's Pagliacci, isn't it? You make believe you hate him, but at night when this door is closed, you like his jabs. He's not so bad looking any more.

Filumena I keep the peace is what I do . . . pigmouth. (*She slaps him.*) Wait. Look at me. Swear on the Saint that you won't leave me here stuck alone with him.

Sebb You got Blaise.

Filumena Blaise is in his diapers, you sonofabitch. Swear.

Sebb Ma, I'm sick of this house. It smells like Sicily, from the cellar to the roof.

Filumena How do you know what Sicilia smells like? Sicilia smells like the sun. It smells like lemons. It smells like fresh air. All right . . . I'll wear your dress and the coat. Tomorrow's Sunday . . . I'll go to ten o'clock Mass if you take me.

Sebb You swear it on the Saint. Touch him.

Filumena I swear that I'll really try. We're a good family, Sebbie.

Sebb And no mention of Doogan, Ma. Do you hear me? Please.

Filumena Swear you won't leave me.

Sebb (*hesitates, then slyly*) Hey, Saint Anthony, I swear I'll stay in this house with her forever, if she only comes with me to the ten o'clock Mass tomorrow.

Filumena I can breathe now. Remember when you were an altar boy? You used to look deep in my eyes and give me a Hollywood kiss, after you did my hair? Kiss me.

Sebb Offah. (*He gives her a quick kiss and moves to go.*)

Filumena Like a chicken he kisses.

Sebb You don't need my kisses, Ma. Pagliacci's home. Here . . . (*Hands her a lipstick forgivingly.*) Put some lipstick on.

Filumena Offah.

Sebb *runs into* **Blaise**.

Blaise Sebb. He's gonna force me to go back to school, I know it. What am I gonna do?

Sebb Sit on his face . . . wait . . . you really want to bring him into line? Make him tell you what happened in the Holland Tunnel.

Blaise I don't wanna know about that.

Sebb I'll be in Pizella's. Lemme know what happens.

Blaise I ain't goin' into no funeral parlour.

Sebb The dead don't bite. (*He exits.*)

Blaise Oh, yeah? I'll meet you in the candy store.

Rocco *enters the u/s area.* **Filumena**, *in her room, lights candles.*

Blaise (*hands* **Rocco** *the mister*) I . . . I got a job. Workin' with Sebb. I'm a mechanic for Alphonse.

Rocco The Texaco Station? You quit Brooklyn Tech? My own doctor was tellin' me . . . he couldn't get his son in there.

Blaise I didn't know you knew where I went to school . . .

Rocco Then I went and got all proud and come home and find you a grease monkey.

Blaise   How come you never hit me? Oh, I got a slap here and there, but you never made me black and blue like you did her and Sebb. He said you once broke every dish in the kitchen, one at a time, like Frisbies. Psssh. Psssh.

Rocco   Knock it off.

Blaise   You threw him against the wall like he was a football when he was a kid, he told me.

Rocco   Please . . .

Blaise   How come you never was interested in me enough to throw me against the wall?

Rocco   Blaise . . .

Blaise   I got left out of everything.

Rocco   Talk about going back to school.

Blaise   Talk about the Holland Tunnel.

Rocco   Okay, wise guy.

Blaise   You never knew the difference between Brooklyn Tech and a reform school. The tunnel, Rocco. C'mon. What you do in the tunnel that night?

Rocco   It's none of your business.

Blaise   So it's none of your business if I work or go to school or whatever the hell I do . . .

Rocco   Who let you know about the tunnel?

Blaise   Everybody in the neighbourhood says something else about the tunnel. I wanna know the truth.

Rocco *turns away in shame. Tears come.*

Blaise   Pa, you okay? Shit. You don't hafta tell me anything . . . you want a tranq? Look, I got three of 'em. I'll get you some water.

Rocco   Come back. Jus' stay here.

Blaise   Forget the tunnel. I'm too young to know . . .

Rocco   You're not too young. You . . . you changed a lot, Blaise. You got some girlfriend?

Blaise   A couple.

Rocco   You're not gonna be able to keep that thing in your pants much longer.

Blaise   That was last year.

Rocco   Here.

Rocco *hands* **Blaise** *the wrapped book and mists the plants.* **Blaise** *unwraps the book.*

Blaise   'The Personality of Plants'?

Rocco   By Doctor Arthur Studebaker. He gave me these. They're species orchids out of the wild. They live on air. And he sent this for you.

Blaise (*reading inscription*)   'To my brother Blaise? Each of us is a bud that will bloom in its time'? Obviously.

Rocco He was my friend up there. I helped him with these plants. They can sense your presence. Really. They like music and you can talk to them.

Blaise (*suspiciously*) Yeah, awesome.

Rocco Next month that book's gonna be in the 'Scientific American'.

Blaise I know the magazine.

Rocco I met a lotta nice people at that place.

Blaise Did you?

Rocco *uncovers more orchids.*

Blaise My God . . . (*All plants have identification tags.*) Phael . . . phaelen-opsis? And brazzalaelia? Y'mean like plants are expressing themselves these days? Like emotions?

Rocco Well, they're trying to prove it. Show that book to your biology teacher. (*To the plants.*) They're scared. Okay. Shhh . . . you're safe. (*To* **Blaise**.) Hey, now open that latch.

Blaise *takes a dining chair and walks d/s into the red box area, taking the two steps in a leap, places the chair precisely d/s/c, and stands on it.* **Rocco** *follows him and stands on the chair next to* **Blaise**. *They look up. The light is concentrated only on their faces. There are stars above their heads.*

Rocco Jesus, look at them stars tonight.

Blaise Oh, my God . . .

Rocco There's a breeze from the river. You feel it?

Blaise Yeah. I smell it, too.

Rocco Big Dipper.

Blaise Where's the Big Dipper?

Rocco (*pointing*) You kidding? It's right there. See the bright one?

Blaise There?

Blaise *points.* **Rocco** *places his hand over* **Blaise**'s *pointing hand.*

Rocco Now follow your finger. (*He guides* **Blaise**'s *hand.*)

Blaise Oh. I got it. It's upside down. Big mother. Yeah. Pa, why'd Studebaker . . . say in the book . . . 'To my brother Blaise'?

Rocco I was his father sometimes. They usta conduct these role playing sessions . . . like make believe I'm your father. You and me . . . now . . .

Blaise Sounds disgusting. So that must be north.

Rocco Say 'Welcome home, Dad.'

Blaise Oh, my God. I called you Pop all the time.

Rocco Just once. Like the American kids.

Blaise Dad? Like that? Welcome home, Dad?

Rocco Thanks.

Blaise Just don't put me through it too many more times, huh?

Rocco (*he stares, as if secure for the first time, to remember*)   This country puts a lotta pressure on people like us. I had a psychotic episode, Blaise . . . is what they call it . . .

Blaise   Forget it, it's okay.

Rocco   Blaise, you know how I usta hate to talk to anybody? Shy? You know, around here, anywhere? It was the same where I worked, except for one guy . . . this Kenny Farrell. He usta bring me a peach every day. I don't know where the sonofagun got 'em, even in winter, him and his peaches were the only things made me talk a lot. He was my – I had something with Kenny like I never had with nobody else before. So they gave me this retirement party at the Canal Street factory . . .

Blaise   It's okay, Pa.

Rocco   Pink champagne and Lorna Doone cookies . . . and this plaque for your coffin that said thirty years . . . and Kenny . . . I think it was when he starts comin' toward me with this bag . . . He's got a whole bag of peaches, I tell myself. Well, at first I'm really kiddin', ya know . . . I grab the bag and start throwin' peaches around the room . . . They looked shocked at me. I'm embarrassed. I turn red, so I make believe I go to my locker. All I can think of is . . . I don't wanna go back in there and I don't wanna come home here to get old, where nobody talks to me. And all of a sudden, when they ain't lookin', I take a quart of milk out of the refrigerator, I go to the medicine cabinet, and I swallow everything in there with the milk, and I go jump off the loadin' platform into the streets and . . . I'm throwin' peaches at the buses and trucks. I'm punchin' taxi cabs and I walk into the Holland Tunnel, two lanes, and I tell myself: Jesus, Mary, and Joseph, help me close my eyes . . . Close 'em, Rocco, you poor goddamn sonofabitch . . . sonofabitch . . . an' I'm waitin' . . .

Blaise   Shut up, Pa.

Rocco   Not one of those goddamn trucks hit me . . . not even a motorcycle . . . just cops grabbin' me, puttin' me in handcuffs.

Blaise (*shouts*)   Shut up.

Rocco   I tried to kill myself, Blaise. No more. Now you know. Just look up. Up.

They look up.

Rocco   . . . Millions of worlds. All kinds of worlds. Each one waitin' to be discovered. You know something, Blaise? They used to call this room the fern room, the Victorians? They used to keep their fern here in the north light. We could clean up the glass in here. And take off these curtains, and you know what we got here? Guess what we got here.

Blaise   A greenhouse?

Rocco   Yeah, a greenhouse. (**Rocco** *and* **Blaise** *return to the u/s area.* **Blaise** *replaces the chair.*) How would you get back into Tech? Say you wanted to . . .

Blaise   Too late to get back into Tech, Pop.

Rocco   Did you try?

Blaise *nods yes.*

Blaise   I got kicked out finally. Wanna see proof?

Rocco   I believe you.

Blaise   I'm sorry, Pop.

Rocco   You'll be okay.

Blaise   Pa, you gotta meet this girl of mine – Mercedes.

Rocco   Just don't knock anybody up.

Blaise   Pa, this son of your's got brains. Trust me.

Rocco   Just make sure you wear a rubber over them brains next time you use 'em. C'mon, beat it now, and let these things breathe. (**Blaise** *exits.*)

Rocco *turns down the lights. The orchids are hanging, beautiful, in the soft light of night, including the budded brazzalaelia.* **Rocco** *gathers two small plants that need sun by their metal hangers and starts upstairs.*

Rocco   Thanks, Studebaker.

Scene Four

Rocco *enters* **Filumena** *'s bedroom. They ignore one another shyly.* **Rocco** *lifts the shades and hangs the plants on the shade rollers of* **Filumena** *'s window.*

Filumena   What are those?

Rocco   Orchid plants that need the sun. This is a south window.

Filumena   But I keep the blinds down in the day so I can see my candles, Rocco. Get those creepy things outta here.

Rocco   They remind me of you, these orchids. They don't like the cold out there. They need warm air and the sun . . . like Sicily. (*Opening a drawer.*) What's these here cigarettes?

Filumena   Who put cigarettes in my drawer?

Rocco   Maybe Saint Anthony.

Filumena   Okay, sarcastic.

Rocco   Maybe your doll Marie Antoinette smokes when you ain't lookin'. Hey, Marie, these your Winstons?

Filumena   Sebbie playin' tricks on me . . . or Blaise.

Rocco   C'mon, Filumena, I been smellin' the smoke in here the past fifteen years now. (*Finding it funny, laughs.*)

Filumena   Ask your son.

Rocco   Go ahead – smoke!

Filumena   You think the little one don't smoke? You should smell the pot.

Rocco   Smoke if you like, Filumena. I want you to be free here; I want you to smoke.

Filumena   It ain't me. I told you.

Rocco   Lipstick?

Filumena   Gimmie that. Sebbie got it for my chap lips.

Rocco   C'mon. Wear lipstick . . . it'd be good.

Filumena   Smoke. Wear lipstick. They did a good job on you in the nut house.

Rocco *laughs, teasingly, seductively.*

Filumena   Stop laughin', clown . . .

Rocco   Clown, huh? You miss me, Filumena? Eh?

Filumena   Next thing you'll tell me you're glad I cut my hair.

Rocco   Never. You'll always be my cigna nivura . . .

Filumena   Oh, you remember that . . .

Rocco   That's the only way I could remember things these past months, the way they used to be a long time ago.

Filumena   Help me turn down the bed.

Rocco   C'mere.

Filumena   What for? You do your side. I'll do mine.

Rocco *rises.*

Filumena   Don't open the door.

Rocco   It's musty in here.

Filumena   I don't want no draft . . . I gotta thing in my neck.

Rocco   A thing? Where? (*He touches her neck.*)

Filumena   No. Ow . . . Ugh . . .

Rocco   Right there?

Filumena   Oh, my God! He touched right on the spot.

Rocco *rubs.*

Filumena   Agggh.

Rocco   Tomorrow I'll help you wash your hair . . . when the kids are gone.

Filumena   Leave go my hair. Get the Vicks over there if you're gonna rub.

Rocco *gets the Vicks. She takes off her dress.*

Filumena   You should put some up your nose now that the heat's back on.

Rocco   I can't with the Vicks.

Filumena   It opens your head up. Ou, the pain is travelin'.

Rocco   It's travelin' where?

Filumena   Down my back . . . (**Rocco** *rubs.*) Yeah . . . (*Then suddenly, as if* **Rocco**'*s rubbing has pushed the pain through her chest.*)

Filumena   I think it's goin' to the front now.

Rocco   Here? (*Her breasts.*)

Filumena   Ou, yeah. You need more Vicks.

Rocco   But the menthol . . . it'll burn your nipples . . .

Filumena   I don't care. I . . . you wanna rub or not? Whatsamatta?

Rocco *kisses her.*

Filumena   What are you doing?

Rocco   Kiss me, please, Filumena.

Filumena   What are you talking about? We don't kiss.

Rocco   I can't do this . . . no more with the Vicks.

Filumena   Where's my dress?

Rocco   You get a cramp, I rub. How many times have we gone through this ritual of the cramp, then close the door . . . and it's terrible for me. I feel abused . . . We go from a cramp to biff, bam, boom with nothin' in between.

Filumena   Take a walk, Rocco.

Rocco   We're done. You roll over and snore. I lay awake tryin' to figure out how we did all that without one single kiss. Kiss me, Filumena . . . why not a little kiss?

Filumena   Don't feel like it. (*She's getting dressed again.*)

Rocco   I wanna show you how much like dogs we are.

Filumena   Well, dogs don't kiss.

Rocco   That's what I mean . . . we're like dogs, Filumena. The young people, they don't do it like this anymore.

Filumena   Get out. I gotta say my prayers. (*She takes out books and a prayer book tied with a rubber band.*)

Filumena   Sant' Antonio Caru, Oatri di li poviri e di li malati, io povera piccatrici, chiedu u to aiutu e u to cunsigghio e chiedu la cura e protezioni tua. Abbi pieta' di sta povera criatura, picchi' la manu di lu signuri mi tucco', e la divina giustizzia me culpi pi li me piccati. Oh amatu prutitturi, talia la miserabili cundizzioni mia e l'amaru turmentu di lu me cori. Intircidi tu a lu me amatu ridinturi, finu a quannu stu calici

Rocco   I'm sorry, Filumena . . . what're you hoardin'? You're gonna explode if you don't give it to somebody. Give it away for crissakes, before they put us in the ground. Filumena, I . . . I have a confession to make to you. Filumena, I never loved you. I never loved you. I found out I shouldn't'a married you. I thought I would learn, but I never learned. That's what the big mistake was. But now I wanna try to learn . . . to take

amaru possa passari dinni mia, sia
fatta ancora la vostra volonta' a la to
povera servitrici. Amen.

care of somebody. We gotta turn this
joke of you and me into somethin'
human . . .

Filumena   This joke of me and you? Rocco . . . please . . . don't say you didn't love me in the beginning because that, that would really do it for me.

Rocco   Who cares how we started out . . . look what we turned into . . . make love like dogs . . . rubdowns with Vicks . . . children born with no kisses.

Filumena   Who started with no kisses? Me? You're the one jus' now tellin' me you never loved me.

Rocco   I admit it. I admit it. I started it off that way.

Filumena   Twenty-two years went by. The fireman comes to the fire twenty-two years too late . . . now you want kisses? Take these plants outta my house . . . he never loved me . . . good. Good. Now I know the secret of my misery in this house. (*She throws the plants on the floor.*)

Rocco   You sonofabitch.

Filumena   You forgot the days you used to put your face in my pillow and . . .

Rocco   Huh?

Filumena   Open her legs, one, two, three, up inside me, ready or not. That's how my kids were born.

Rocco   I'm not that man anymore . . .

Filumena   No. Now you're the man who kills himself, then comes home and says he never loved me, and then demands a kiss for it? Who do you think rules over this house? You? (*She points to Saint Anthony.*) Him. Il Santu. He gets my lips. He's the one took care of this family while you were eatin' and fartin' alone in the kitchen and puttin' your money in the bank . . . him, the Saint. (**Rocco** *takes the statue from its place.*)

Rocco   The Saint don't feel, the Saint don't bleed. This is chalk. (**Rocco** *drops the statue. It falls between* **Filumena**'*s fingers as she tries to catch it.*)

Filumena   You crazy sonofabitch. You broke it!! Don't hit me. Don't you touch me. He'll punish you. The seagulls make a ring around this house.

Rocco   'Cause there's a garbage dump down by the river, three blocks, but you've never walked far enough to see it. Instead, you turned this bedroom into a mausoleum. You keep your shades down so no light comes in and keep your door closed so your wax fog doesn't creep down the stairs. But me? I ain't sleepin' in this room with you, Filumena. No, not without a kiss . . . no . . . (**Rocco** *takes his orchids and leaves Filumena's room. He enters the u/s area.*)

Filumena *kisses the head of the broken statue as she picks it up; then she weeps.*

Rocco (*speaks to his plants in the dark*)   Easy . . . don't be scared. Shhh. Shhh . . . you're safe. I won't let nothin' happen to you. It's not their fault. Sshh . . . shhssshhsshh.

Rocco *exits u/r and returns with a blanket. He settles down in a chair to sleep. A suggestion of the passage of time.* **Sebb** *and* **Blaise** *are heard offstage.*

Sebb   That Pizella. He paints their face like a birthday cake.

Blaise   Don't talk about it.

Sebb   I swear I saw her eyelash move in the casket.

Blaise   Sebbie, I won't sleep tonight.

Sebb *and* **Blaise** *enter.* **Sebb**, *seeing his father sleeping downstairs, runs to check on* **Filumena**.)

Blaise   Pa, you sleeping down here?

Rocco   I'll sleep with my plants tonight.

Sebb   Ma!

Blaise   Should I clean this shit up?

Rocco   No, I'll do it; I'll take it down the cellar.

Sebb   Ma!

Rocco   Go to sleep.

Filumena   Go away, I'm okay.

Blaise   Goodnight.

Sebb *goes to his room, switches on the radio, and lights a joint.* **Blaise** *follows slowly behind.*

Sebb   Get in here, Blaise.

Blaise *starts to play with* **Sebb**'s *darts, casually throwing them at a home-made Saint Sebastian dart board.*

Sebb   Somethin' happened around here. I smell danger. C'mon. Leave go them darts.

Blaise   Between him and her? Gimmie. (*Joint.*)

Sebb   Two tokes.

Blaise   Cheapskate.

Sebb   Chip in for some of this shit now that you're workin'. And what are them Playboys doin' in here. . . ?

Blaise   The electric car . . .

Sebb   Cheesus.

Blaise   I mean it. There's a thing in one of them about the engine.

Sebb   You're full of shit.

Blaise   You know what Caputo tol' me? You and Doogan are fuckin' one another.

Sebb   Oh, yeah? That's interestin'.

Blaise   And Doogan's pissed 'cause you ain't goin' with him to Texas.

Sebb   Caputo's a real special investigator, isn't he?

Blaise   Can I ask you a personal question?

Sebb   No.

Blaise   Sebbie . . . What ya think of when you jerk off?

Sebb   Get lost . . .

Blaise   It reveals the deep, deep truth about ya.

Sebb   Just don't wipe your fingers on my face cloth.

Blaise   I don't use a face cloth.

Sebb   Out.

Blaise   I'm just tryin' to talk to ya.

Sebb   Did you bring up the Holland Tunnel to the old man?

Blaise   Oh, yeah . . . He made me feel sorry for him.

Sebb   Feel sorry for your ol' lady. She'll turn to penicillin if we don't get her out in the sunlight.

Blaise   Would you be mad at me, Sebbie, if I quit Alphonse?

Sebb   Do you love your mother?

Blaise   I don't really hate her.

Sebb   You just wish she had bleached blonde hair and wore high heels.

Blaise   I got over that. Now I jus' wish she'd go to the corner to buy a quart of milk.

Sebb   Look . . . if we don't keep on workin' and savin' up, we'll never get her to that place in Denver . . .

Blaise   You should talk to the ol' man about it. He learned a lot about that stuff.

Sebb   Oh yeah, sure – in between his delusions.

Blaise   Don't tell me it don't suck, what he's been through. Funny, they got married, two people like that. You know, I betcha now he makes it up to her.

Sebb   How you gonna make it up to somebody after you blow their brains out? Huh? How's he gonna give her back twenty-five years? This is the post mortem, man, what d'ya think this is?

Blaise   I feel like a hundred years old . . . (*Yawns.*) Tired. Tomorrow's Sunday and I'm gonna do everything in my power not to wake up at seven o'clock. (**Blaise** *rises.*)

Sebb   Go ahead, finish it!

Blaise *sits and smokes.*

Filumena *has put the broken Saint Anthony statue in the bottom half of the coat box. She stands up, holding it. She leaves her room, descends the two steps to the u/s area. She sees the orchids. She puts the broken statue on the floor and exits u/l to the kitchen. She re-enters with a bottle.*

Filumena Here, drink . . . drink. Have a nice drink. Drink some more. Drink it all. I had poison poured in my heart too . . .

Blaise (*to* **Sebbie**) Goodnight!

Blaise *descends the two steps to the u/s area.*

Blaise What've you got there, Ma? Huh?

Filumena That's my business.

Blaise What's that smell? Jesus! It's ammonia. Sebbie! Sebbie! (**Sebb** *enters the u/s area.*) She poured ammonia on his orchids.

Sebbie Crazy sonofabitch . . . you wanna hatchet in your head?

Filumena I'm crazy?

Rocco (*calling from o/s*) That you up there, Blaise?

Blaise Uh, yeah, Pa.

Sebb You are crazy!

Filumena I'm crazy. Right. You don't know what that man did to me.

Sebb Ma. But you gotta be careful, Ma. I can leave. You gotta stay here.

Filumena Oh, now you can leave? Ohhh . . . Did you see the broken statue on the floor there . . . throw him in the garbage, you. (*To* **Blaise**.)

Blaise Christ. Saint Anthony.

Rocco (*entering*) What's going on here? What happened?

Sebb You . . . brainless gorilla . . . stupid Sicilian.

Filumena What? What am I?

Rocco She what? Jesus! No.

Filumena Why? These should enjoy my house and I should be spit on? Let them put us both in a straitjacket . . . I'm dangerous too. Okay?

Rocco Water, Blaise.

Sebb You really want him to kill you? That's what you really want! Don't expect me to come between you. Have your bloodbath without me. You two. You deserve one another. I pronounce you man and wife.

Filumena Now you got your excuse to leave, eh, Sebbie? I know what you're up to even with no brains! I know what's cookin' in that mind of yours. Go to Doogan, Judas . . . Now you got your excuse. And while you're at it . . . tell your father about how you don't like girls. Tell your father about Doogan, your boyfriend. Go. Put on a dress for your father. Put on a dress. Judas.

Curtain.

Act Two

Scene One

The time is early the next morning, Sunday, approximately 9.30 a.m.

Blaise *enters. He's carrying a container of coffee, the five-budded orchid, and the book* **Rocco** *gave him.*

Blaise   Pa, did you put these orchids outside on top of the garbage pail?

Rocco   Oh, Blaise, please . . .

Blaise   . . . with the snow fallin' on them half the night?

Rocco   They're dead.

Blaise   Hold it . . . the book, the book . . . Neglect . . . Neglect . . . Here, Neglect. (*Reading.*) 'Hobbyists often inquire why some species bloom under conditions of neglect, while others do not bloom when fed, misted, and fanned . . .'

Rocco   Blaise, that's different.

Blaise   'Orchid plants have been known to live over one hundred years . . .'

Rocco   Not if somebody . . .

Blaise (*still reading*)   'Sensing they cannot recover, an orchid will sometimes set seed in order to regenerate itself.'

Rocco   Blaise . . . neglect is not ammonia. Ammonia is death. You know what ammonia does?

Blaise   I'm bringin' them in.

Rocco   I don't want them in my sight, okay? And what's this?

Blaise   I got you coffee from Scambatti's.

Rocco   Oh. I can't. I got heartburn.

Blaise   What is heartburn? I keep hearin' people sayin' heartburn, heartburn . . .

Rocco   Gas. And a pain here.

Blaise   Gas. That's how else they describe it. God, look at this poor orchid. You go sixteen years bored, passin' the same garbage . . . leftovers, empty milk containers, coffee grinds . . . an' it all changes in one day. There's Saint Anthony all broke up next to the downers and the rigatoni . . . and on the garbage pail cover, like funeral flowers, are these murdered orchid plants that it's snowing on top of. Now that can give you goosebumps. (*He belches.*) Gas and a pain here?

Rocco   Yeah.

Blaise   I got heartburn.

Rocco   Blaise . . . will ya . . . help me figure somethin' out?

Blaise   Sure.

Rocco I wanna know how come your mother can ... can ... come up with this information about Sebb.

Blaise What information? Oh. Okay. Pa, she ain't stupid. She knows everything that goes on.

Rocco Oh? She knows the. . . ? How though. . . ? How does she know?

Blaise Maybe Sebb told her himself.

Rocco And how do you know?

Blaise Louis Caputo spilled it to me.

Rocco Louis Caputo? Spilled what?

Blaise What? What we're talking about.

Rocco What're we talkin' about?

Blaise Nothin' . . . I don't know.

Rocco Someone tells you your brother's queer and you believe it? You don't punch 'im in the mouth?

Blaise Caputo's a liar. What ya want from me?

Rocco Sebbie can't be that way. He's a car mechanic, not a hairdresser.

Blaise He does her hair. I don't know what I'm talkin' about here . . . Don't get me in trouble, Pa . . .

Rocco Why don't you bring that coffee up to your mother?

Blaise Pa, it wasn't my intention to come in here and disrupt anything.

Rocco Don't worry . . . Does she know he's packin'?

Blaise Why? Who?

Rocco Your mother.

Blaise Who's packin'?

Rocco Your brother. He dragged a bag outta the cellar and he's up there banging drawers.

Blaise Christ. Sebbie!! (*He runs up the two steps and shouts.*) Sebbie, open. Sebbie, it's Blaise, Sebbie. Sebbie, open this door or I warn ya . . .

Sebb It's open.

Scene Two

Blaise *comes into* **Sebb**'s *area.*

Blaise What in the fuck do you think you're doin'?

Sebb It's called leavin' home.

Blaise And who'd you consult about doin' this?

Sebb Blaise, take a walk.

Blaise You're leavin', now . . . that you lit the fuse and they're all set to blow up?

Sebb Fuck him. Fuck her. Doogan's gonna pick me up in ten minutes.

Blaise You gonna Texas?

Sebb All the way.

Blaise What kinda guy don't hang around for his grandmother's funeral?

Sebb That's Doogan.

Blaise I think I'm gonna have a heart attack or else I'm jus' gonna vomit. You're gonna leave me here with them two on the brink of bloodshed?

Sebb Maybe this'll put them over the brink.

Blaise You're sticking me here with the problem.

Sebb I paid my dues. I came outta her first. (**Blaise** *is stealing a joint from* **Sebb**'s *little box.*) I'm the sonofabitch they named Sebastiano. I caught all the arrows.

Blaise (*lighting the joint*) Here.

Sebb No.

Blaise Relax a minute. You're all hopped up.

Sebb *succumbs and takes the joint, but continues packing.*

Blaise He's an outpatient, you know.

Sebb So what?

Blaise So you read in the fuckin' newspapers 'Man Kills Self and Family'? Sebbie, maybe there's really a screw loose deep in him.

Sebb Of course there's a fuckin' screw loose deep in him.

Blaise Sebb, you're makin' me sick to my stomach and it's the kinda thing I'm not gonna get over . . . You . . . you can't go to Texas on me. She's gonna die here . . . Jesus, I can't even imagine what she's gonna do when she finds this out . . .

Sebb Wanna tie?

Blaise I'll take your Cardinal Hayes jacket.

Sebb It's yours.

Blaise Naaa . . .

Sebb I don't think Cardinal Hayes is gonna appreciate his name splattered all over the gay bars of Texas.

Blaise Maybe he'd love it. Aw, come on, Sebb, you two go to Texas, getta suntan, act like a couple cowboys down there, you come home and we go back to Alphonse's . . . I'll go in tomorrow, okay? 'N' tell 'em you hadda . . .

Sebb You better wake up, Blaise. You just don't get it do you? Don't expect to ever see me in this house again. This is it, kid brother.

Blaise But it's startin' to snow.

Sebb So don't hold me up.

Blaise Last night you wanted us to drag the ol' lady to Colorado.

Sebb Today I say let her blow up like a big tumor till she explodes. I can't help her . . .

Blaise Hey, calm down a minute and look at me here . . . I'm your brother. I'm your brother.

Sebb Not now, Blaise.

Blaise And when? Fifty years from now? You're walkin' outta here after talkin' to me about it for five minutes . . .

Sebb I'm not married to you.

Blaise Oh, yeah? Remember that old movie we saw on TV with James Mason and whatsername . . . the blonde chick who was the piano player?

Sebb Ann Todd. Get outta my way.

Blaise Remember how she played lousy till he started hittin' her hands with a stick and all of a sudden Da-doom, Da-doom, Da-doom, Doom, Daaaa-Bll-eeee, Doom . . . (*Rachmaninoff's Third.*)

Sebb Okay, so . . .

Blaise She fell in love with him.

Sebb You're in love with James Mason?

Blaise He's dead. It's . . . you – I don't know how to get along here without you.

Sebb You'll get the knack of it.

Blaise Jesus, Sebbie, I was jus' startin' to talk to you . . .

Sebb You and me are two totally different stories . . .

Blaise Shit! I know girls so hot for you they have to wash out their panties after you pass them on the street. Sebbie, it's heaven in there. Who's to stop you from diggin' chicks? Doogan? I'll put an end to him with one punch.

Blaise *surprises* **Sebb** *with the amount of power he puts into punching his own hand.*

Sebb Get outta my way, you little creep.

Blaise (*screams*) Who's to stop you?

Sebb Me. I'm to stop me.

Blaise Only you? Then tell me, why are you doin' this to yourself?

Sebb Blaise, you're givin' me a headache.

Blaise   Hold it. Hold it . . . somebody's rippin' me off here. Okay? Me. Was I gonna be your best man?

Sebb   Best man? What has that got to do?

Blaise   I get cheated outta bein' your best man 'cause you say you're gay. You know that? I get cheated outta bein' godfather, bein' an uncle for your kids. Instead, I get them. And what happens if he hurts her?

Sebb   He won't hurt her any more.

Blaise   Maybe she'll kill him . . . or what happens when they die on me? Huh? I gotta put on some bomber's jacket and go drag you outta some goddamn weird bar?

Sebb   You little sonofabitch. You'll never find me in one of those bars, okay? Now get out . . . and here . . . (**Sebb** *flings 'Playboy' into* **Blaise***'s face*.) Take your Playboys. You won't have to sneak them in here any more.

Blaise   Jus' like the ol' man in the old days. You're gonna be him all over again. You motherfucker . . .

Sebb   I nearly killed somebody for that word.

Blaise   Cocksucker.

Sebb   You . . .

Sebb *slaps* **Blaise**, *but* **Blaise** *overcomes* **Sebb** *and pins him to the floor.*

Blaise   C'mon. Surprise, huh? The kid grew up. Now say 'uncle'.

Sebb   Get off me.

Blaise   'Uncle' . . . 'Uncle'.

Sebb (*after a pause*)   Uncle.

Blaise   Again.

Sebb   'Uncle.' Uncle. Okay? Blaise? (**Blaise** *softens, and cries*.) Whatsamatta?

Blaise   I don't wanna be your uncle . . . Oh, God, Sebbie! I hate them . . .

Sebb   No, ya don't.

Blaise   I'll hate it here alone with them. Please don't leave me here. I wouldn't do it to you. I could never do it to you.

Sebb   Yes, you would, kid brother . . . you would hafta. You would just hafta. Hey . . . You woulda been my best man.

Blaise   Huh?

Sebb   You woulda been my best man.

Rocco   Sebbie?

Blaise   Come in, Pa.

Rocco (*entering Sebb's area*) Oh, Blaise. (**Rocco** *carries a pack of money in a small, brown paper bag.*)

Blaise 'Scuse me. This coffee's cold. How d'ya make it with the percolator? Never mind, I'll figure it out. (*He exits via the u/s area to the kitchen u/l.*)

Sebb Pa, just do me a favor and don't lay any of your shit on me, okay?

Rocco I won't say anything.

Sebb You gonna stand there and watch me?

No response.

Sebb Pa, lemme pack.

Rocco Pack. (*Pause.*) Where ya goin'?

Sebb Fort Worth.

Rocco Fort Worth?

Sebb That's right. Texas. My friend Doogan's uncle's got a big garage down there.

Rocco You got some girlfriend to take with you?

This shocks **Sebb** *a little.*

Sebb Pa . . . you didn't get married till you were way past thirty. What're you up to, Rocco?

Rocco You a homo?

Sebb Are you?

Rocco I'm askin' you . . . Are you a homo?

Sebb Go ask the black swan. (*Pause.*) I'm queer . . . that's right, Rocco.

Rocco What exactly is the meaning?

Sebb Pa, I'm queer. I'm a fairy. Gabeesh? I ain't gonna marry no Alice in Wonderland. It's just you were the last to find out around here!

Rocco Mary Ann Benedetto . . .

Sebb Who is she?

Rocco Didn't you and her . . .

Sebb Pa, three years ago I took her to my prom.

Rocco Jesus, it makes me laugh. I mean, in the hospital we had a men's support group. We weren't afraid to show . . .

Sebb Out.

Rocco What I say?

Sebb You think you got somethin' I need you can give me? An ol' man with his hair and teeth fallin' out?

Rocco Hey, come on.

Sebb Half-alive corpses don't bounce their sons on their knees, you shitball.

Rocco I'm only tryin' . . .

Sebb   I'm hip to what you're tryin'. You want to put lipstick on the corpse and dance with it, but it's dead between you and me . . . there's no life, no love between you and me.

Rocco   Listen to me as a bump on a log or a goddamn radio . . .

Sebb   Spit it out.

Rocco   I was puttin' aside money, I dunno . . . in case somebody would need it, and now that you're goin' I think it's only fair . . . I got eight thousand here.

Sebb   The King of Too Late. Pa, I'm almost twenty-two now and this is the first thing you ever done for me.

Rocco   No. First thing was my stayin' alive for you.

Sebb   What nerve you got . . . far as I'm concerned, you shoulda gotten your way in the Holland Tunnel.

Rocco   Sebbie . . .

Sebb   We'd get that money in your will.

Rocco   Don't do this.

Sebb   Keepin' yourself alive. Who gives a shit? I've got hair under my arms almost ten years now. I'm leavin'. You're in a time warp. Your life was. There's no more gonna be. Keep your fuckin' money.

Rocco   Have it your way. (*He puts the money back in his pocket.*)

Sebb   Wait. Gimme the money. I got a good use for it.

Rocco   What . . .

Sebb   All mine now? No strings?

Rocco   No strings.

Sebb *starts tearing up the money.*

Rocco   Sebb . . . Sebb . . . Gimme that. Don't rip it up. Gimme, you little bastard.

Sebb   It's mine, and this is what I choose to do with it, just like you did what you wanted when it was yours, and we lived in one room . . .

Rocco   I lived in one room half my life. I was a father when I was eleven 'cause my father died. We had to take baths in the kitchen. I hadda see my mother . . . ashamed . . . I was a father at eleven years old, cleanin' the toilets in the sweat shop my mother worked in, for a dollar and a half a week.

Sebb   You're the same kind of father to me that yours was to you, so don't worry about me.

Rocco   Nowhere near . . .

Sebb   I woulda liked to have turned down goin' to college, okay? I went to a good high school. I got marks in high school.

Rocco   There's no comparison anyway. Thousands of kids put themselves through college.

Sebb That's not my point. You had that rotten money all the while. I saw those bank books in your black iron box . . .

Rocco Sebbie, when I was a kid at night, I'd close my eyes and dream of bein' an aviator . . .

Sebb (*scoops out the bottom of an empty drawer, picks up pictures, and flings them at* **Rocco**) Instead, here's what you turned out to be. Pictures of us on the fire escape . . . with our monkey faces. Those were the days when you were sockin' us if we moved in bed, and that gorilla in there used to hang on to me like she was drownin' . . . oh, my God, get out.

Rocco Sebbie, please.

Sebb You can't pay, don't you understand? I don't want you to think you're paid up. Ever. Money is the least you owe this family.

Rocco You only remember what you wanna. You know how many times, when you were little, I was dyin' to bend down and hug you? But . . . I . . .

Sebb But what? You were ashamed? Eh, squeaky?

Rocco Maybe ashamed is the word . . .

Sebb 'Shamed in front of who? Your wife? Ashamed of me, a little boy? Did I do somethin'? Was I ugly?

Rocco You were an angel.

Sebb Aw.

Rocco She was like a tiger with you. She gave me the message from the beginnin' she wasn't gonna be too happy if I got too close to you.

Sebb So she wouldn'ta been too happy.

Rocco Well . . .

Sebb You were scared of her?

Rocco Who was scared?

Sebb Pa, you shouldn't marry someone you're gonna be scared of. You shoulda taken the route I'm takin' . . . gabeesh? Not fuck up the world with fucked-up kids. You're more queer than I am.

Rocco No, Sebbie . . .

Sebb Okay them, lemme take my shower.

Sebb *holds out his hand to shake and* **Rocco** *takes it.*

Rocco (*leaving the money on a shelf*) You take the money.

Sebb (*screams*) Oh, no. (*Flings the money.*) No payment.

Rocco *picks up the money, as* **Sebb** *undresses for his shower.*

Sebb Pa . . . I'm behind schedule . . .

Rocco You remember when your mother was in the hospital havin' Blaise?

Sebb Pa, I had my limit.

Rocco   Bear with me. I took you to Mount Carmel Feast with that big ferris wheel? You remember that ferris wheel?

Sebb   No Pa.

Rocco   Sure you do. Blaise was just born . . . and . . . okay . . . I won you this. (*He reaches for the Pinocchio puppet.*) Tell me you don't remember where you got this Pinocchio.

Sebb   Pa, I swear to God, I don't.

Rocco   You don't remember ridin' the ferris wheel with me? Scared, inside my jacket jus' like a little mouse? Remember what you asked me?

Sebb   Pa . . .

Rocco   Go along with me.

Sebb   What'd I ask?

Rocco   You went, 'Pa, what happens if we fall offa this thing?' and I said what?

Sebb   What you say?

Rocco   I said, 'Sebbie, if we fall, I'll jus' turn over on my back so's you land on my soft tummy.'

Sebb   That was nice . . .

Rocco   You remember?

Sebb   Sorry, Pa . . . I don't.

Rocco   I was wearin' that plaid mackinaw . . . What am I gonna tell ya? I didn't come in here only to drop this money, Sebbie.

Sebb   (*he is totally stripped now*)   What else did you come in for? Don't stand there like chocolate pudding . . . you wanna hug me and tell me you love me? Like those people in your hospital? Nurturing . . . you know?

Rocco   Cover yourself.

Sebb   Why, whatsamatta? I'm gonna take a shower.

Rocco   Don't make a fool of me, Sebb.

Sebb   Is that your excuse to cop out on me now?

Rocco   What am I copping out of? I don't follow you.

Sebb   The love. What're you ashamed of? We're men, for crissakes. (*He wraps a towel around his waist.*) I'm sincere . . . you send me a letter expressing your feelings if you're so ashamed here.

Rocco   You're being sarcastic.

Sebb   See? When your chance finally comes, you muff it.

Rocco   What am I muffing?

Sebb   I want proof. I have a right to it.

Rocco   I don't understand. What proof?

Sebb   Proof that you cared about me, like you said.

Rocco   I feel it in here. How does a person prove such a thing?

Sebb   You go down on your knees and swear it to God.

Rocco   You're makin' a joke of it.

Sebb   I'm sincere, you dope. You kneel.

Rocco   Don't make a fool outta me now . . .

Sebb   I swear on Christ on His cross. I won't Pa . . .

Rocco (*kneels*)   What do you want me to say?

Sebb   Swear to me you always . . . you know?

Rocco   Cared about you?

Sebb   Exactly. I wanna take that with me.

Rocco   What do I say?

Sebb   Just say I love you . . .

Rocco   I love you.

Sebb *removes his towel.*

Sebb   You wanna suck it? Go ahead . . .

Rocco   Fuckin' pig . . . you fuckin' pig . . . tou . . . tou . . . tou . . . (*He sprays spit into his son's face.*)

Sebb *smiles into the spray. He enjoys it. He wipes some off his face and looks at his hand.*

Sebb   Thanks for givin' me somethin' to remember you by . . .

Rocco (swings at **Sebb**)   I'll split your head open.

Sebb   Yeah! We got the ol' Rocco back. He splits. He hits. He spits like the old days . . . Hit me, motherfucker . . . (**Rocco** *head-butts* **Sebb**.) Good. Now here's somethin' to remember your son by. (**Sebb** *grabs* **Rocco** *by his throat.*)

Rocco   No, Sebb . . .

Sebb   I hate you, you silly motherfucker. You don't deserve to have me for a son. You didn't pay for it. You didn't pay for it. You didn't pay for it.

Rocco   Sonny . . . no.

Sebb   You didn't pay . . . (*He is nearly choking* **Rocco**.)

Rocco *senses he should yield.*

Rocco   You're hurtin' me.

Sebb   You didn't pay. You didn't pay.

Rocco   I'm sorry, Sebbie.

Sebb   You didn't pay. (*He weeps.*)

Rocco *composes himself a little as* **Sebb** *grabs for support, disoriented.*

Sebb   I'll always hate you. Nothin', nothin' could ever change it.

Rocco   I know. It's okay. Put your robe on.

Sebb   Pa, I feel dizzy. Sick.

Rocco   Huh?

Sebb   I think I'm gonna . . .

Rocco   What kinda sick? Sit. Sit. (**Rocco** *guides him into a chair.*)

Sebb   Weak . . . I feel faint . . .

Rocco   Put your head down. Put it down.

Sebb   No. (*He leans back in the chair – throws back his head, facing the ceiling, eyes closed.*)

Rocco   You're sweatin'. Lemme wipe your forehead. Here.

Rocco *stands behind him and sweeps his hand over* **Sebb**'*s brow, back over his hair several times.*

Sebb   Okay . . . okay. Leave me alone, Pa, and I'll be . . .

Rocco   You sure?

Ignoring him, **Rocco** *continues wiping* **Sebb**'*s brow caressingly several more times.* **Sebb** *breathes deeply.* **Rocco** *bends, kisses his head, embraces him.* **Sebb** *struggles, allowing a small part of it.*

Sebb   Yeah. I'm all right now.

Pause.

Rocco   Can I leave the money?

Sebb   No. Jus' lemme alone. Please . . .

Rocco   Splash your face with some water.

Sebb   Okay.

Rocco *exits.*

Scene Three

Blaise *enters the u/s area from the u/l door and* **Rocco** *enters it from Sebb's bedroom. They meet.* **Blaise** *has coffee.*

Blaise   He gonna leave?

Rocco   Bring him that coffee.

Blaise   Thanks for bringin' home all this good luck. (**Blaise** *goes to the steps before* **Sebb**'*s room.*) Sebb? Sebb? (*Receiving no answer, he turns to* **Filumena**'*s area.*) Ma? I got some coffee here.

Filumena (*her hair is down, she pulls* **Blaise** *inside*)   Get in.

Blaise   Ma . . . whattya doin?

Filumena   I don't know. I don't know. But I gotta do somethin'. Count this.

Blaise   Where'd you get all this money?

Filumena   Did you take our passports outta my drawer?

Blaise   I never touched the passports.

Filumena San Antonio! Blaise. You stay here with your father, if . . . if . . . I go 'way with Sebbie. Where in the manage a diavolia madonna are the friggin' passports? (*Searches frantically for the passports.*)

Blaise Ma, looka me. Doogan's comin'. Sebbie's goin' with Doogan to Texas. You know where Texas is?

Filumena Yeah. In bluff land. Take a hundred. Go to Pizella's. Tell him to have a black car here in five minutes to take me to church . . . me and Sebbie . . . but tell him we're really goin' to the airport.

Blaise The airport? Ma, have you been takin' them diet pills again?

Filumena I'll slap your face till it bleeds. Go get the car.

Blaise Sebbie's goin' to Texas I told ya.

Filumena He swore on San Antonio he'd take me to church today. Okay? He won't go to no Texas when he sees me dressed for church. I know my son. Then we get in the car and I tell the driver: to the airport. Don't you dare tell your father. Let him wait ten years for me to come back from church.

Blaise Ma, number one, you're the one who's bluffin' 'cause you ain't gonna make it even to the sidewalk and you know it.

Filumena Don't worry . . . I'll make it.

Blaise Number two . . . Sebbie'll never go to Sicily in a million years.

Filumena You know how many times he begged me to run away with him? Now he gets his wish. Where's my mother's gold ring?

Blaise Would you act like this if I was leavin' home?

Filumena Hey, I'm gonna be trapped here with a nervous old man and you, you little jerk. He likes you.

Blaise Trapped with me and a nervous old man? But if Sebbie stays, you're not trapped, eh? You take the cake.

Filumena You with your girlfriends. You'll be gone in a couple years and then where am I? Stuck in this country.

Blaise This is your country. You're married.

Filumena I spit on this country. I hate it.

Blaise Then why'd you come here?

Filumena Another traitor. Help me.

Blaise You're the traitor with your . . . Italian mouth . . . with your stink and your sweats an' . . . an' . . . your Sicilian face. This country don't want you. Look in the mirror. That's the traitor. The Sicilian jungle woman. Don't expect me to brush that hair when he's gone.

Filumena Gesu Maria aiuta . . .

Blaise Ma . . . I'm sorry I said that, but . . .

Filumena Shhh. Jus' make believe you're my friend then.

Blaise Jesus, Ma, I'm your son. You would leave me here and go away with Sebbie? Why am I always second? You're killing me. What are you tryin' to do to me. You want an abortion – go ahead. Put a knife in me.

Filumena Okay. Sebbie was my favorite. It's just the way it was. In my mind . . . (*She stares a moment.*)

Blaise No. I don't want to hear this. (*Holding his ears.*) I ain't . . . (*Grabbing her face.*) Look at me. I wanna be your favorite now. Say something.

Filumena I . . . can't lie.

Blaise Say something . . . I love you, Ma. Ma?

Filumena I slept with my face to the wall 'cause your father wouldn't talk to me in Italian. Hadda learn English. I wanted my mother's house so bad. Every night I prayed to the saints, Christ, His mother, anything: get me outta here. My answer was I got pregnant. I wasn't alone in America anymore. I had Sicily inside me. I named him Sebastiano after my father. But you, you're not like us. You're Amerigano. Look at your face.

Blaise Noooo! . . . Sebbie won't go with you.

Filumena I'm the boss of Sebbie, not Doogan.

Blaise Why don't you take a walk before you fly over the oceans? We'll take a walk tomorrow.

Filumena Don't baby me.

Blaise Funny that you could go all the way to Sicily but you're scared to go to Scambatti's. Your stockin's are fallin'. (*Laughs.*)

Filumena You think I'm a faker? What you think I been prayin' to that saint for all these years? (*She cries.*)

Blaise So don't cry. You want me to help ya?

Filumena Sure I'm scared. I open the front door, and I can't put my foot down, not even one step.

Blaise You jus' drop the foot down.

Filumena I get dizzy. I feel like I'm dyin'. I look at the house across the street. I see the cars and kids yellin', and I feel my bones melting.

Blaise Ma, you can trip on a rug.

Filumena You don't wanna see what he's doin'. He got rid of Sebbie, and next you. Mark my words.

Blaise He's not gettin' rid of me, Ma – you are.

Filumena He'll send you to college. He'll pay for it. Then he'll close in on me. Get Pizella. Don't let that sonofabitch sneak outta here without me. Don't trick me, please . . .

Doogan (*off*) Hey Sebbie!

Filumena Who's that?

Sebb (*calling*) Blaise?

Blaise Doogan's here with the car.

Sebb (*calling*)   Tell him I'll be right down.

Filumena   Go, you get Pizella first. Go fast and I'll love you. I swear.

Blaise *exits u/l.*

Sebb *moves from his area to* **Filumena***'s. He carries two bags.*

Sebb   Ma? Ma?

Filumena   Ohhh . . . the undertaker face.

Sebb   Ma . . . what're ya dressed for?

Filumena   Ten o'clock Mass. You're takin' me to church, right? The lipstick okay?

Sebb   Huh?

Filumena   Here. Help me with my hair. C'mon, don't make such a fuss. This dress is not long enough. You think we'll look okay walkin' down the aisle together?

Sebb   Ma, I came to say goodbye.

Filumena   You not takin' me?

Sebb   I'm leavin', Ma.

Filumena   Who's gonna take me?

Sebb   Ma . . . I . . . uh . . . hafta . . .

Filumena   Okay. Don't tell me. Weakling.

Sebb   Don't call me that, Ma.

Filumena   Yes, you are. You let Rocco win. But he won't win with me. I'm goin' to Sicily.

Sebb   Right this minute?

Filumena   Laugh at me, you sonofabitch, and I'll stick this nail file in your face.

Sebb   Put that down.

Filumena   You think I can't go to Sicily?

Sebb   Sure you can.

Filumena   You think I can stick this in my throat?

Sebb   Gimme the nail file.

Filumena   And that's the way I can throw myself out the front door when the time comes. This house is a worse coffin than the plane. So go. Be proud that you tricked me.

Sebb   How'd I trick you?

Filumena   You swore on Sant Antonio you wouldn't leave me if I went to church today. (*Suddenly, for sympathy.*) Looka me gettin' ready.

Sebb   Ma. I'm sorry.

Filumena   Sebbie . . . you . . . you're Siciliano. The lemons grow this big . . . the sun is always shining. I got money . . .

Sebb   Ma, I can't live in Sicily.

Filumena   I'm ready . . . look, Sebbie, I really am.

Sebb   Ma, lemme . . . lemme finish your hair. Sit. Go ahead. That feel good? What you cryin' for?

He brushes her hair, gently, affectionately.

Filumena *melts under his tenderness and cries, realising her defeat.*

Filumena   You're gonna leave.

Sebb   I gotta . . . Ma.

Filumena   There's young people in Sicily . . .

Sebb   No. Ma.

Filumena   And what about gogathatz . . . goom a si chiam . . . where they'll cure me?

Sebb   Colorado? Ma, there's snow there. You hate the snow. Someday, I swear . . .

Filumena   No someday, please, please. You're makin' me scared.

Sebb   Ssshhhhh.

Filumena   I'll die . . . I know. (*She clings to him, hard.*)

Sebb *tries to pull out of her grip.*

Sebb   Ma, lemme go now. Doogan's gonna get mad.

Filumena   Sebbie.

Sebb   Ma . . . leggo, Ma. Jesus! (*He pushes her off to break her grip.*)

Filumena *responds by pushing* **Sebb** *violently away.*

Filumena   And when they bury me, don't you dare come across the ocean. I want none of youse. I got my passport.

Sebb   Huh? What're you tryin' to prove with the passports?

Filumena   Go. You think God is gonna bless you for trickin' me?

Sebb   I don't need God's blessing.

Filumena   He don't need it.

Sebb   Yours I want.

Filumena   Where's the nail file . . . here . . . take it in your cheek. (*She jabs* **Sebb** *in the cheek with the nail file.*)

Sebb   Ow! You're crazy . . . God . . . You're crazy.

Filumena   You turned me into Christ, Judas. You put me on the cross.

Sebb   You poor crazy women.

Filumena   Now you can remember me whenever you look in the mirror, remember me . . . even when I'm dead. I was your mother. (**Filumena** *turns to her mirror.*)

Sebb *turns to his area.* **Doogan** *enters u/l.*

Doogan   Sebb? (**Doogan** *looks around the room cautiously.*)

Blaise *enters u/l and watches.*

Blaise   Doogan! I think he planned to meet you outside . . .

Doogan   That's okay.

Blaise   We don't have guests.

Doogan   I just wanted to see the place. Smells interesting.

Blaise   Garlic.

Doogan   I love Italian stuff.

Blaise   Then I'll tell you something I never told a soul . . .

Doogan   It's alright . . . (*He gestures no.*)

Blaise   My real name's Biaggio, after the Saint of the throats but my father wanted it Americanised. But the priest wrote it in French 'cause there is no American for Biaggio . . . so I was baptised B-l-a-i-s-e, but I spell it B-l-a-z-e. Like . . . Blaze, the human torch, and when someone trespasses on me, or my brother, I go on fire and destroy them, so I think you better split man.

Rocco *enters u/r.*

Rocco   Who is this?

Blaise   Uh . . . he's, you know . . .

Doogan   The name's Doogan.

Rocco   And what can I do for you?

Blaise   He's waiting for Sebbie.

Rocco   Oh. You travelin' together?

Doogan   Yes.

Rocco   You got some balls walkin' in here.

Doogan   I've been known to have balls.

Rocco   You and Sebbie been together long?

Doogan   Maybe you should talk to your son about it.

Rocco   Look kid, you walked in here and put yourself in my face so don't tell me talk to my son . . .

Doogan   I'll be outside.

Rocco   Come back here you. Have some wine.

Doogan   I'm not one of your sons. I can leave.

Rocco   Take it easy, what's your name?

Doogan   Doogan, Vinnie Doogan.

Rocco   I'm not going to bite you.

Doogan   I'm not worried.

Rocco   Then sit. Blaise . . .

Blaise *exits u/s.*

Rocco   Sit.

Doogan   I'll stand.

Rocco   You seem scared of me.

Doogan   Are you gonna ask me what we do in bed?

Rocco   No, but what are you two? You're what? What do you call yourself? Good friends, what do I tell the neighbors?

Doogan   The neighbors know.

Rocco   Your parents know?

Doogan   Yes.

Rocco   My son has in-laws and I never got invited to the wedding. Just kidding, no, I just want to know what you call yourselves, friends, partners . . .

Doogan   He's my lover.

Rocco   Ou, that sounds so sexual . . .

Doogan   He's my friend first.

Rocco   One hopes . . . And what are you going to achieve? Huh? To have kids? What?

Doogan   I don't know.

Rocco   That simple, you don't know?

Doogan   That's right.

Rocco   It's a dangerous world out there.

Doogan   From what I hear, it's a dangerous world in here, too.

Rocco   Very true. You tell me, what kind of man will my son be when he reaches my age?

Doogan   I hope not like you.

Rocco   See, that's what I worry about. Who'll take care of him when he's old? You?

Doogan   If I'm alive.

Rocco Who besides me has witnessed this promise?

Doogan Your son.

Rocco Only my son? So if you have a little problem, you just walk out on him?

Doogan No.

Rocco You'll be with him for the rest of his life, even if he goes off with a woman, or another one like you, or becomes a drunk?

Doogan Yes.

Rocco People have made that promise in front of priests . . .

Doogan So what do you want from me?

Rocco Make that promise to me. Make it? Can you?

Doogan Yes. I promise.

Rocco That's impressive, Vinnie, very impressive. I admire you. I do.

Rocco *opens the shades in the u/s area.* **Sebb** *walks into* **Filumena**'s *area. She is sitting, stunned, with her back to him.*

Sebb Ma, minavog.

Filumena Go.

Sebb You okay?

Filumena (*nods yes*) I'm okay.

Sebb I ain't a weakling, Ma.

Filumena I know you ain't . . .Go. And don't ever forget me. And don't ever forgive me.

Sebb *kisses the top of her head, then goes with his bags and encounters* **Rocco** *and* **Doogan**.

Sebb I told you to wait outside. (*Gives* **Doogan** *a hug.*)

Doogan Goodbye Mr Lazarra.

Rocco No. Shake hands?

Doogan *is suspicious, yet he risks the handshake. It turns out okay.* **Doogan** *exits.*

Sebb You're a regular evangelist.

Rocco What happened to your face?

Sebb Shavin' . . .

Rocco You guys got snow tyres?

Sebb No. It'll be okay.

Rocco Don't let anybody . . . ya know . . . don't let anybody . . .

Sebb Just take care of her.

Sebb exits. Rocco toasts the u/l door through which Sebb has exited. Filumena picks up her mother's clock and moves to the u/s area.

Rocco   Filumena . . . What're ya dressed up for? Huh? Where are you going with your mother's clock? (*Laughs at her.*)

Filumena   Where's Blaise?

Rocco   I dunno.

Filumena   If you were dead that kid never would have left.

Rocco   Don't you think it's good he left?

Filumena   No. The good man. He knows what's good for everybody.

Rocco   He was old enough to leave home, Filumena. He wanted to go.

Filumena   Sure, to get fucked up the ass.

Rocco   Maybe he's better off than we are.

Filumena   I don't want to be alone with you. I don't want to die with you.

Rocco   Okay . . . I understand what you mean, Filumena, but now I wanna take care of you. I wanna love you . . . whatta you say . . . It hurts.

Filumena   Who started with the hands twenty-five years ago? Who shoved cotton down my throat?

Rocco   Cotton? What cotton. . . ?

Filumena   Speak English, Italian girl. You remember? Eat your love now! . . . love now after your hand hit me, hit your kids. (*She's beginning to tremble.*)

Rocco   Shshhhhh . . .

Filumena   Now he says love when his hair's falling out. Love now that we're old . . . (*She disintegrates into Rocco's arms, punching his back even as she accepts his tenderness.*) Sebbie! . . . Sebbie!

Rocco   Shh . . . sh . . . shhhhh . . . Filumena. Please . . . please . . . please.

There is an exhaustive moment of surrender, which Blaise interrupts. Filumena recovers her anger.

Blaise   Sebb's gone. Pizella's here.

Rocco   Pizella? What for Pizella?

Blaise   Uh . . . Pa . . . the car . . . she wanted the car.

Filumena   I'm goin' home, Rocco.

Rocco   Home? This is your home.

Filumena   No. Sicilia.

Rocco (*trying not to laugh*) Sicilia? Sicily? Filumena, Sicily is different now. They're all dead over there.

Filumena I don't care. Blaise'll take me to the airport. Passports, money . . . and Pizella.

Rocco A kiss goodbye, Filumena.

Filumena Rocco, men like you should never be forgiven. To forgive you would take the last ounce of my strength.

Rocco (*grabbing* **Blaise**) Look at this kid's nose.

Blaise Pa, lemme go.

Rocco This is your father's nose to a tee.

Filumena My father was dead before you met me.

Rocco You usta say you had your father's nose.

Filumena Oh please.

Rocco And this kid's got your nose, so . . .

Filumena So?

Rocco You gonna leave this nose in America?

Filumena Pagliacci.

Rocco Yeah. If you stay, I'll make you laugh, Filumena.

Filumena Clown.

Rocco Yeah. Or make believe I'm your Marie Antoinette . . . stick me on your bed upstairs and put a hat on me.

Filumena Wipe it all away with a little joke? Sure.

Rocco Or make me your saint upstairs. Light candles to me. I'm Saint Anthony, ask me a favor. Go ahead. Ask me a favor.

Filumena Rocco . . . There's a young girl dead in this house somewhere. Some day you may find the body. Do her the favour. Minavog.

Rocco Okay, go. I give up, honest to Christ. Go if you can. I can't live with hate either. You deserve to be free . . . Go. I'll help you down the stoop. C'mon. Wha're we waiting for?

Blaise Pa, she can't really go . . .

Rocco gestures for **Blaise** to be silent.

Filumena (*puts down her mother's clock and slowly, deliberately puts on her gloves, trying to take up the challenge*) The planes take off in snow like this?

Blaise Sure.

Filumena And they sell tickets at the airport?

Blaise Uh-huh.

Filumena What a wind passed through this house . . .

Church bells softly start far off.

Filumena   What's that? Are those bells? (*She knows perfectly well that they are bells for the ten o'clock mass.*)

Blaise (*realising his opportunity*)   Yeah. For the ten o'clock Mass.

Filumena   If we let Pizella's car stop at the church, is there time?

Blaise (*catching on*)   Uh . . . sure.

Filumena   Yep. All right. I'll try to light a candle for Sebbie . . . maybe. We got time, yeah?

Blaise   I said yeah.

Filumena (*trembling*)   But if the priest talks, we get up.

Blaise   Sure.

Filumena   Good. Then maybe we go to the airport or maybe we come back here. If. If I feel like it. (*Points a finger up, gesturing for* **Rocco**.) If!

Rocco   And maybe you'll make coffee for us . . .

Filumena   No. I won't cook for you, talk to you, sleep with you. Never. And no matter how lonely I get or how good you get, I will never kiss you. (*She turns and calls into the house as if there's someone she's leaving behind.*) Filumena? Hey! Filumena Battaglia . . .

Blaise   Huh?

Filumena   I'll never forget you. Mai. Mai. Sulu una pirsuna always loved you from the beginning, and that was me, Puvuredda.

At this point, **Filumena** *exits u/s/l, followed by* **Blaise**. *We hear them o/s.*

Filumena   Look at this one without a scarf. Put up your collar.

Suddenly, with a burst of music, the back wall of the entire set springs open like the outer double doors of the house they live in. All is whiteness. Snow is falling heavily. **Filumena**, *in her purple dress and black coat (herself now the snow orchid), cannot take the first step down towards the street. She is supported by* **Blaise**. **Rocco** *stands at the top step, sadly watching their departure.*

Blaise   Slide that foot . . . off . . . off . . . Pa . . .

Rocco   You help her.

Filumena   Oh, where? Ou.

Blaise   Down here. You should be wearin' your galoshes, Ma.

They come d/s, falteringly, the pace determined by **Filumena**.

Filumena   I don't have any galoshes. Ou, it's slippery. Dio . . .

Blaise   I gottcha. Now step again.

Filumena   Wait. My feet are getting wet. Lemme go back.

Blaise   No. The snow is dry. Step . . . I gottcha.

Filumena   I can't.

Blaise   You can. I got you.

Filumena Hold me tight, Blaise. If God gets me there, I'll light a candle with thirty dollars on the altar. If Gods gets me there . . .

Blaise God'll get us there. Now, step.

Filumena (*slides an inch*) Ou, ooop. Fifty dollars I'll leave, fifty dollars and a candle, right on the altar.

Blaise Good. One more now.

Filumena Ou, it's cold . . . blessed Mother . . . please get us there.

Blaise Step at a time, Ma.

They have reached the two steps up to the red box.

Filumena (*voice fades*) It's cold . . .

Blaise Easy . . .

Filumena *takes the second step, then a third step.*

Filumena Step at a time. A step . . . Sant Antonio . . . San Antonio . . . oh . . . oh.

Lights out.

End.

Snow Orchid

In its early stages, AJ Antoon, the director, told me that he found *Snow Orchid* fascinating but that he wished I would make the characters less cruel and more loving toward one another. Up until recently, I was offended that this director couldn't see that through the abuse, they all truly loved one another. I had run across such characters in my own life and believed I understood them. But recently, after reading the galleys for this volume, I too was shocked and also embarrassed, that I could ever have taken this much familial cruelty for granted and the play, like a ghost of myself, spoke to me, and I could no longer hide from the personal truths about my own life, that it was placing before me.

Such a play could never end happily, which I had tried so hard to make it do. So I did just a little re-writing with a good deal of respect for what I had accomplished in writing what had come before. For me, now, *Snow Orchid* remains both crude and graceful, both naïve and wise, the most difficult play of my life to write.

At the Eugene O'Neill conference, Martin Esslin, my dramaturg, felt that the bitter rebellion of Sebbie made for a new sort of breakaway character, a man on the threshold of a whole new sort of independence. It must be remembered that in 1979, when this play was written, there was hardly any sort of gay liberation.

I had never intended to make it a 'gay play'. I thought I was writing about the new America seen through the eyes of Filumena Lazarra, an immigrant bride who was brought to the United States largely against her will. The New World encroaches upon this poor, agoraphobic girl in the form of her American husband's violent machismo, and later, her first son's homosexuality and her younger son's total Americanism. But it is impossible to separate homosexuals from the heterosexual marriages from which they emerge. After all, gay people are born of straight parents. That's the rule, generally. They make an odd triangle, two parents and their gay offspring, just as siblings, straight and gay, have a peculiar relativity. Gay male existence does not begin with parades and bars. The most difficult years of gay life take place early, in the home, where homophobia can make life hell and where the gay person faces the first, tortuous separations of his life.

My difficulties must have been greater than I ever could admit to myself, for this play to have come out of me. In it, the gay son is a ferociously vengeful and angry auto mechanic who hates his father. His straight kid brother is worshipfully in love with the gay brother who turns him away with teasing and ridicule. The father is a repressed, woman-hating, psychotic. The mother is besieged by hysterics and fear, assaulted by phobias and shame and eventually resorts to the physical abuse that had been heaped upon her in her life. I see now, that the collision of these ancient forces with new ideas, exploded in this play, and hopefully made it a better work. Perhaps *Snow Orchid* was my attempt to harness these undisciplined energies in characters whom I had known in my life, people who were at once, extremely dangerous to one another and madly, incestuously, in love with one another.

Plays with strong gay characters have been taboo for most of our dramatic and literary history. Back then, I thought I was writing a classically realistic, retro-style play, imitating the styles of Inge and Williams, full of lyrical realism and symbolism, as if to infuse gay enlightenment into the politically unenlightened past. With the extraordinary help of Tim Luscombe and some of the most gifted artists and theatre technicians that ever worked with my material, *Snow Orchid*, at the Gate in Notting Hill, was the realisation of my highest hopes for this play.

Joe Pintauro
New York, 1994

Joe Pintauro is a playwright, novelist and poet. He is best known for works such as *Raft of the Medusa, Beside Herself, Cacciatore* and *Men's Lives*. The entire collection of his twenty-two, one-act plays was published by Broadway Publishing in New York in 1989 under the title *Plays by Joe Pintauro*. Other plays have been published in various collections, including *Wild Blue* in *Gay Plays: Four* by Methuen. *The Dead Boy*, soon to be produced in New York, was given a public workshop by Stephen Daldry at the Royal Court in 1992. Pintauro has written several novels including *Cold Hands* (Simon and Schuster, 1979) and *State of Grace* (Times Books [New York Times] 1983), as well as several award-winning books of poetry, published by Harper and Row, 1968–73. He is currently working on a new novel and a three-part play in collaboration with Lanford Wilson and Terrence McNally.

London Gay Theatre Company production

It was because of plays like *Snow Orchid* that I formed the London Gay Theatre Company in 1991. Neither commercial producers nor decent rep. companies would consider producing the gay plays that I was sending them: many, many plays over the years; all, I thought, excellent. They would be happy for me to come and do another Noël Coward revival, perhaps a Priestley. What about a little-known Maugham? My choice! But a play about gays – forget it. I was only able to direct plays that I felt really properly connected to by doing them for free on the fringe. A fine state of affairs. So I thought I'd consolidate all this work, formed the LGTC with actor Adam Magnani and now, three productions later, the experiment seems to have become a way of life.

I wanted to do *Snow Orchid* as our first production. It is an exquisite play by Joe who seemed to be the most exciting gay playwright coming out of America, the country writing the most exciting gay plays.

I always thought *Snow Orchid* was a sexy play; red blooded, fierce, passionate, ludicrously funny and complete; the tense and clever structure invisible, and the four main characters given equal share of the spectacular big numbers, duos and foursomes, sparring with every permutation, colouring the play all colours.

Snow Orchid explores honestly the taboo-ish subject of intra-family sexuality, against a backdrop of domestic violence, fear and claustrophobia. Italians running riot with their emotions and neuroses is great material for a play of explicit confrontation and rapid verbal violence.

The trouble was, it really wasn't gay enough for a company called the London Gay Theatre Company, at least not for a *first* production, by which I supposed people would gauge our aims and judge our politics. The strands of sexuality are very complex in *Snow Orchid*, and gayness hardly seems top of the agenda of sexual issues. There are so many other issues than that of sex and sexuality. Filumena's agoraphobia, her decayed, impossible marriage with Rocco, these are what the play's mostly about. Secondly, in 1991–2 *Snow Orchid* seemed to lie in that odd no-man's land of old new writing. Written in 1979, it was neither old enough to be a classic worth reviving nor recent enough to be considered new writing. This state was then exacerbated by the fact that between its writing and the present, AIDS happened, changed everything and dated all that had been said before it.

As AIDS has jolted us into a new era of thinking about ourselves and our sexuality, it has changed the way Joe writes his plays. Since *Snow Orchid*, his work has demonstrated the most open, wise, sensible, strong attitude to gayness and its place in society and the family but *Snow Orchid* is a pre-AIDS play.

Of course, it's possible to do a play about gay issues and not mention AIDS, but at the time it seemed irresponsible to inaugurate the company so. It was formed not only to give me a chance to direct the plays no one allowed me to, but because we wanted other gay people to see them! And it seemed that the company should address the issues that affect us most, and AIDS has got to be the big one.

So we started with five short American plays (two by Joe), all but one about AIDS, and having done that we followed it with something English, fearing the critical response to two American plays on the trot. That production had nothing to do with AIDS and everything to do with the Eurovision Song Contest. Then finally in February 1993 we'd finally cleared the way for *Snow Orchid*.

I visited Joe in Sag Harbor to learn from him about the play and to get to know him. We talked about a few cosmetic alterations in accordance with my concerns, but what I really wanted was Doogan, Sebbie's boyfriend, in the play. And Joe provided it. I was thinking about a scene between Sebbie and Doogan (perhaps at the wake), but Joe cleverly gave me Doogan confronting Rocco and Blaise.

I had a thousand questions for Joe: how do you pronounce 'lookit', what's a fern room, have Sebbie and Filumena ever made love? He disappeared into the cellar one day and came up with an old box full of drafts (maybe fifteen, twenty; dusty as hell and incredibly varied: Rocco was gay, straight, unsure, gay again, in love with Kenny Farrell, on a lake fishing with Kenny Farrell, straight again) and some dead orchids. We sat in coffee shops all over Sag Harbor and Joe talked about the constraints, manners, idiosyncracies of the Italian New Yorkers from his youth. We visited his Sicilian friend Antonina who hooked us up by phone with her friend in Florida who corrected my attempts at Sicilian pronunciation, explained the swear words and read Filumena's prayer, all from her Florida poolside.

During an electric storm, and way into the night, Joe worked out the new Doogan scene. In the end, I fell asleep to the sound of Joe and his word processor working and reworking next door.

We talked so much that we ran out of time, and, when I had to leave, Joe hadn't finished the changes he wanted to do (for example, changing all the valiums to prozacs), so he came with me to New York, and in the back of the bus that took us there (called the Hampton Jitney), he scrawled fairly illegible stuff in red ink into my copy, reading it to me as he did with full characterisation, particularly Rocco, though his Blaise was best! In New York he showed me the house he imagined the Lazarras lived in. I drew a sketch for Rob who was going to have to put it into the Gate Theatre!

Of course, when we were in the thick of rehearsals, my thinking switched from gay-political idealism to fusing the play with actors, designers, etc. The Doogan scene was massively worthwhile, I thought. I found the actor easily, Rob dressed him from Camden Market and Clone Zone, and we had a real 1993 Act-Up American, with 1993 clothes and 1993 sideburns!

I know it's not the job of a theatre company to be politically correct – a good play's a good play whether right-wing, left-wing, straight or gay – but there's a consideration to be made in gay theatre because gay theatre, like the whole gay community, faces a particular problem. One of the ways society's oppression of us expresses itself is in the lack of ways we're allowed to show ourselves or see ourselves in the public arena. If there was a great new gay play opening every week expressing increasingly varied aspects of our lifestyles, then there'd be no reason for a gay theatre company to think about its responsibility to present positive images of ourselves. But there isn't, so we do.

Sebbie in 1979 could be seen in equal measure as self-hating, or quietly stoic in his assertion of his gayness, the former in accordance with the old school of much gay writing, reflecting both the prevalent emotional environment of subjugation and defeat and life in the Lazarra household. I felt the LGTC had a responsibility to show the boyfriend, suggest a positive outcome for Sebbie and, even if after the play one imagines the Sebbie/Doogan relationship failing, at least we'd have shown an alternative attitude – a modern, positive, aggressive pride, which Doogan represents.

In the end, in separating gayness from the other sexual issues of the play, and worrying that its place was not central enough, I was denying one of the main tenets of the theatre company: that sexuality is fluid, and that in our hearts we cannot completely separate gayness from any other form of sexual expression . . . Yet we are an oppressed minority and in our *heads* we recognise that our sexuality deserves separate consideration. We are, simply, in the way straight society sidelines us, separate, we are feared and in most places we are invisible. Doogan speaks for a future when this will not be the case.

And what I'd feared about Sebbie's self hatred,

Blaise . . . or what happens when they [the parents] die on me? Huh? I gotta put on some bomber's jacket and go drag you outta some goddamn weird bar?
Sebb You little sonofabitch. You'll never find *me* in one of those bars, okay?

seemed to be overcome by the strength of Adam's performance and by the fact that what you really hear through the play is the author, through Sebbie, saying I'm gay; it doesn't matter how or why; the details are unimportant; and damn the lot of you, I'm off to live with Doogan in Texas!

My other great fear, this one self-imposed, was that what Joe had so beautifully built up might be ruined by what I'd manoeuvred. But as it turned out the play was so robust, Jonathan, Roger and Jude played the scene brilliantly and with Doogan the audience got a welcome breath of cool air from the snowy New York street, blowing across the bright red volcanic ash still settling from Paola's last scene!

Particularly impressive to me, as well as the beautiful acting (which, though Italianate, in the best sense of its honest confrontational emotion, concerned itself with detailed realism and truthful characterisation, so that my need for orchestration, heightened in such a small space with such proximity to the audience, was easily satisfied) was Rob Howell's gigantic doll's house set, miraculously giving us a feeling of space, claustrophobia, perspective and specific locations at once, Jason Carr's breathtaking music and Paul Arditti's sensational offstage St Anthony parade.

Tim Luscombe
Artistic Director
London Gay Theatre Company

Printed in the United States
67957LVS00006B/114